BEING

BIBLICAL

How can we use the Bible in constructing ethics today?

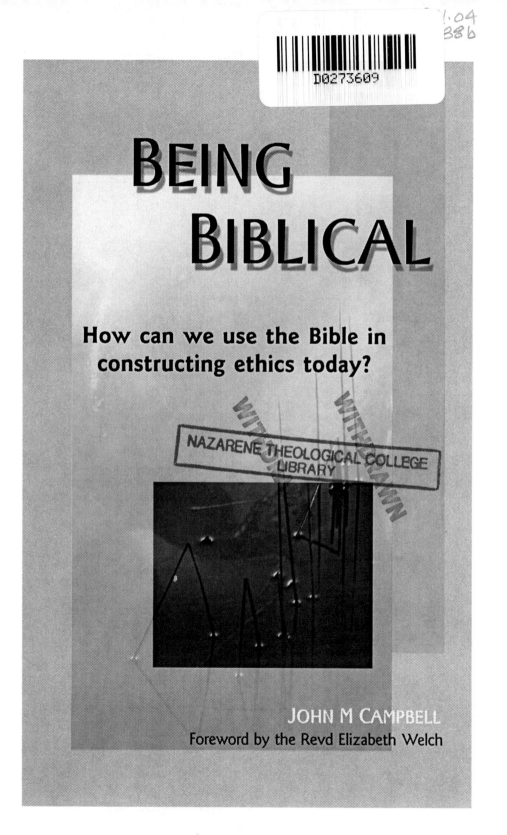

JOHN M CAMPBELL

Foreword by the Revd Elizabeth Welch

The
United
Reformed
Church

Being Biblical
by John Campbell
ISBN 0 85346 216 X

© The United Reformed Church
First Edition 2003
Reprint 2006

Published by The United Reformed Church
86 Tavistock Place, London WC1H 9RT

Produced by Communications and Editorial, Graphics Office
The United Reformed Church, 86 Tavistock Place, London WC1H 9RT

FOREWORD

by Revd Elizabeth Welch, Moderator of West Midlands Synod of the United Reformed Church

I'm delighted to be invited to write a foreword for this book.

I have known John as the minister of the inner city church of South Aston since I became West Midlands Synod Moderator in 1996. I was grateful that he agreed to take on the Bible Studies at Assembly in 2001, when I was national Moderator of the United Reformed Church. His combination of wisdom and wit, interwoven with an ability to think carefully through complex issues, has continued to impress me.

The time is right for this book. It arises out of the discussions on Human Sexuality that have occupied the United Reformed Church for a number of years. General Assembly agreed in 2000 that there should be a moratorium on resolutions on matters of sexuality, while encouraging a period of further thought and reflection. This book is a timely contribution to that reflection.

In my role as Convenor of the Core Group taking forward the discussions on Human Sexuality in the United Reformed Church from 1997 to 1999, I was aware that one of the underlying issues with which we needed to get to grips was that of the authority of the Bible (taken up by the Working Group on this subject).

This book helpfully points us to the need to look at the 'How' questions with regard to the study of scripture. How do we go about interpreting the text? What tools do we use? How come there are so many different interpretations? How do we come to an agreement in the church about the way we interpret scripture together?

In the questions raised, we are pointed to the issues that we need to discuss together and the way in which it would be helpful to discuss them, in order to take forward not only issues of human sexuality, but the variety of ethical issues that face us at the beginning of the third Millennium.

This book lays out complex issues from our history and our present life, in a way that is clearly accessible. The layout of the book, with its format including both chunks of text to make the argument and regular summaries to highlight where the argument is up to, give a study guide that could be usefully used by both individuals and groups.

I warmly recommend this timely book to all who are interested in the question of the way we interpret the Bible when faced with the complex ethical issues of the 21st Century.

Elizabeth Welch

ACKNOWLEDGEMENTS

I'd like to thank the Cheshunt Foundation for funding a term of research and writing at Westminster College in Cambridge. Also the staff, students and visiting scholars at Westminster for their friendship, understanding and support through autumn term 2000. I'd note especially David and Joy Coster from Dunedin, New Zealand and Clifford Wilton from Nottingham, who shared the hospitality and comradeship of the Autumn 2000 Cheshunt Fellowships.

Particular thanks to Lance Stone who gave me wise and encouraging discussion and supervision both during my term at Westminster and subsequently. Thanks, also, to all the Stone family who welcomed me as one of their own whenever I was in Cambridge.

I'd add a big thank you to the people of South Aston United Reformed Church and everyone who has helped them through the time I was away on sabbatical and subsequent shorter periods of study leave. Thanks for managing so well and so uncomplainingly and for allowing me to keep writing until the book was written.

Thanks to Neil Messer for helping with the development of the idea in its earliest stages and for facilitating the sabbatical I was able to take in Autumn 2000.

Thanks, also, to all the others who've read various parts of the book, commented on drafts and made suggestions for improvements, including David Cornick, Keith Forecast, Martin Forrest, Edward Furness, Ruth Packwood, Gill Paterson, John Proctor, Keith Steven, Maureen Thompson, Janet Tollington, Wallie Warmington, and Barry Welch.

Thanks to Elizabeth Welch for her interest throughout the Project and kindly agreeing to write the Foreword.

Thanks to Graham Cook (Convener) and Carol Rogers (Secretary) of the United Reformed Church Communications and Editorial Committee and the members of the Publications Board for their interest and practical support. Also thanks to Sara Foyle for her skillful work on layout and design.

Finally, a special thanks to my Mother and her kind husband Max who both contributed massive quantities of emotional support to the whole enterprise for as long as they could, but who died, some six months apart, whilst this book was being written. One of Mother's most persistent questions as her memory failed and her grasp of our shared reality faded was, "Has John finished his book yet?" Later, Max, when I told him in our last conversation together that the United Reformed Church had asked for a synopsis and a sample chapter, forced himself to sit up in his hospital bed, shook my hand and said, "Well done!" (like the blessing of a dying Isaac). Thanks, both of you, for being there for me for as long as you possibly could. I sense your encouragement still.

J M C Epiphany, 2003

This book is dedicated to

two Aberdeen Biblical Scholars

WILLIAM JOHNSTONE
who tried to make me think
and
HOWARD MARSHALL
who tried to make me thorough

with sincere thanks.

CONTENTS

Foreword   iii

Acknowledgements   v

INTRODUCTION: ASKING THE "HOW?" QUESTIONS   xi

PART ONE - LESSONS FROM HISTORY?

1   SEEING WITH "REFORMED" SPECTACLES

1.1   Big ideas with hidden expectations   3
1.2   Luther and Scripture for us all   3
1.3   Calvin and the unified Word of God   6
1.4   1646 - old friends on English soil   9
    1.   The 'Presbyterians' gathered in assembly   9
    2.   The Independents on the march   10

2   CRITICISM & REACTION

2.1   The Rise of the Modern World   13
2.2   "Assured results" of Higher Criticism   15
2.3   Warfield and the Evangelical Reaction   19
2.4   A century of impasse?   23
2.5   Lessons from History?   24

PART TWO - ENCOUNTERING THE BIBLE TODAY

3   READING AND MAKING SENSE TODAY

3.1   The Fall of the Modern World   29
3.2   What's happening now?   30
    1.   I can construct my own truth   30
    2.   I can invent and re-invent myself   31
    3.   Consume, consume, consume!   31
    4.   There's a lot of pain and despair in this   31
    5.   Major evils are still to be addressed   32

3.3	And what can we learn from the text?	33
	1. The impossibility of objectivity	33
	2. The spiral of learning	36
	3. The importance of suspicion	38
	4. The liberation of listening	40
	5. The ubiquity of violence	43
	6. The judging of meanings	44
	7. The recovery of story	49
3.4	Are we simply following fashion?	50
	1. A reasonable risk	51
	2. A real problem	52
	3. A helpful ending	52
	4. An accurate description	53
	5. A believable account	54
	6. A greater awareness of sin	55
	7. A more honest appraisal	56
3.5	A personal journey	56

4 SEEING THE BIBLE WITH FRESH EYES

4.1	Two ways of seeing the Bible	63
	1. Approaching the Bible in bits	63
	2. Approaching the-Bible-as-a-whole	64
4.2	What have we got in the Bible?	68
	1. A diverse library	68
	2. A particular story	71
	3. A kitchenful of ingredients but no recipe	72
	4. A strange rule book	74
	5. A choice of many mansions	76
4.3	Why don't we get what we expect?	77
4.4	What might the Bible be trying to say?	79
	1. Defeating domestication	79
	2. Challenging closure	83
	3. Finding friendship	85
	4. Valuing vulnerability	88
	5. Creating community	89
	6. Always anew	90
4.5	Where does this leave us?	91

PART THREE: BIBLICAL ETHICS FOR TODAY

5   HOW DO WE DECIDE WHAT GOD WANTS US TO DO?

5.1	Biblical Ethics	97
5.2	By what Authority?	98
	1. Resistance to authority	98
	2. What sort of authority?	100
5.3	Trying to Answer the 'HOW?' Question	103
	1. What have we got to interpret?	104
	2. How has this been done in practice?	107
	3. Can we devise a reliable method?	108
5.4	Entering God's Conversation	111
5.5	Seven proposals for Conversationalists	115
	1. Allow for real argument	116
	2. Admit our need of others	118
	3. Accept the Bible as it is	121
	4. Allow the Bible's own methods	123
	5. Keep talking about ethics	125
	6. Affirm God's underlying purposes	127
	7. Allow for the role of God's Spirit	129

6   CONFLICT IN CORINTH – A CASE STUDY

6.1	Church Conflict in Corinth	135
6.2	Paul in conversation	138
	1. Paul and the power of persuasion	139
	2. Cherishing competing contributions	139
	3. Hearing all God's Word?	143
	4. Master of many methods	143
	5. Conversations concluded or commenced?	144
	6. Paul's twin imperatives	145
	7. Paul and the Spirit	148
6.3	1 Corinthians as a 21st Century text	148

7   OUR DEVELOPING CONVERSATION

7.1   A Reformable Revelation?   151

7.2   Unfinished Business?   155

7.3   Moments of meaningful change   161

    1.   *Was God against the Atlantic Slave trade?*   161

    2.   *Was God against American Chattel Slavery?*   165

    3.   *Was God against South African apartheid?*   168

7.4   The struggle continues   172

AFTERWORD: THE VIEW FROM HERE   175

FOOTNOTES   178

INTRODUCTION

Asking the "HOW?" Questions

This book has its origins in the bruising and difficult debates about homosexuality that consumed so much time and effort in the United Reformed Church for several years up to the summer of 2000. But it's not about sexuality; it's about how Churches in the Reformed tradition should go about finding God's truth in the Bible.

I have always been fascinated by the "How?" questions - the ones about method and technique; pre-suppositions and practice; hidden assumptions and smuggled baggage. In a previous career as a plant geneticist, I was amazed at the ease with which scientists rushed unreflectively into their laboratories to experiment. It worried me that they never seemed to stop and look carefully at this "Scientific Method" that was supposed to enable them to find 'truth'. Few of them seemed ever to have done a course on it or read a book about it. Most seemed to have only the haziest of ideas as to what the built-in assumptions of the method might be - or where the limits to its reasonable application might lie. Indeed, the more I read about the History and Philosophy of Science, the less certain its certainties seemed, the less unquestionably secure its truths. Yet, the scientific research I witnessed in the 1970s seemed propelled by an unthinking certainty of progress that asked no questions of itself or its methods. I was always suspicious that this was dangerous, both for the scientists themselves and for wider society. As a result, I still find myself wary of leaving the ethical dilemmas of genetic engineering entirely to geneticists - even geneticists who are not employed by profit-driven multi-nationals.

Indeed, trying to study anything without considering the "How?" questions of methods, goals and pre-suppositions seems dangerous to me - a bit like trying to drive a car before you've even got a rough idea what the various switches, levers and pedals do.[1] So, as my own denomination (the United Reformed Church) hurtled through a fraught debate on what God might be saying to us about "human sexuality", I've frequently felt a bit like a passenger driven off by a first-time learner before the instructor has arrived. I've kept wanting to lean forward and ask, "Are we sure we know what we're doing?"

Eventually, the United Reformed Church discussions came to a halt. We crunched and crashed our way through about three years of difficult debates at General Assemblies, regional Synods, District Councils and local Church Meetings to the point where the July 2000 General Assembly accepted a "lack of agreement"[2]. Assembly then proposed a voluntary seven year pause in policy-making about human sexuality in the councils of our church. Phew!

We were invited to use this pause for "reflection, praying and sharing"[3]. I, for one, felt I needed to go back and sort out my grasp of some of the "How?" questions. I wanted to look more carefully at how we use the Bible to discover what God is saying to us.

Like other English-speaking Reformed denominations across the world who had had broadly parallel debates on these issues, we had been provided with copious supplies of Working Group Reports[4]. These included one from a Working Group on Biblical Authority. I found this a strangely unsatisfying report. The Working Group had clearly had vigorous debate and sharp disagreement about the Bible passages where they felt direct reference was made to homosexual practice, but if they worked together on the prior question of how we should try to develop Christian ethics from the Bible in the 21st Century, they largely failed to put any indication of their various ideas or approaches into their Report.

They did however, suggest that these "How?" questions are at the root of our difficulties. They concluded that underlying their own sharply different interpretations of the texts they studied was the way that each of them approaches Scripture. They talked of different 'patterns' or 'schemes' of viewing Scripture, noting that "those who have found a significant message in the Bible" have always used some sort of interpretative 'scheme'. They accepted that they could not agree on what the four texts they considered 'mean' because they were using different schemes through which they viewed all of Scripture. Indeed, they say:

> "We would view the current interpretative conflict as lying largely in the… different schemes used by those who have taken part."
>
> *United Reformed Church Human Sexuality Report. 1999. A 6.5*

So, they appear to be claiming that the heart of our disagreements about the meaning of Scripture is to be found in the "How?" questions. They make the case that what you find when you get to the Bible depends to a significant extent on the way you approach the Bible. Reapplying our learner driver analogy, we keep bumping into one another at important intersections in the Bible because we all have different 'Highway Codes' and 'Driving Manuals'. We're all driving by different rules.

This is crucial. It means that, if we are ever to 'agree' or even 'understand' one another when we come to consider the Bible together, we have to look together at the "How?" questions first. So, did the Working Group go on to offer us any help with the "How?" questions? No. They simply commented:

> …conflict between interpretative patterns [or schemes] cannot be speedily resolved, but rather can only come about through persistent, humble attention to what is before us in the Bible.
>
> *United Reformed Church Human Sexuality Report. 1999. A 6.6*

After this, they devoted the remaining five pages of their Report to urging us all with evident passion to engage in more Bible study and prayer and to 'cultivate a delight in the Scriptures' by daily meditation. Now, I would never argue against more Bible study and more prayer and the cultivation of 'a delight in the Scriptures', but if we are to grow together around the Bible, I would propose that we cannot avoid looking together at how we use the Bible. I cannot see spirituality as an alternative to a shared pursuit of knowledge and understanding. I am bold enough to hope that both are part of God's will for us all. So, with the recklessness of a D I Y novice who's desperate for new shelves but cannot find a carpenter, I decided to explore the "How?" questions myself.

As a result, I spent a sabbatical term at Westminster College in Cambridge in the autumn of 2000 reading up on some subjects I had barely touched since my divinity studies in Aberdeen some twenty years before and other subjects that hardly existed at that time. I have grappled with church history, with Christian ethics, with Biblical and secular hermeneutics, with epistemology and with theories of modernism, postmodernism and postcolonialism. Since then I have tried to squeeze the process of reading and writing into the gaps in my real life as the minister of a busy, multiracial, inner city United Reformed Church in Birmingham. I am no expert in the various fields of study through which this book takes a hasty tour. Still, I wonder whether my 'learner' status might help in two ways:

because I've really struggled with the language and ideas myself, I am going to try to put all of this over as simply as possible (without, I hope, "dumbing down")

because I'm not an "expert", it should be easier for everyone to disagree with me without feeling any need to bow to my "expertise".

I'll try to share with you the questions and issues I've uncovered and invite you to consider them for yourself. You could see me as a bit like a learner driver (who's had one or maybe two lessons) sharing a few proudly-remembered ideas about driving and road safety with another one. Hear me carefully, but critically, as I try to assemble some answers to the "How?" questions, in a way that might help you to clarify what *you* think. I'll simply be trying to share my understanding of the theory, so you and I have a slightly clearer idea of what we can and cannot do when we turn to the Bible. Yes, I'm bound to be biased, but I'll try to be honest about my biases and what has shaped them. I'll also encourage you to make up your own mind, but to do so with a similar openness to seeing what you are doing and why… and where your biases lie.

The basic question the whole of this book seeks to address is this -

> How do we, in a Reformed Church at the start of the 21st Century, go about finding God's truth in the Bible to help us construct Christian ethical responses to the issues we face?

Let me, then, invite you to step back from the fixating issue of "What the Bible tells us about sexuality" to look afresh at the "How?" questions. In fact, I think we'll need to take three steps back:

Before we are able to look properly at what the Bible says about a particular ethical issue, we need to take a first step back and look at how we might reasonably use the Bible to seek God's guidance on ethical matters in general.

Before we are able to look properly at how we use the Bible in deciding about ethical matters in general, we need to take a second step back and look at how we use the Bible as a whole, today. The last twenty years have produced a great flowering of new understanding of what is happening when we look at *any* text and what happens when we look at the Bible in particular. We need to get some sort of a grasp of all that before we can look at the specifics of using the Bible to construct our ethics.

Before we are able to look properly at how we use the Bible as-a-whole today, we need to take a third step back and look at how our Reformed traditions have approached the Bible through their history, since the Reformation. For strong underlying attitudes to the Bible, inherited from our faith forebears, set the whole tone of how we approach this foundational book. It is our history that has generated the particular "schemes of interpretation" that we unselfconsciously use when we approach the Bible.

So, the whole structure of the book that follows is constructed around the idea of these three steps back. We'll begin (three steps back) with some history, then move (two steps back) to a look at how we may reasonably interpret the bible today, then (and only then) consider (one step back) how we can rightly handle the Bible in addressing ethical issues. I would argue that if we do not take these three steps before we discuss a particular ethical issue, we cannot claim that we're being "Biblical" in our approach.

In **Part One – Lessons from History**? I'm going to put to you an interpretation of how the Bible has been handled by our Protestant and Reformed traditions since the Reformation. Firstly, Chapter One will look at two of the big, bold, beautiful ideas of the Reformation that also dragged unfortunate assumptions about what the Bible *should* be like along behind them. Chapter Two will do the same for two exciting ideas from the period since 'the Enlightenment' that also smuggled in assumptions about what the Bible *should* be like.

We'll look in **Part Two – Encountering the Bible Today** at how we handle the Bible now. Chapter Three will look first at how we read and make sense of texts (any texts) *today*. After a brief preparatory look at the 'fall' of the modern world and the nature of the emerging 'Post-modern' world, we'll take quite a bit of space to look at the new developments in the study of how we find meaning in texts ('hermeneutics'). This study is central not only to recent understandings of how we make sense of 'reality' but also to the specific task of approaching the Bible today. So, as we go, we'll keep stopping to think how each idea about reading texts in general might specifically affect our approach to the Bible. I'll also take the opportunity, at this point, to tell how my own particular experiences over the last thirty years have shaped the way I see the Bible. After that, Chapter Four will be looking directly at the Bible itself. It will look at what we hope to find when we go to the Bible, what it actually offers us and some possible explanations as to why the Bible is the way it seems to be.

Then (and only then) we'll begin to think in **Part Three - Biblical Ethics** about how we can realistically address ethical questions by seeking the Bible's guidance and help. In Chapter Five we will look at the nature of 'Biblical Authority' and how it seems to work before considering at length the practicalities and possibilities of using the Bible to construct 21st Century Christian ethics. Then, in Chapter Six, we will see how all this works out in a Bible case study – the ethical debates we can observe in *1 Corinthians*. Then, in Chapter Seven we will look briefly at selected examples of the ethical debates that have raged through Christian history. Finally, in a brief Afterword we will seek to look back at the road we have travelled and present some summary conclusions.

Perhaps we will see more clearly how we can "rightly handle the word of truth" (*2 Timothy 2:15 RSV*). Perhaps this will allow us to enrich one another with fresh understandings of God's Word even if we don't agree on every aspect of interpretation. Anyhow, I hope you are able to find this quest as exciting, challenging and spiritually stretching as I have done. Let's go…

BEING BIBLICAL

PART ONE

LESSONS FROM HISTORY?

CHAPTER ONE

SEEING WITH "REFORMED" SPECTACLES

1.1 Big ideas with hidden expectations

Have you ever found yourself saying, "What I didn't realise when I started this......" or "It seems obvious now, but..." or "In the beginning I was so excited that I didn't stop to think about..."?

Even some of our best and most exciting ideas smuggle in problems that we don't notice until it's too late. It can happen on the small scale - that clever way to skip three steps in the assembly instructions that means that the bookcase will always lean slightly to the left because the "holding sprocket (6b)" won't now do its job. It can happen in the big decisions of life - like moving house, or getting a new job, or marriage, or... whatever.

I'd like to propose that two of the biggest and most impressive ideas of Luther and Calvin, the great 'fathers' of the Reformation, smuggled in assumptions about the way we can use the Bible that are still in danger of tripping us up as we approach the Bible today. Let's start with Luther......

1.2 Luther and Scripture for us all

Something of enormous consequence happened to Martin Luther as he wrestled with the meaning of the Scriptures; but something of equal consequence happened to the Scriptures themselves as a result of Luther reading them.

For centuries the hand-copied text of the Latin Scriptures had been effectively confined to the world of scholars, scholars who themselves were effectively confined by the canons, traditions and hierarchy of the Church Catholic. The Scriptures were controlled by the Church. They were revered as the very Word of God, but confined within that reverence. They were protected by a surrounding collar of tradition and beliefs that had been gradually built up by the Church over the centuries - traditions that prescribed the very nature of permissible interpretation, in the defence of orthodoxy. For social, political and religious stability all depended on the stable interpretation of the Word of God. All legitimate interpretation took place within the faith community of approved Christian scholarship and dogma with Bishops, Archbishops and Pope as the ultimate arbiters of truth and defenders of the Holy Word of God.[5]

With Luther all that changed. Driven by his encounter with the text of Romans, Luther swept aside the whole edifice of Church control and all the encrusting layers of received dogma. He disregarded the canons, traditions and power of the Church, standing alone before the bald text of the Bible. He allowed himself but one controlling idea to unlock these otherwise autonomous Scriptures - in his margin notes for his

> Here the door is thrown open wide for the understanding of Scripture,
> that is, that everything must be understood in relation to Christ
>
> *Luther's Lectures on Romans 6*

lectures on Romans in the summer of 1515, opposite Romans 1:3, he writes:

By the time he came to defend himself and his opinions in debate with Johann Eck at Leipzig in 1519, he not only debated in German (the language of everyday living) rather than Latin (the language of monks and scholars), but 'allowed only the Bible to be used as an authority in their dispute'.[7] Indeed, during the dispute he maintained that 'a simple layman armed with the Scriptures was superior to the pope and councils of the church'.[8]

This clean, fresh way of seeing the Scriptures as able to stand on their own as the one needful authority available and obvious to everyone ('*Sola scriptura!*' ie 'Scripture alone') was attractive, even exhilarating, to many others beside Luther. Three years later, in 1522, Ulrich Zwingli, the Swiss reformer, published a treatise '*On the Clarity*

> The Word of God, as soon as it shines upon an individual's understanding, illuminates
> it in such a way that he understands it"
>
> *quoted in McGrath, 1999, p.162 9*

and Certainty of the Word of God', in which he maintained:

And in 1523, when seeking to set up public debates on possible reforms in the church in Zurich, Zwingli was able to insist in his turn that the 600 clergy and laymen assembled use vernacular German rather than scholarly Latin and 'allow only the Bible as an authority in argument'.[10]

By that time Luther had begun working on a German translation of the New Testament determined, as Owen Chadwick puts it, 'that the Bible should be brought to the homes of the common people'.[11] He deliberately exploited all the advantages of the new printing technology that vastly improved the availability and affordability of books and pamphlets. Luther and the printing press turned the Bible into the People's Book. Now 'everyone'[12] was free to read and comment. All sorts of ordinary folk could decide for themselves what God was saying. The Scriptures were loose among the people.

What an exciting idea! It spread rapidly through the towns and cities of Northern Europe, giving birth to a multi-form, unstructured movement often referred to as Anabaptists or 'the Radical Reformation'[13]. Their liberated, affordable (if not exactly cheap) Bible seemed to allow a near limitless ferment of interpretations. Everything from simple, peaceful, proto-Congregational groups with a commitment to 'reading the Bible from the standpoint of the powerless'[14] to Thomas Münzer's apocalyptic prophecies that helped to stir up the German Peasants' War of 1524-51[5] and John of Batenburg's beliefs that the unconverted ought to be killed, churches should be plundered and polygamy was a good thing[16].

Indeed, the vigour and uncontrolled nature of this movement began to worry Luther. He increasingly had significant doubts about the helpfulness of letting ordinary people read the Bible for themselves, thinking, as Christopher Hill tells us, that 'catechising by ministers was safer than unrestricted Bible-reading'[17]. Yet, this People's Bible was a pre-condition for the growth of Independency from which our Congregational traditions grew[18]. It is still of fundamental importance to us that the Bible is for everyone and everyone should read the Bible. Each time we encourage someone to "Read your Bible!" we are sharing in Luther's first flush of enthusiasm for the Bible as the People's book. "Here", we say, "is truth for *your* life; centre your spirituality on what you read here."

Yet, I would contend that this glorious Reformation idea that the Bible is God's Word for everyone, has somehow smuggled in with it the idea that everyone should be able to interpret it by themselves for themselves. We assume all too easily that each of us can form our own opinions, find a Bible verse to support them and claim that what we say must be true "because it says so in the Bible!" The Bible is not always clear in what it says. Its truths are not always obvious. This assumption is plausible because we want the Bible's message to be clear to each and every individual who reads it, not because that is what is actually there page by page or book by book. As we shall see in Part Two, we need to work on the Bible's meaning together and employ all the inherited wisdom, subtlety, understanding, debate and prayer we can muster if we would rightly apply it to our lives and times.

Luther's Big Idea:
THE BIBLE IS GOD'S WORD FOR EVERYONE TO READ

The hidden assumption often smuggled in with it:
EVERYONE CAN MAKE SENSE OF THE BIBLE FOR THEMSELVES

1.3 Calvin & the unified Word of God

In the generation after Luther, one above all others set himself the task of proving that the Bible Alone, in the right hands, could provide a clear and stable basis for a Godly, sober and civilised society. This was the senior pastor of the small Swiss city of Geneva - John Calvin. For some 28 years between 1536 and 1564 he led Geneva's efforts to be a city run according to Scriptural principles. He seems to have been every bit as wary of the great ferment of unguided Bible study that had spread across Europe as Luther had become in later life. He set out to do something about it and he was very, very thorough. All his efforts were built on the assumption that "Scripture has its authority from God, not from the church"[19], being authenticated to the believer by the inward work of the Holy Spirit. Yet this did not stop him from using his own powers of reason, or, deny him the wealth of insights of the Church Fathers who had commented on Scripture down through the centuries. But Reason and Interpretative Tradition were always to be seen as subsidiary to the self-authenticating Scriptures. The primary means of elucidating any difficult text was always other, clearer Scriptures.

Although he is best remembered for his major work of dogmatic theology, *"Institutes of the Christian Religion"*[20], which he developed and expanded over more than twenty years, between 1536 and 1559, this was only one of the three related phases of his work with Scripture. He also put huge amounts of effort into producing careful commentaries on most of the books of the New Testament and slightly over half of the Old Testament between 1540 and his death in 1564.[21] Also, throughout his pastorate he preached each weekday morning on the Old Testament, each Sunday morning on the New Testament and each Sunday afternoon on the Psalms[22]. Any one of these strands of work (his Commentaries, the '*Institutes*' and his Sermons) would have been remarkable in themselves, but for Calvin it was the integrated effect of all three that seems to have constituted his core strategy for building a Bible-based citizenry.

Gerald Bray[23] argues that Calvin saw correct Scripture Interpretation as requiring three necessary stages, none of which could be omitted without risk of distortion:

> **1st : CAREFUL STUDY OF THE TEXT,** verse by verse and book by book
> *seen in Calvin's writing of careful commentaries on Bible books*
>
> **2nd : ASSEMBLING A COHERENT TOTAL PICTURE OF GOD'S SELF-REVELATION**
> *seen in Calvin's work on 'dogmatics' - "The Institutes of*
> *the Christian Religion"*
>
> **3rd : PREACHING, SO THE MESSAGE COULD CHANGE PEOPLE'S LIVES**
> *seen in Calvin's prodigious number of sermons putting the Bible*
> *to the people*

We might suspect that, in practice, the three stages are in constant 'conversation' as the years go by. In other words, Calvin's developing understanding of 'the total picture' shapes his thinking when he tries to understand a particular book or passage, whilst, at the same time, his in-depth study of particular passages is gradually re-shaping his 'total picture'. Added to that, the process of preaching to the people is constantly putting fresh questions and perceptions in his mind as he returns to work on his Commentaries and the 'Institutes'.

There is something truly magnificent about Calvin's attempt to bring scholarship and reason, system and method, balance and care to full flower in the service of God's Word. I wonder whether Biblical Scholarship, Dogmatic Theology and Pastoral Preaching have ever been as carefully and systematically integrated as they were in this one man, through nearly thirty years of ministry in Geneva? Indeed, his approach has proved so persuasive that he single-handedly brought about the 'Reformed' tradition[24]. The cohesiveness of his account of the faith and the form of Church governance that he claimed to have found in the Scriptures attracted a sincere and persistent following. And yet......

There is a driven quality about this towering intellect; a determination that the truth of God is clear and unified and that the Scriptures will yield up a cohesive 'Reformed' message because Calvin will not be denied. Writing of Calvin as a religious and community leader in Geneva, Owen Chadwick says this:

> .....he pursued with a single mind what he believed to be the truth; he extorted that reluctant admiration and discipleship which is given to consistency, to courage and to decisiveness. He always spoke and wrote with a magisterial force, knew what he wanted and where he was going, was devoid of pomp or cant or sentimentality. He impressed Geneva with the stamp of his mind.
>
> *Owen Chadwick. "The Reformation". Penguin Books. Harmondsworth. 1964. p.91*

I would suggest that the heroic stamp of his mind was most clearly seen in his work with the Bible. Even in his commentaries he 'knew what he wanted and where he was going'. Apparent discrepancies and disagreements between the Gospel writers are swiftly explained away and a unified, coherent Gospel according to Calvin is persuasively produced.[25] Indeed, Calvin is in full agreement with his bitter opponent Cardinal Sadolet when he says that Truth is always "bright and clear" and that "Truth is always one, while falsehood is varied and multiform"[26] Perhaps the very extent of the threat of division and dissent which the Bible in the hands of the people seemed to have unleashed, helped to create in men like Calvin and Sadolet a determination that God's truth must be clear and evident to their determined intellect (even if they disagreed totally on what that truth might be). Perhaps the fear of social disintegration and anarchy that might so easily follow on the heels of all this disagreement left them little choice but to seek and find clarity of doctrinal and moral guidance in the Scriptures - a clarity that to other minds in other times is not evidently there at all.

To an extent that he would probably have found hard to accept, Calvin's whole edifice of Biblical scholarship was shaped and infused with his own culture and character; infected by the fears and concerns that pressed in on him in Geneva; layered with the shared assumptions of his day and age. Here, rather than in the nature of the Scriptures themselves, can we find the origins of Calvin's urge to try to tame Scripture into tidy, timeless, obvious truth.

Along with his awesome thoroughness as a scholar of the Bible, his singular success in writing persuasively systematic theology and his persistent pertinent preaching, Calvin has infiltrated an assumption. He seems to assume all too readily that Scripture must have the sort of innate coherence we would expect of the work of a single author. In the 'Institutes' he talks of all Scripture being from God - the earthly writers are but God's 'secretaries' (each had their own style and message which a commentator could seek to understand, but they were, in every respect, faithful to the very mind of God)[27].

I think we need to be wary of that assumption. Even now, we can easily presume a coherence in Scripture (particularly when we are looking for 'doctrine' or ethical guidance) that is only there because we impose it, distorting the messages of the various books as we go along. This assumption is, if anything, more pervasively attractive within the Reformed tradition than the assumption that we can all mine the Scriptures on our own and always find truth. Somehow, we seem to have a deep need for 'closure', for some sort of parental figure who gives us a clear ruling on what the truth of the matter must be. Indeed, when Reformed Christians take issue with Calvinism, they delight to do so by claiming that the Calvinists have betrayed the insights of Calvin and that they themselves are being faithful to the master and his magisterial, all-embracing theology.

Calvin's Big Idea:
BIBLE STUDY, THEOLOGY & PREACHING CAN WORK IN HARMONY

The hidden assumption often smuggled in with it:
THE BIBLE FITS NEATLY INTO A UNIFIED, COHERENT THEOLOGY

1.4   1646 - old friends on English soil

Let's move on a whole century and turn our attention to England. Here we find an intriguing mix of the same issues are now at the heart of an intense struggle between different strands of the developing English-speaking Reformed tradition.   Indeed, in 1646 we find a revealing moment, in the midst of the English Civil Wars, when ancestral 'Presbyterianism' and early 'Congregationalism' briefly vied for control of England. Here the same strengths and dangers in the way the Bible was viewed that we found in the times of Luther and Calvin are just as evident.

In 1646 King Charles is all but militarily defeated. A parliament sitting in London, with a moderate 'Presbyterian' majority, is living in uneasy co-existence with its victorious army, in whose ranks are many Bible-carrying Independents who see Presbyterianism as but another potential imposition on their God-given freedoms.[28]

I.   THE 'PRESBYTERIANS' GATHERED IN ASSEMBLY...

In Westminster, the Assembly set up by Parliament in 1643 to reform the English Church and bring uniformity of religion between England and Scotland (to win Scottish political and military support in the struggle against the king) is still sitting. Its 121 divines, ten peers, twenty members of the House of Commons and some very influential Scottish 'commissioners' or advisers, have already produced a 'Directory of Worship' to replace the Prayer Book, the Larger and Shorter Catechisms and proposals for a Presbyterian form of church governance for the English national Church.[29] The Assembly, with its built-in 'Presbyterian' majority, has now turned its attention to producing a Confession of Faith. After its publication the following year (1647), it will come to be known as "The Westminster Confession". It will be widely influential, probably the most influential Confession in the history of English-speaking Reformed churches.

David Cornick describes the confession as a 'stringently Calvinist' account of the Christian faith[30], that lays out more succinctly than Calvin's *Institutes* what is deemed to be the faith of the Bible. Intriguingly, parliament sends it back to have scriptural proof-texts (footnotes giving Bible references for each point) added[31]. Some of these footnotes refer to texts whose relationship to the point being made in the Confession is hard to determine. Working in the tradition of Calvinist systematising and scholarship, the text of the Confession is anxious to clarify, even control, the correct interpretation of the Bible. The Assembly seems to be driven by fear of the very variety of interpretations that are currently being put on the Bible's meaning by unlearned Bible readers. As John M Ross wrote, revealingly, in 1982, whilst explaining the Presbyterians' persisting interest in retaining the Westminster Confession as a 'Subordinate Standard' of the faith alongside the Bible as 'Supreme Standard' - from a Presbyterian perspective:

> The Bible contains such [a] variety of attitudes and implications that it can be used in support of almost any doctrine.
>
> John M. Ross, 'The Westminster Confession in the
> Presbyterian Church of England, in A. I. C. Heron (ed.) p.89

Here, once again, is Calvin's systematising, caution and care (albeit with a bit more systematising). Here, also, is this too-easy assumption that the Bible can be shaped by Reformed men of learning into something as neat, orderly, definitive and "one-voiced" as this Confession without significant distortion happening in the process. Again, we can sense that the 'Presbyterian' party need a clear authority for their sort of order that will allow them to resist the King without surrendering to the competing interpretations out there among the Independents and unlearned street preachers. They are looking for a king-free basis for political stability that gives due place to learning and a central role to gentlefolk. But, on what basis can they tell that their interpretative scheme is superior to any other? Is it likely to be superior when its very learned neatness might be forcing significant distortion onto what is there in the text of the Bible?

2.   THE INDEPENDENTS ON THE MARCH...

Even as this assembly of educated scholars, with the backing of the educated gentlemen of Parliament are trying to settle things with due order, events are sweeping past them. The mass of their victorious army is not made up of gentlemen or 'Presbyterians'. It is, in the main, an army of Bible-believing Independents, for whom the Bible is the source of their hope for freedom and justice. And it is this army that will determine the political and religious shape of the next dozen years, not the 'Presbyterian' majority in parliament, nor the soon-to-be-executed king.

Out here, in the army of Fairfax and Cromwell in 1646, and in the wider world of Independency, the Bible operates differently. It has all of the freshness and presumed accessibility of the Bible of Luther's early days as a reformer or the Bible of the German, Swiss and Dutch Anabaptists in Calvin's time. Here, where anyone may be a Bible interpreter, there is a fine ferment of ideas - spiritual, political and spiritually-political. Out here the Bible is the friend of ordinary, literate but unlearned people. Christopher Hills tells how, in the 1640s:

> ...uneducated men and women read back into the Bible themselves and their problems, and the problems of their communities, and found Biblical answers there, which they could discuss with others who shared the same problems.
>
> Christopher Hill, 'The English Bible and the Seventeenth
> Century Revolution' (Penguin, Harmondsworth, 1994) p199

In addition, the collapse of censorship has allowed anyone with anything to say to coax a printer into printing it if they can persuade them that it might sell and make a profit. By 1646 England is awash with pamphlets addressing every aspect of life and politics based on a cornucopia of Bible texts and stories all interpreted in a rich and ingenious variety of fashions.

As with the earlier European Anabaptists, the celebration of the availability of God's Word to everyone has brought with it the too-easy assumption (even the certainty) that everyone, under God's Spirit, can find the true spiritual meaning of any Bible passage. Christopher Hill tells of wide respect amongst uneducated preachers for Cobbler How's sermon published in 1640 on *'The Sufficiency of the Spirit's Teaching without Humane Learning'*.[32] How's central point is that 'unlearned persons' are preferable to scholars in the pulpit, since the Spirit's teaching is all that matters for understanding 'the mind of God'. Indeed, everyone should read the Bible and decide for themselves what it means.

Clearly, at times, the very social position of unlearned preachers can lend special insight as to what the Bible is saying. When Radicals in Chelmsford are said to think that the relation of master and servant had no grounds in Scripture and that they find no basis in nature or Scripture why one man should have £1,000 a year and another £1, we might be inclined to think their case should at least be heard.[33] Yet we equally cannot assume that they will always and everywhere find the 'truth' of every Scripture. They must not be ignored or sidelined, yet they must not be presumed correct in all that they say. These readings are as infused with the situation and expectations of the readers as any reading done in the Abbey at Westminster by the august members of the Assembly of learned divines and lesser gentry.

Even before the complexities of the modern age have emerged, Luther, Calvin and these competing worlds of English 'Presbyterians' and 'Congregationalists' in 1646 have clearly demonstrated that we all bring acknowledged and unacknowledged expectations when we come to the Scriptures - expectations that may too easily affect what we are able to find in the Word; expectations that restrict what we can hear of the voice of God. So far, we have found that neither of the two main Reformation approaches to mining the truth of God's Word is guaranteed success. Neither allowing everyone to read the Scriptures and decide for themselves nor keeping Bible interpretation as a task for careful scholars would seem to ensure definitive access to God's truth. There must be more than either of these approaches involved in rightly handling the Word of Truth. We'll need to take care!

But first, we'll need to look at the rise of the modern world. For, developments from the 18th to the 20th Centuries fractured the different parts of Calvin's three-fold method. Bible scholars, theologians and Church interpreters set off in different directions leaving the ordinary reader not a little bemused. Did this 'modernity' simply create division and diversion... or did we somehow learn other important things about the Bible and how we might understand God's Word today?...

CHAPTER TWO

CRITICISM AND REACTION

2.1 The rise of the Modern World

Opinions vary as to when 'The Modern World' began. The French Philosopher and literary critic, Michel Foucault, dates 'The Modern Age' from the end of the 18th Century.[34] Richard Middleton and Brian Walsh, on the other hand, find a significant starting point for the Modern World in Columbus' famous voyage to Cathay in 1492, on which he accidentally "discovered" the already-inhabited Americas instead.[35] We will roughly 'split the difference' by looking at a pamphlet with a whole range of ideas that came to be central to the Modern World that was published in 1660.

To resolve the political crisis caused by the death of Cromwell, Charles Stuart, the son of the executed King, has been invited to return from exile and be crowned Charles II. But, what will this mean for religion in England? At this moment of uncertainty, Robert Boyle, the renowned chemist (remember 'Boyle's Law'?), discusses his concerns for the future with his friend Peter Pett. They agree Pett will write a pamphlet outlining the advantages of a religious settlement that relies not on "retaliation" but on "liberty of conscience". As J R Jacob tells it[36], their concerns are rooted in an intriguing circle of interlocking ideas and a confident sense that their ideas will work:

+ the Reformation is best served by the success of ENGLAND at home and overseas

+ success is most likely in an atmosphere of religious TOLERATION (within limits)

+ toleration will BALANCE THE POWER of king, bishops and clergy in the church

+ such a balance will best preserve the FREEDOMS of gentry, clergy and merchants

+ freedom of gentry, clergy and merchants will best serve their SELF-INTEREST

+ the self-interest of gentry, clergy and merchants IS the national interest

+ the self-interest of gentry, clergy and merchants is best served by TRADE

+ trade is stimulated both by SCIENCE and by the development of COLONIES

+ colonies can be used as a base to CIVILISE and CONVERT unbelievers

+ ALL of THIS is driven by human SELF-INTEREST channelled through WORK

+ by these means there will be steady PROGRESS towards God's Kingdom

The concerns of Robert Boyle and Peter Pett as explained by J R Jacob (see note 37)

Here, in embryo, is an account of most of the central concerns of the 'modern' world, yet still, for now, rooted in a strong post-Reformation Biblical faith. Here is a vision of human progress built on self-interest, trade, colonisation, imperial civilisation, missionary work and science. Acquisitiveness and curiosity are to be unleashed so as to bring in a richly-material version of the Kingdom of God with a fierce inevitability. All this is seen as an urgently necessary bulwark against the perceived twin threats to the freedom of progressive gentlemen of science and their allies in trade and commerce:

+ **ANARCHY caused by religious sectarianism running unchecked among artisans**

+ **AUTHORITY re-imposed by re-installed Catholicism or the divine right of kings.**

It didn't work out exactly as Boyle and Pett predicted. Religious toleration did not begin to arrive in England until William and Mary's 'revolution' in 1689. Boyle's beloved science was not immediately fruitful in supporting trade; but its lowly cousin technology proved more than adequate until developments in science began to have major effects on trade and capitalism in the early 19th Century. Again, this list of ideas is innocent of all the violence, coercion and cruelty that such a route to 'progress' did, in practice, require, both from self-interested individuals and from the state apparatus.

Yet, here is an expectation of progress in knowledge, well-being and civilisation, that will flow naturally from the development and propagation of the ideas, the values and the faith of the English gentry and merchant classes. Even though this privileged group is a tiny minority of the world's population, their idea of progress is seen to be progress with a capital letter, Progress as an absolute; their idea of Progress is presumed to be appropriate for everyone, whoever they are, whatever their circumstances. Moreover, it is carried along on an unquestioned confidence that the world is just waiting to be known, and the process of discovery is simple, clear and straightforward... It seems to say 'I bring no baggage'; 'I have no hidden agenda'; 'I have a scientific mind'.

Intriguingly, the world view that shaped my own primary school education in Glasgow three hundred years later was substantially that of Boyle and Pett. Certainly, there had been some changes - the voters' franchise had been extended to the entire adult population; the state had become largely secular; missionary endeavour was only discussed in church; we now talked of colonies becoming 'independent' because we had successfully 'civilised' them; science had by this time delivered technologies, industries and urbanisation way beyond Boyle's possible imaginings. And yet, at root, my primary school teachers would have been intellectually 'at home' in the company of Boyle and Pett even if they would have insisted in taking along supplies of pungent carbolic soap and strong Education Department toilet paper and made certain that they boiled the water.

None of the intervening years, no pogroms or holocausts, not the slave trade, nor the Great Depression, nor the invention of trench warfare or the atom bomb, no Atheism, no Rationalism, no Romanticism, no Marxism, no Socialism, no alternative world views... none of the pain and injustice of the real world, had seriously shaken this 'modern' faith in our human ability endlessly to engineer our own progress. Such was the seductive attraction of the unquestioned assumptions of "The Modern World" that my primary school teachers still dutifully & vigorously put before eager young minds in Glasgow in the 1960s.

So what happened to the Bible in the 300 years of this 'modern world' between Boyle's conversations with Pett in 1660 and my primary education in Glasgow around 1960?

2.2 "Assured results" of Higher Criticism

Not that long after Pett's pamphlet, in 1687, the mechanical 'Laws' of Isaac Newton, another English scientist, successfully explained the motion of absolutely everything[37] (or so it seemed). Now, the confidence of this new world in its powers of objective reason, cried out for application to every area of study, including the Bible. The earliest, strenuously-resisted, attempts appear to have been made in England in the first half of the 18th Century by authors such as John Toland and Anthony Collins, who were to become known as the English Deists.[38] But it was the Protestant universities of Germany in the 19th Century that became the home of sustained and serious attempts to study the Bible with the critical confidence of the modern world - developing what Albert Schweitzer called "the science of historical theology".[39]

In Germany and German-speaking Switzerland, there were twenty-one universities which all had multiple posts for professional Bible scholars[40]. In a unique way, this allowed the development of approaches to the study of the Bible that were focussed on being academically respectable rather than spiritually helpful. The Bible was to be given no privileged position; it was to be studied as would any other ancient text, as history, by scientific Bible historians. Gerald Bray puts it like this:

> Textual anomalies which had been ignored or explained away by earlier generations now became essential clues in the attempts to reconstruct the historical evolution of both the written text of Scripture and the religion which it proclaimed.
>
> G. Bray, "Biblical Interpretation Past and Present" (IVP, Leicester, 1996) p.222

For example, in 1845 **Ferdinand Christian Baur** argued that only four of Paul's Epistles in the New Testament (*Romans, I & II Corinthians and Galatians*) were written by Paul himself, also that the Book of Acts was quite untrustworthy as a source for historical reconstruction of the New Testament Church[41]. He had earlier elaborated a theory of early church history from I Corinthians which argued that there had been an enormous, lengthy dispute between Jewish and Gentile Christians in the New Testament Church; this was not entirely evident in Acts[42].

Again, in 1878 Julius Wellhausen published an account of the first six books of the Old Testament (*Genesis to Joshua*) that proposed that they had been constructed by the complex interweaving of four distinct source documents (which he labelled J, E, D & P). He was preparing to write an evolutionary account of the development of Israelite religion.[43] Other German professors challenged the proposals of both Baur and Wellhausen. Baur's ideas did not survive the challenges unscathed, but by 1900 Wellhausen's theory had become one of the "assured results" of the Higher Criticism.

I suspect that, even today, reports of this sort of 'critical' work on the Bible leave the average Christian believer with two main feelings:

- **A sense of slight BEMUSEMENT...**
  "Where is all this going & how can it possibly help?"

- **A growing, hard-to-articulate FEAR...**
  "Are these people trying to destroy the basis of my faith?"

Yet, as with Luther and Calvin, I would argue that we have here a hugely important idea, with an unfortunate smuggled assumption hidden with it. Let me explain...

If we truly believe that the Bible is God's Word for us and our Church's one true "Authority"[44], we need to be sure of what we have. As John Barton puts it:

> The idea of reading the Bible critically is not derived from an interest in history... it is linked with the Reformation insistence on the authority of the Bible, read freely, over the Church. Christian believers, according to Reformation principles, have the right to ask whether the Bible really means what the Church says it means.
>
> *John Barton, "Historical Critical Approaches" in "The Cambridge Companion to Biblical Interpretation" p16* [45]

Someone has to be out there trying to see what the Bible is actually like. What sort of text has God actually given us to be our Scriptures? How might it have been constructed? How might its human authors have been understood in their own day and age, and is that important? How might the Bible have come to have the shape it now has? Does the Bible speak with one voice or many? How serious are apparent disagreements between different bits of the Bible? Do we understand how God can speak to us from this sort of book?

The Bible needs our 'heads' as well as our 'hearts'. Scripture, to be Scripture, needs to be approached with a constant stream of probing, uncomfortable questions as well as reverence and respect. Without the uncomfortable questions, we will only hear God speak in the ways we want to hear God. If the Church insists on silencing the uncomfortable questions, it will acquire a muffling authority over Scripture, rather than be constantly called to listen afresh to what we have from God.

Certainly, some of the ideas put forward by critical scholars are wrong, others clearly ridiculous, yet others downright obscure, but historical criticism has already helped us to get a clearer idea of what the Bible is actually like:

- **TEXTUAL CRITICISM** has meant that we have a much more accurate agreed TEXT of the Greek New Testament than was true before, and some improvements in the accuracy of the Hebrew text of the Old Testament.

- **ARCHAEOLOGY** means we have a much clearer idea of the sorts of lives people lived all over the ancient Near East and the cultures that came and went as well as important documents and records of contemporaneous cultures and religions.

- **LANGUAGE STUDIES** of 'popular' Greek, and of Hebrew and related Semitic languages (some only recovered by archaeology) mean we have a much clearer idea what words in the Bible may (or may not) mean and how the Bible languages work.

- **SOURCE CRITICISM** (which tries to reconstruct the possible pre-history of the books in the Bible) means we have a clearer idea of how the material in the Bible may have been assembled, including the relationship between the four Gospels.

- **FORM CRITICISM** (which thinks about how and why particular sorts of stories and sayings might have been used and memorised) means we have a greater sense of the purpose and quality of oral transmission of stories and other items that ended up in written form in the Old Testament and in the Gospels.

- **REDACTION CRITICISM** (which looks at how assemblers and editors handled the materials they inherited and what they were trying to say) means we have much greater respect for those who assembled Biblical books from earlier material (written or oral) - both for their sensitivity to their material and for their own theological and social vision. For example, we now see more clearly the distinct perspectives on the Jesus story of Matthew, Mark, Luke and John.

- **ALTOGETHER** we have a much better grasp of what our Scriptures are actually like (and how, therefore, God may and may not have chosen to speak to us), than was possible in 1660.

The BIG idea is that, when we approach the Bible, we need to look as carefully and as critically as we can at what is there. We cannot simply assume that the Church already knows exactly what it's got. After all, it was this very idea of looking carefully at what is there in the Bible that set Martin Luther wrestling with Romans, in defiance of what the Church told him he would find. It was the same idea that fuelled Calvin through 28 years of exacting Bible studies.

Yet, as with Luther and Calvin, I think we have here some smuggled baggage that needs to be declared. The practitioners of the new historical critical method believed themselves to be objective historical scholars standing unencumbered before the text. In refusing to be restricted by Church Dogma when they came to the Bible, they thought they were free of all dogma. In fact, they had, by and large, imbibed all the prejudices and assumptions of the modern world. They saw their world as inherently superior to all previous tradition-burdened worlds. They saw history as a single progressing story leading by developmental stages towards their own enlightened, rational world. They could not see the distortion that imposing such an assumption might bring. Walter Brueggemann talks of how this "thin objectivism", when applied to the Old Testament led scholars to "distort or deny the most defining characteristics of the text itself"[46] Indeed, even Wellhausen's "assured" results may have been driven by a need to shape and tell a developmental story. Walter Brueggemann again:

> The Wellhausian synthesis that has governed Old Testament scholarship reflects the spirit of the age. In that synthesis, it was possible for scholars to agree upon early (J & E), middle (D) and late (P) documents, which in turn reflected Israel's religion: early-primitive, ethical monotheism, and "degenerate legalism."
>
> *Walter Brueggemann, "Theology of the Old Testament". p.12f*

In other words, Wellhausen and his colleagues saw what they wanted to see, but seem to have believed it to be pure, objective, historical truth.

Similarly, in the study of the New Testament, a succession of scholars seemed to have seen only what they wanted to see. Albert Schweitzer's classic (1906) account of various 19th Century attempts to 'recover' or 'reconstruct' the life story of Jesus (published in English in 1910 as "*The Quest of the Historical Jesus*") concludes:

> The historical investigation of the life of Jesus did not take its rise from a purely historical interest; it turned to the Jesus of history as an ally in the struggle against the tyranny of dogma. ... Thus each successive epoch of theology found its own thoughts in Jesus... [and] ...each individual created Him in accordance with his own character.
>
> *Albert Schweitzer. "The Quest of the Historical Jesus"*
> *(Eng. trans. A & C Black. London. 1910) p4*

In the process, much of the vitality of the Gospel text is excised. With vivid imagery, Schweitzer tells how, when the scholars have selected the bits of the Gospels they want to include in their own 'life of Jesus', "Many of the greatest sayings [of Jesus] are found lying in a corner like explosive shells from which the charges have been removed." [47]

Some of the bemusement and fear so often aroused in Christian believers by this sort of critical scholarship is a necessary unsettling of old certainties induced by valid critical questioning. Yet, we may suspect that much of it is an entirely legitimate fear that something dangerous and unacknowledged is going on.

The same danger of smuggling-in assumptions and fixed ideas whilst proclaiming that we have an open mind as we approach the Bible is real for all of us. We all have 'beams' in our eyes that we like to think are not there, even as we fuss over the specks we see in the eyes of others (Matthew 7:1-5). That is one of the mighty reasons why we must not only read the Bible for ourselves and in the company of like-minded people. We all need folk whose assumptions are so different from ours that meeting them over the Bible highlights both their smuggling and ours. "Oh dear, did I really have *that* in my bag?"

The Big Idea of Critical Scholarship:
CRITICAL QUESTIONS HELP US SEE WHAT GOD HAS GIVEN US

The hidden assumption often smuggled in with it:
SCHOLARS CAN BE OBJECTIVE AND FREE FROM ALL DOGMA

2.3 Warfield and the Evangelical Reaction

Although the German critical scholarship gradually spread through the universities and colleges of Britain and North America towards the end of the 19th Century, the churches reacted badly to it. For example, John Campbell, the late 19th Century editor of two popular magazines for Congregationalists in England and Wales, felt it necessary to reassure his tender Christian readers that they 'need fear nothing from Germany'. He assured them that, as their careful editor, he had 'burned... reams of a speculative nature.' [48] Elsewhere, professors were dislodged from their posts because of church disquiet with these methods. In the United States the Presbyterians, after a long and complicated process, revoked the ordination of Charles Briggs of Union Seminary in New York in 1893 for suggesting that: Scripture contains error, Moses did not write the Pentateuch and Isaiah wrote only half of the work attributed to him [49]. In Scotland, the General Assembly of the Free Church of Scotland (also Presbyterian) had earlier removed William Robertson Smith from a professorship at its Aberdeen college (in 1881) because of the content of his article on "Bible" in the 1876 edition of the Encyclopaedia Britannica. [50] Indeed, even Julius Wellhausen himself, the doyen of German critical scholarship on the Old Testament, was persuaded to resign from his professorship at Greifswald in 1882 by the force of church objections to his views on the pre-history of the Pentateuch (J, E, D & P), which he had published some four years earlier. [51]

In the face of such widespread church disquiet with the new methods coming over from Germany, another American Presbyterian, Benjamin B. Warfield of Princeton Seminary, began to construct a reasoned defence of the Inspiration of Scripture. He published a series of articles between 1880 and his death in 1921 that have been acknowledged by evangelicals and by their critics as the classical statement of the 20th Century evangelical doctrine of 'Biblical Inerrancy'.[52]

As with Luther, Calvin and the German Critics themselves, I would argue that Warfield has grasped something of central importance, but smuggled in a damaging assumption along with it.

I have already spoken of the mixture of bemusement and fear that I suspect are still widespread today when believing Christians hear that their Bible is being cut and pasted for what seems to be no obvious reason. By extrapolation, I can sense the late 19th Century outrage as persistent rumours of strange theories in Germany start to be echoed by disturbing accounts of professors saying similar things in our own theological colleges and seminaries. How do you respond to these people who claim they are being objective and rational, serious and scientific? What's to be done, especially if you suspect that they are not as objective as they say; that they must have some hidden purpose for what they are saying? Why, they can only be out to undermine our belief that the Bible is the Word of God!

Warfield determines to defend that central, apparently-threatened, idea… that idea without which none of the rest of this makes any sense. Either we are looking to the Bible to offer us THE WORD OF GOD, or we can all walk away and leave Christianity and the scholarly study of the Bible as a waste of everyone's precious time. Either we have come to meet God here, or why are any of us hanging around? For me, Warfield's BIG idea is that we must never lose sight of why we go to the Bible - first and foremost, we are longing to hear the voice of God speak to us from this book.

But as he prepares to defend that which is the *sine qua non* of Christianity, I reckon that Warfield is smuggling in a huge hidden assumption. As he builds a defensive wall to keep out these anarchic and apparently Godless ideas, he buries an enormous pre-supposition in the foundations. He assumes that he knows, in advance, what a Word from God has to be like. Steeped in the scholasticised Calvinism of François Turretin and the 'common sense' philosophy of the Scottish Enlightenment that had shaped Princeton theology for generations[53], he is looking for God's Special Revelation (i.e. the Bible) to be as objectively knowable to him as God's General Revelation (i.e. the Natural World) was then presumed to be.

> By all means let the doctrine of the Bible be tested by the facts and let the test be made all the more, not the less, stringent and penetrating because of the great issues that hang on it. If the facts are inconsistent with the doctrine, let us all know it, and know it so clearly that the matter is put beyond doubt.
>
> *Benjamin B. Warfield, "The Real Problem of Inspiration"* [54]

In other words, Warfield argues that the Bible has to be 'true', and testably so, in every particular. It has, *a priori*, to be 'inerrant'[55], and the rules against which it is to be tested are the truth standards and methods of the natural sciences. My problem is not that this seems to leave Warfield with the Bible standing or falling on one proven factual error[56]. Nor is my problem simply that I cannot follow Warfield into his apparent confidence in the scientific method.[57] My problem is that Warfield has decided in advance what ways and according to which ground rules God is to be allowed to reveal himself to us[58]; God, according to Warfield, is giving us "doctrine" and "law".

Gerald Bray quotes Warfield explaining his concept of scriptural authority in these terms: "The Scriptures are simply the law-code which the law-givers of the Church gave it".[59] To adapt Walter Brueggemann's telling phrase about Warfield's German opponents[60], I struggle with the "thin" legalism that this idea of Scripture seems to imply. Even when I turn to Matthew's Gospel, where we are arguably invited to hear Jesus, like a second Moses on the mountain, giving us a New Law (*Matthew 5-7, "The Sermon on the Mount"*), Jesus gives us something much more richly-textured and dramatic than a "law-code". Even here in the most 'Law-like' part of the most legally-aware gospel, Jesus uses irony, rhetoric, and a whole range of other subtle and creative verbal skills and strategies (that would never make it into an act of parliament) to turn 'law' into challenge; safe statute into the danger of God speaking directly to me; dead letter into living Gospel. I fear that, in his efforts to protect the Scriptures from the dangers of Wellhausen, Warfield may have closed himself off from something of the danger of God too.

Indeed, I don't think Benjamin Warfield, or I, or anyone can predict what the Word of God has to be like or define in advance how God may or may not choose to speak to us in the Bible. Do we not have to allow that God may speak with subtlety and surprise, opening ourselves to the possibility of depth and richness, of conundrum and challenge, paradox and passion, even playfulness, in what God may choose to say? I think we have to keep on encountering the Word of God to find out how God chooses to speak to us. Surely God must be allowed to surprise even those of us schooled in a precise, carefully-organised Scottish Presbyterian tradition? For, even within the Biblical narratives themselves, there are plenty examples of people being surprised by God (e.g. Moses, Elijah and Paul).

I suspect Warfield's core problem is that he is every bit as immersed in Enlightenment assumptions as the movement he seeks to oppose. He has as much, perhaps even more, confidence that he has straightforward access to objective truth and that he brings no distorting pre-suppositions with him. He is as committed to the logical and linguistic simplicity of hearing God speak as his Princeton predecessor Charles Hodge who said:

> The Bible is the word of God. That is to be assumed or proved. If granted; then it follows that what the Bible says, God says. That ends the matter.
>
> *Charles Hodge, cited by A. A. Hodge, "The Life of Charles Hodge" (New York, 1880)* [61]

Thus, in trying to defend us from the ravages of this dangerously 'modern' scholarship he has stood his ground in a place that is every bit as dangerously 'modern'. God is as worryingly trapped within the neat, exacting, imposed system of the Princeton theologians as he ever was traduced and abused by the worst high-handedness of 19th Century critical scholarship. The Bible is as much denied the right to speak challengingly and freshly with the unnerving voice of God by Warfield's protective glass case and stern museum security as it ever was by the eager dismembering of its pages by the trendy wide boys of German critical scholarship.

The same danger of suffocating the very thing we are trying to preserve is a real risk for all of us. God cannot be preserved and allowed to be alive. Attempts to keep-the-Bible-safe only end up making the Bible itself "safe" and unthreatening and leave us sitting around faithfully like museum staff waiting for nothing to happen. Yet God (if the Bible is to be believed) is never safe and has a habit of breaking out to be dangerous. The prophet Jeremiah asserts that it was God who was behind the destruction of the holy temple of Jerusalem and the exiling of God's people to Babylon; the apostle Paul proclaims that the desperate death of Jesus on a savagely cruel cross is the central act of God's saving purposes. In both cases, those who thought they knew what God was about were deeply scandalised by these events and their interpretation as God's deliberate purpose. Yet, I would argue, these acts get closer to defining the nature and purpose of God than almost anything else in the Scriptures. The God of the Bible refuses to be contained by our ideas of what is right.

However much we would wish it, there does not seem to be a way of eliminating risk in our dealings with God without 'quenching the Spirit' or inventing our own idol.

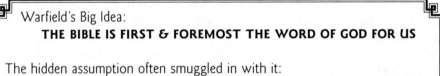

Warfield's Big Idea:
THE BIBLE IS FIRST & FOREMOST THE WORD OF GOD FOR US

The hidden assumption often smuggled in with it:
GOD'S WORD IS OBVIOUS, NEAT DOCTRINAL PROPOSITIONS

2.4 A century of impasse?

The painful, distrustful stand-off between academic study of the Bible and 'Bible-believing Christians' that Wellhausen and Warfield helped to establish and entrench, has had an enormous impact on the way the Bible has been handled in the churches through most of the 20th Century.

Even where trained ministers had been persuaded in college of the value of the critical methods, often and often they would be wary of how much of that way of seeing they should dare to expose to their congregations as they preached Sunday by Sunday. On the other hand sincere believers would sometimes get desperate with the dry, distrustful accounts of gospel story that they heard from the pulpit. Other times theological college lecturers would sigh at the prospect of a fresh intake of eager students with whom, yet again, they would have to battle for some sort of 'conversion' if these students were to accept a scholarly view of the Bible as part of their understanding.

Sometimes churches or denominations would split over a particular issue, when the underlying mutual distrust about these two competing ways of seeing the Bible may have been the true cause of disagreement. Indeed, a persistent 'evangelical' versus 'liberal' tension has affected, in one way or another, just about every denomination in the Western world through much of the 20th Century. For many Christians the 'Liberal' or 'Evangelical' label seems to come closer to defining who they are than their own particular denomination.

Yet, by 1980, when I went to train for the ministry in Aberdeen, I was schooled in the historical critical method by a respected evangelical New Testament scholar, Howard Marshall, who had a whole clutch of Evangelical research students happily applying historical critical method to the Bible in defence of interpretations that were acceptably conservative and evangelical. The oil and the water had started to mix.

Intriguingly, Gerald Bray, in his 1996 book on the history of Biblical interpretation for Inter-Varsity Press, a conservative evangelical publishing house[62], indicates that in recent years evangelical biblical scholars have been getting a little restive with the full panoply of inerrancy theory.[63] It is the systematic theologians that continue to argue for its importance, not those who are working closely with the actual text of the Bible. And from the other side, newer critical methods such as redaction criticism (which looks at the theological slant of author/compilers of bible books) narrative criticism (which seeks to highlight the author's main interests in telling their story), rhetorical criticism (which looks at the techniques an author uses to make their telling effective) and sociological criticism (which asks an exciting new range of questions about the social setting of letters and gospels, and how they might relate to what was said)[64] seem a lot more attractive and relevant to believers seeking understanding than "J, E, D & P". In important ways we seem to be coming closer together around the

Bible - not necessarily agreeing, but able to take each other's stances and interpretations seriously - even though the divisions may have got seriously arthritic and hard to shift in the churches themselves.

Indeed, as the 20th century turns into the 21st and the 'Modern' world seems to be in the process of being replaced with the still ill-defined and unsettling 'Postmodern' world, there may be a special opportunity for new and exciting interaction with one another and with God as we try to approach the Scriptures together.

See what you think, as we look at how we approach the Bible TODAY, in PART TWO, but first we need to review where we have reached at the end of PART ONE.

2.5 Lessons from History?

With considerable boldness and not a little cheek, we have re-told, in a very particular way, the story of how the Bible has been handled since the Reformation. We have found something to celebrate in the way the precursors of both Presbyterianism and Congregationalism have handled the Bible and, in both cases, important assumptions of which we should be wary. Again, we have rejoiced at the insights on how to handle the Bible of the antecedents of both the liberal and evangelical 'wings' of the church, as well as noting assumptions in each case (rooted in the Modern world view) that bring significant dangers with them.

The balance of joy and warning we found in each story is not accidental. One of the possible 'Lessons from History' that I would put to you is that we all have assumptions that we knowingly or unknowingly smuggle in along with whatever creative insights we bring (and that *clearly* includes me, even whilst I am writing this book, so be careful!). Perhaps we need a way of approaching the Bible that allows us to bring all our baggage with us and is happy for us all to help each other unpack it - the sort of approach that some scholars have suggested as an alternative to the uncomfortable assumptions that held sway all throughout the time of the 'Modern World'.

This, for me, is a particularly important concern at this point when the 'Modern World' is being radically questioned and the alternatives that some call 'Postmodern' are still so vague and so various. We are at a point as dangerously rich with diverse possibilities as Reformation Germany or England in 1646. The difference this time is that most people are not directly interested in what *we* do with the Bible and, indeed, many of the ideas in circulation can take on a profoundly anti-Bible slant. That, for me, means that how the church responds now is even more important. What will *we* do with the Bible now?

So, with the memories of these past crisis moments in the history of the Bible still fresh (whether or not you agree with my particular interpretations of them), let us press on. Let us look carefully at what the world is like today and how, in a world like this, we may best approach the Bible to meet with God and find how God would have us live. Part Two, which follows, will look at Encountering the Bible Today.

Chapter Three will look briefly at the 'fall' of the Modern World and some of the 'Postmodern' ideas that seem to be replacing it before considering recent crucial work on 'hermeneutics' (how we find 'meaning' in texts when we read them). This 'hermeneutical' work is at once a major factor in the current sea change in how reality itself is viewed and directly relevant to the question of how we approach the Bible (which is, after all, a great big complex 'text'). Indeed, as we look at each of the new ideas about how we read texts we'll stop to think about how they impinge directly on Bible reading. After that, **Chapter Four** looks at the Bible itself in the light of the history we have reviewed and the new developments in our own exciting and challenging times.

BEING BIBLICAL

PART TWO

ENCOUNTERING THE BIBLE TODAY

CHAPTER THREE

READING & MAKING SENSE TODAY

3.1 The Fall of the Modern World

As the 20th Century drew to a close, there were hugely-significant changes to long-accepted ideas about the nature of knowledge. In particular, the glorious certainty about science, truth and progress that my enthusiastic 1960s primary school teachers seemed to have in common with the 1660 pamphleteers Robert Boyle and Peter Pett[65], is getting more than a little tattered after 300 years. The Modern World and its assumptions are being deeply questioned and, like Belshazzar at his triumphant feast, found wanting[66].

Whilst both science and technology continue to be significantly productive in a wide variety of fields, the idea of science-led human progress has been severely battered by the history of the 20th Century.[67] From the Great European War of 1914-1919 with its stalemated trenches of death, through Nazi racial 'science' and the holocaust it engendered, and the application of the new physics to the production of nuclear bombs and warheads, to a world threatened by technologically-induced ecological catastrophes on a global scale and unnerved by the risks of cloning and genetic engineering the evidence *against* the old certainty that science is an unmitigated good is piled high.

As the certainty was shaken, the assumptions that surrounded it have begun to be questioned with ever-increasing vigour. The key assumption, that unencumbered observers could generate objective truth (that went right back to Descartes in 1619[68] and seemed to be taken for granted by everyone including Wellhausen and Warfield), began to be seen for what it was - an assumption.[69] People were now free to admit that the truth looked different depending on where you were standing and that everyone but everyone was lugging around a whole suitcase full of assumptions, experience and traditions that could deeply affect how they saw what they saw. It has become impossible to presume *any* observer to be innocent and entirely objective.

Dissident voices that had had to be silenced whilst the key group of white, Western, educated men (and their respectful allies and hired 'muscle') had been building this modern world, could now begin to be heard. The general culture in 'The West' has begun to reflect the insights and attitudes of women, black people, people with disabilities, foreigners...... not well, not exclusively, but to some extent. Even in the cinema, the few 'Westerns' now being made have begun to show native Americans (the 'Indians') and Mexicans as three-dimensional people rather than things to be killed or to be left looking ridiculous and the heroes (the 'cowboys'), whilst still mainly white and male, are increasingly left ambiguous, troubled, uncertain[70]. The full extent of the violence and cruelty that modernisation had required, from the vast Atlantic slave trade through lists of long-forgotten atrocities of imperial expansion and warfare, to the unscrupulous plundering of natural resources, the wholesale expropriation of land and the systematic exploitation of labour, can, at last, be taken into account in assessing the costs of the modern world and openly acknowledged in the general culture of 'The West'.

Indeed, it could now be admitted that the whole idea of 'the modern world' was not a simple, incontrovertible 'fact' but a very particular controlling idea or 'interpretation' that brought huge costs for some even as it richly rewarded others. The persuasive 'reality' in which we had all been invited (or forced) to live for hundreds of years could now be seen to be a clever manipulative construction, not a given truth. Some may still 'squat' in decaying parts of 'the great myth of the modern world' as if nothing has changed or even be adding on speculative new wings and floors; others have evacuated it, never to return.

As a result of the ending of the absolute sway of 'the modern world' we have all been left uncertain and a little chilly in a world with a number of competing explanations, no assured access to objective truth and no agreed certainty as to where we go from here. As the title of Walter Anderson's book tells us, *"Reality isn't what it used to be"*.[71]

3.2 **What's happening now?**

There's always a thrill of freedom about the collapse of an old certainty - an exhilarating moment packed with promise, like the night the Berlin Wall was breached. Something of that exhilaration still seems to hang in the air for those who would have us welcome the new 'Postmodern' world - they savour the joy of destroying what was. But what is to happen now - now that the old certainties have been brought down to size as but one theory among many, rather than the unavoidable absolute truth? Let me try to summarise the summaries of Richard Middleton and Brian Walsh's book *"Truth is stranger than it used to be"*,[72] as their explanations seem to make good sense of my own limited experience and observations. I would, therefore, list five major effects of the collapse of the big idea of progress that seem to have been let loose in our increasingly 'Postmodern' world. These, I propose, are the key observable effects that shape this emerging 'Postmodern' world that seems to be overtaking us all:

I.   *I CAN CONSTRUCT MY OWN TRUTH.*

People now feel that each of us has a freedom to construct our own truth. If nothing is 'given' then I can decide for myself what I believe and no-one can say that I'm wrong. Middleton and Walsh describe how reality now seems to be an enormous 'carnival' with lots and lots of side-shows but no central circus[73]. They also use the image of a *'smorgasbord'*[74] - a huge buffet from which you can select what you like and leave the rest (and *no-one* can tell you what you have to eat). We can all choose our own plateful of 'truths to live by' and seek out our own agreeable companions to eat with. This gives a world where all centralised organisations (like church denominations, trades unions and political parties) tend to lose their committed membership base. Instead, we find an endless flux of 'interest groups' with variable levels of commitment and a swirl of forming and dissolving alliances and moments of joint action… all helpfully served by the Internet and mobile 'phones (so, anyone for a demo, or would you rather share some spirituality in the woods?).

2. *I CAN INVENT & RE-INVENT MYSELF.*

People now feel that each of us is free to invent and re-invent ourselves. If all of 'reality' is to some extent 'constructed', then I can construct and re-construct the image I put across as 'me'.[75] Here is the triumph of style over substance… the world where the beautician's 'makeover' is supposed to do the business. We may have become adept at spotting when governments and politicians are trying out a new image, but running successive or simultaneous 'takes' on who I am is all part of where it's at. We are endlessly encouraged to believe we can be who we'd like to be - and try again if we find we don't like what we've become! And if we want just a momentary escape to another self, there's a plethora of 'virtual' realities available from computer games and theme parks to mind-altering drugs, that invite you to some sort of 'hyper-reality', only to leave your actual underlying feelings seeming all the more flat and depressing on your return (so, who else d'ya wanna be?).

3. *CONSUME, CONSUME, CONSUME!*

Capitalism has responded vigorously to this new choice. "Consume, consume, consume!" is the endless challenge put to us all, as the market seeks ever new ways of persuading us that we *need* to try things we never knew we needed[76]. As Roger Lundin puts it, "the ideal of the self disinterestedly seeking truth has given way to the idea of the self as a unit of consumption seeking to slake its unquenchable thirsts."[77] Like the proverbial insect whose sexual performance is supposedly improved by having its head bitten off, the removal of its central 'myth of progress' seems to have liberated the modern world into ever more rampant feats of production and sales to sensation-hungry, self-reinventing, rudderless postmoderns desperate to shop for image… if only they have enough cash or credit (OK, let me buy that on one of my *other* credit cards).

4. *THERE'S A LOT OF PAIN & DESPAIR IN THIS.*

But all this possibility without clear direction leads to a lot of pain and despair. There is, after all, a real comfort in knowing what's expected. If there are no expectations, only possibilities, life can be cruelly difficult. Underneath this fascination with image and possibility there is a deep, dark, desperate sense of loss, of grief at the death of certainty and direction, of personal pain at the difference between what I feel I am and what I'm supposed to project. There's a brittleness about some of the brightness, a fighting-for-forgetfulness about some of the fun, a homelessness about some of the hyped-up happiness. It can be tough being a postmodern, but you're not supposed to say.

5.   MAJOR EVILS ARE STILL TO BE ADDRESSED.

D espite the excitement of the new, there's still a mass of unaddressed evil. Certainly, there's room for lots of *personal* morality in this new world. You or I can decide to be a 'green' campaigner or join the 'Drop the Debt' protests. There's room for a lot of grass-roots democracy in single-issue protest groups and broader alliances, but the really big failures of the Modern World have still to be properly addressed. These new choices are all for those who can afford them. The big evils of economic injustice have come through the move from Modern to Postmodern almost unaltered. The great engines of modern capitalist consumerism seem almost *more* at home in this world of insatiable appetites and growing markets, but no direction. Old evils like racism and xenophobia seem ever-ready to develop new and disturbing forms to supplement the older, entrenched forms of injustice. How do we co-ordinate resistance to great moral evils, when we're all supposed to work out for ourselves what is right and what is wrong? The dangers of this brave new world lie as much in what it doesn't do, as in what it does.

That, 'in a nutshell' is a quick, crude, wildly-interpretative account of the emerging Postmodern world. I suspect that quite a few of these ideas underlie the perplexing differences between the way church-going grandparents and their texting, trainer-wearing grandchildren seem to see the world. Postmodern ideas are among the commonly-accepted assumptions of the young, even as they feel disturbingly 'different' to many of us who are older. Eventually the dissonance and tension, the pain and frustration that young people themselves will find in postmodernity will lead them into fresh and exciting critiques of things they now assume to be true. But, whilst they grow, this is the way the world is, in the same way that the 'modern' world, with its confidence in progress and 'The Triumph of the West'[78], was the one I and my generation had to accept or learn to resist as we grew up.

So, what happens when we try to read familiar texts in this startlingly different postmodern world? Will the whole fuss simply pass texts by, or do we have to read them differently? Intriguingly, "Hermeneutics", the study of how we find 'meaning' in what we read (or watch or hear) has been at the very eye of the storm blowing away the thought-structures of the modern world...

3.3   And what can we learn from the text?

Over recent years the study of how we find 'meaning' in what we read (hermeneutics) has been greatly developed by people like Paul Ricoeur, Hans-Georg Gadamer, Michel Foucault and Jacques Derrida. They have produced a diverse array of important ideas about how we read and make sense of texts[79]. These ideas, which have seriously questioned, even 'deconstructed', the whole of the Modern World View, have been at the forefront of our current cultural change. We need to share at least a summary of where their work seems to be taking us before we turn to see what effects it might have on our relationship with the Bible. Whilst it will be hard for us to agree fully with all of these ideas (the authors of these ideas often strongly disagree amongst themselves), I think there are SEVEN KEY IDEAS about how we might approach *any* text that we'll need to note. So, here is another quick, crude, wildly-interpretative account by me, and although we are talking, for now, about how we approach *any* text, most of our illustrative examples will have something to do with the Bible, and each will be followed by considering the question, "How might we (as Christians trying to read the Bible) respond to this?"

I.   THE IMPOSSIBILITY OF OBJECTIVITY

Whenever we pick up a book and start to read, or stop to try to understand a poem or even glimpse a headline on someone else's newspaper, we can't help bringing along the effects of ALL OUR PAST EXPERIENCE - the way of seeing that we've gradually, subtly assembled since the day we were born. We bring assumptions we've picked up unquestioningly from people we trust and the way things 'just are' in our own culture and tradition. We bring the scars of past hurt, the strengths of past relationships, the effects of things we've read before. We bring conscious and sub-conscious prejudices and perceptions that may be big, deep and hugely important to us even though we never talk of them, never even acknowledge them to ourselves. All of that is already there when we pick up the book or try to make sense of the poem or squint at the headline. Much of it is held in common with our wider community, culture and tradition in a way that makes it feel so certain that it seems objectively 'true'. No conscious effort to be freshly, newly "objective" can switch all of that off; nor is it possible to 'put on' objectivity like a white lab coat as we approach a text.

Reviewing (with hindsight) the work of countless authors from the last three hundred years who clearly assumed that they were being objective and universal in their pronouncements, quickly reveals how culture-bound and context-fettered they almost always are. They spoke with the voice and opinions of their time, their place, even their social group. We have already picked up on some of this with Calvin, Boyle, Wellhausen and Warfield.[80] Because they shared the assumption that they could and should make universal, timeless, objective pronouncements of truth, they simply became expert smugglers, hiding their particularities and prejudices from themselves and each other. This was easier than it might sound because through most of modern times the ranks of those ALLOWED to deal with 'universal' issues were quite limited and those to be admitted to the world of letters were thoroughly schooled into the great myth of Western progress. To be considered 'civilised' you had to conform to the codes, expectations and aspirations of this particular Western 'civilisation' with its imperial notion of 'progress'. For example, Frederick Douglass, the 19th Century black American anti-slavery campaigner (an ex-slave himself) discovered, there just didn't appear to be any other way to be taken seriously. Wilson Moses[81] argues that Douglass was strongly against any kind of multiculturalism or cultural pluralism because, according to the only accepted view of progress-through-science-and-reason then available, that would imply settling for some sort of second best for African Americans. For Douglass, as for most English-language commentators of his day, the American & European, white, Protestant view of culture *was* "Culture" and the American & European, white, Protestant view of progress *was* "Progress".

In recent times, it has become possible to acknowledge openly that our assumptions, our prejudices and our tradition are part of what we are and are inevitably there with us when we approach any text. Rightly recognised, they can be an important contribution of gifts, insights and skills that help as well as hinder. Objectivity, according to this new way of seeing, has always been both impossible to achieve and profoundly unhelpful - even though it may have sounded like a really sensible idea at the time. This realisation that there is no objective, easy access to the truth or to the meaning of any text (without all our baggage of ideas, experience and cultural assumptions coming into the picture) is central to the new world of ideas. It changes everything.

How might we respond to this?

THE IMPOSSIBILITY OF OBJECTIVITY........

✦ In **ORDINARY LIFE** we readily accept that how people view things is shaped by **who** they are and **where** they've come from. We regularly account for people's opinions with reference to a whole host of factors from their present and their past. .... *"You men just don't understand..." "Africa totally changed her outlook..." "Remember, he's been trained to think like a lawyer..." "I blame her mother..."* We don't seem to imagine that our experiences **determine** in any absolute way how we view things, yet we easily accept that every individual is a complex fusion of factors and effects that **help** to shape how they make sense of what they see. We seem to assume that no-one is without biases, no-one is able to be 'objective'. Indeed, we 'read' other people by weighing the various factors that seem to have shaped them. Having biases and showing them is an important part of being human, as the script writers of any TV 'soap' would be happy to tell you.

✦ But what happens when we come to **READING THE BIBLE**? We can accept that other people with a different understanding of the faith from us might be 'biased' in how they read the Bible, yet we all find it hard to accept that we ourselves may be every bit as much shaped by our past and the preconceptions we have generated along the way as they have been by theirs. We like to think that if we open ourselves to God, it is God's undistorted voice that we will hear speaking from the Bible's page. We tend to have a grammar that operates:

THEY are deeply biased in their approach.

> **YOU** sometimes allow your experiences to distort what you read.

> > **I** am carefully objective and open to God.[82]

✦ Yet **JESUS KNOWS US WELL**. Remember his telling remark about leaving the tiny specks in the eyes of others until we have dealt with the roof-beam sticking out of our own eye *(Matthew 7:3-5)*? He seems to be addressing this very tendency. Jesus clearly knows that we *all* tend to deny the factors that distort our own vision, even whilst we are eager to recognise possible distorting factors in the viewpoints of others.

✦ **THE DISTURBING THING** about accepting that we're none of us objective *even* as we approach the Word of God (the problem that Jesus' highlights) is that this means God is harder to hear. If I can only hear God through my own distorting 'noise' or see God past my own obstructing 'beam', then I can be less certain that I've heard God aright or seen God at all. Yet none of our other relationships with real persons is straightforwardly objective, why should knowing God be so neat, clinical, tidily precise... so impersonal?

✦ You might then want to argue that **THE SPIRIT OF GOD** is there to help us know God aright. OK. But how does God's Spirit operate? Does the Spirit download instant enlightenment about everything, or lead us through pathways of discovery? The evidence of our own experience of spiritual growth and the obviously diverse experiences of God's people surely suggest that God's Spirit helps us *gradually* to learn and grow in hearing and insight, rather than instantaneously removing all the obstacles to spiritual 20:20 vision. Might not our clarity of spiritual vision always be 'work in progress'? In this life, might we all see even God "through a glass, darkly..." *(1 Corinthians 13:12)*? Even, perhaps especially, when reading the Bible, direct, objective access to the meaning of the text is impossible. There is always the risk that we will find new layers of meaning and new ways of seeing as we try to ascend the spiral of learning....

2. THE SPIRAL OF LEARNING

So if we can't leave our prejudices and assumptions behind, how do we learn from the text rather than simply impose our own prejudiced reading on to what we read? Hans-Georg Gadamer talks of bringing together and fusing 'two horizons' - the horizon of the text and the horizon of the reader - by a spiralling set of exchanges between the two of them, a sort of developing dialogue between reader and text[83]. Roger Lundin helpfully interprets this idea for us by suggesting the picture of the reader "befriending" the text. When two people meet they both bring the whole history of prejudice, assumption and experience that makes them who they are. They sit side by side and talk, questioning each other about things that are important as they see it. They begin to find "points of fusion in their understanding"[84]. Some prejudices may even be shaken or altered by the encounter, some assumptions exposed and challenged. That is what needs to occur between reader and text if those who read, without suppressing who they are, are going to understand the text, hear what the text is saying to them, even risk being changed by what the text says.

Clearly, this process is fraught with the same risks and possibilities as getting to know another person. Of course we can be so trapped in our own prejudices that we never get to know the other - be it person or text. Or we can think we know them, but find later that there are whole new ways of seeing who they are and what they are about that we never saw before. Sometimes, the act of 'getting to know' may profoundly change us. Jesus, the roadside storyteller, seems to have had an acute sense of just how powerful a text or a story could be. Why else did he tell a story like "The Good Samaritan" (*Luke 10:25-37*) to that niggling, distrustful lawyer? The story, even on brief acquaintance, extracted an admission that things might be very different from what the lawyer had always assumed. It may not be easy. It may rarely be so sudden and sharp, but texts and stories can cut through our assumptions and prejudices and effect real change, if we risk engaging in this dialogue of befriending.

This may be a lot less objective, scientific and certain than you or I think it ought to be, but living life and forming relationships has always been more of an art than a science - why should getting an understanding of a text be any different?

How might we respond to this?

THE SPIRAL OF LEARNING....

✦ In **ORDINARY LIFE** we've all watched someone 'getting the wrong end of the stick' and seen how difficult it can be for them to let go of their 'wrong' understanding. What seems so obvious to everyone else may take several trips round the story before the clouds of puzzlement are suddenly blown away by a new way of seeing.... relief, then shared laughter! We have probably all experienced that same puzzlement for ourselves on many occasions. Again, we've known a gradual dawning of realisation that there's a lot more to what someone is saying than we first thought. This 'spiral of learning' describes a world we know, it suggests that we read texts the same way that we hear and befriend each other.

✦ When we turn to **READING THE BIBLE**, the idea of a gradual process of befriending the text and being changed by the process again describes a common experience. Preachers can return year after year to familiar texts and each time find something new in them to share with the people of God. Sometimes we find whole rich depths of meaning that we can't believe we never saw before. The reality of Bible reading is that it is a life-long task of being befriended, a task that we never complete, a friendship that's never exhausted.

✦ If the Gospel accounts of the step-by-step developing understanding of Jesus' disciples (classically Peter) reflect their 'spiral of learning' as they seek to befriend Jesus, then, clearly, **JESUS KNOWS US WELL** and how grasping a *bit* of the truth doesn't mean we understand it all (yet). Remember Peter's confession of Jesus Messiah and Jesus' subsequent rebuke on the road near Caesarea Philippi *(Mark 8:27-38)*.

✦ **THE DISTURBING THING** is that this account of how we read seems to imply that the truth is more distant, harder to know, more of a struggle. But is that really such a bad thing? Both Jesus and Paul regularly present the difficulties of following God as an integral part of its ultimate glory and joy *(e.g. Matthew 7:14, 2 Corinthians 4:7-11)*.

✦ For me, as we approach the Bible, this idea of a spiral of learning is exciting. It promises truth that's always bigger and deeper. It gives a clear ongoing role to **THE SPIRIT OF GOD** as our guide in the process of befriending, our helper on the stairway of learning, the bearer of a healthy suspicion about our settled ideas of the truth...

3. THE IMPORTANCE OF SUSPICION

When we meet strangers we are inherently at least a little suspicious. Part of the process of establishing a basis of trust involves carefully checking things out. "What's his game?" "Why is she asking me this?" "Is this conversation leading somewhere I don't want to go?" We are often a little less comfortable when we detect that someone else is being carefully suspicious of us, but our possible motives and interests have to be investigated too. A similar use of careful suspicion about motives and any possible pay-off is only appropriate as we build a relationship with a text. But, again, this must not only be suspicion of what the text may be trying to say to us, but also suspicion as to how your particular interpretation or mine may be serving *our* interests (whether or not we would acknowledge it).

Craig Gay illustrates this with a story from Mark's Gospel.[85] The story in Mark 7:1-2 & 5-13 shows Jesus exposing the subtle, self-deceiving hypocrisy of some Pharisees. It seems they were using the idea of 'Corban' (property dedicated in advance to God, but still able to be used by the person who had dedicated it) as a means of simultaneously looking pious and getting out of the expense of looking after their parents in old age. "Sorry, Mother, you know I'd like to help you, but all my property is 'Corban' so I can't possibly sell it to give you the money you need." Jesus showed how they were simply effecting a cruel deception on themselves and their parents and misconstruing the texts they sought to live by. Yet, without the suspicions that Jesus dared to put to them (about their motives and their misconstrual of the Scriptures), they were entirely satisfied that they were interpreting God's Word carefully and wholeheartedly doing God's Will. The suspicion other readers dare to share with us provides our main tool to root out our smuggled self-deceptions. Still, as these Pharisees seem to have found, the better the quality of the self-deception, the harder it is to shift.

We all have a propensity to "read our own interests into" a text, especially when, like Scripture, we expect its authority to turn round and prove to the world the rightness of our actions. As Craig Gay puts it, "...we seem to have a natural propensity to use truth, even (and perhaps especially) scriptural truth, to our own advantage"[86] (and here the meaning of 'use' is the one that comes close to 'abuse'). With all the unfairness and value of hindsight, we have already looked with some suspicion on the motives and ideology of Calvin, Wellhausen and Warfield and how unacknowledged ideology may have affected their ways of approaching Scripture. Any right we may have to do so must involve a willingness to have our own ideology and motives questioned by those who can see us from sufficient distance to be rightly suspicious. So, suspicion, creatively used in dialogue with the text and with other interpreters who have distinct standpoints, can help us all to declare our undeclared 'baggage'. In this way, between us, we get a truer and fairer picture of what our text is saying to each and to all of us. Suspicion is a necessary and important tool in helping us, albeit painfully, to get past our ideas and find what the text might be saying.

How might we respond to this?

THE IMPORTANCE OF SUSPICION....

✦ This one is never comfortable. In **ORDINARY LIFE** we prefer to think that suspicion is for strangers and trust is for friends. Yet, the biggest, toughest, most dangerous deceptions in our lives are usually the ones we perpetrate on ourselves, especially if our friends share the same self-deceptions. We bury our own (individual and shared) self-deceptions deeper and turf them over more elegantly than any other deceptions. As a result, we are more likely to succeed in forgetting that they are there at all and digging them up again becomes a very painful business. I have sat and watched the pain on the faces of gentle Afrikaners who were trying, at last, to see how apartheid looked from a South African black perspective. Acknowledging the underlying evil of something that had hitherto seemed obviously to be justified by the good it did for your Christian friends and family is deeply, deeply disturbing. This is the real meaning of our casual saying - "The truth hurts". We would *all* rather forget how hard it can sometimes be. I think we'd rather not have to admit the importance of suspicion.

✦ When we are **READING THE BIBLE**, we are entering an area where we are all particularly open to valid suspicion. If we expect 'truth' and 'authority' to reside here, we will be specially anxious that they support our own way of seeing. The very importance to us of the text (when we read the Bible) increases greatly the risk that we will bury big self-deceptions and shared-deceptions under the 'front lawn' of our commitment to the Bible.

✦ Again, **JESUS KNOWS US WELL**. Craig Gay's example of how Jesus confronts some Pharisees and their attitude to 'Corban', is only part of a bigger picture. In their commitment to God, to the Scriptures and to holiness the Pharisees should surely have been some of Jesus' closest natural allies in a threatening and unsympathetic world. Yet it is these passionately religious 'People of the Book' who receive some of his sharpest criticisms. It is their 'front lawns' he seems most determined to 'dig up'. He is unafraid of using his suspicions to help them address their deep self-deceptions about what the Word of God is saying.

✦ **ONE DISTURBING THING** is that the more important something is to us, the more likely we are to engage in protective self-deception or shared deception with those who want to see things the way we do. How, then, are we ever to find 'the truth'? Suddenly, those with whom we disagree are potentially very important. The people whose ideas feel as if they're designed to dig up our front lawn with a mechanical digger, *may* be helping us. Certainly, they may just be vandals, they may have hidden things under their own lawns, but we have to watch carefully to see if they dig up something or nothing. Not easy!

✦ **ANOTHER DISTURBING THING** is that the never-ending risk of self-deception and shared-deception leaves our grasp of 'the truth' as always provisional. However certain we *feel*, we cannot logically *be* certain that we've got it right. That is unsettling. Yet, this permanent risk that we're resisting some aspects of 'the truth', could surely be very helpful. It could be an antidote to arrogance and pride, a spur to humility, an opening for the Spirit of God.

✦ **THE SPIRIT OF GOD** is most likely to be able to help us to the truth when we are open to hearing what other people say - *even* other people whom we may consider less 'holy' or more frequently 'wrong' - as they might be the very people to see and say something that breaks through our own layers of self deceit. Think how inadequate and ignorable Jesus must have looked to those careful, 'correct', self-confused Pharisees. Why should they pay *any* attention to this wandering village preacher? We have to keep listening…

4. *THE LIBERATION OF LISTENING*

Once we have accepted that truth can look quite different depending where you stand, reading has to become a *shared* activity. Yes, I can still read the book on my own, even see the film on my own, but if I am to understand more fully what I have read or seen, I need to find others and ask, "So, what did you make of it, then? Don't you think he was just terrible to her? Didn't the way her mother behaved at the end make you so angry?" And if you are fortunate, you will not find complete agreement, but dialogue, even argument, between yourself, another interpreter and the book or the film. Then you may learn things you would never learn on your own, see things you never saw at the time, grow in ways you could never have done curled up on your own with that book you are befriending or watching that intriguing video all alone with a bag of microwaveable popcorn. Indeed, the greater the diversity of stances, of possible insights, of divergent readings to which we have access the better. We cannot simply shelter within the safe circle of the fellow-readers with whom we feel cosily at home. Somehow we have to hear voices from elsewhere, even from distant times and remote places. Indeed, we ought to give *particular* attention to voices, near or far, that have been silenced or ignored. The victims of violence and repression, the marginalised, the powerless, must have a certain privilege to speak and respond to our text, whilst we listen carefully.

I still remember the shock of reading an article by Robert Allen Warrior, a Native American. He wrote that when he reads the Bible story of the exodus of the former slave people from Egypt and their journey to their promised land, he can't relate to these slaves set free. Rather, he writes, "The obvious people for Native Americans to identify with are the Canaanites, the people who already lived in the promised land." He then notes how theologies of liberation tend to ignore, crucially, "... those parts of the story that describe Yahweh's command to mercilessly annihilate the indigenous population"[87] Ouch! This is a fresh and deeply unsettling hearing of the story which I and many others *need* to catch, even though it hurts. The exodus story has inspired many in South Africa, South America, Central America and elsewhere, with the hope that God is a God who liberates those who are oppressed. Yet even a part of *this* story can cut out others, imposing other silences. We need to hear and think again.

So, we do not need calm solitude to approach a text, we need a clamour of diverse voices, a cacophony of competing insights, but with a real chance for the desperate whispering voices to be heard as well as the loud confident ones.   We must learn how to approach a text *together*.

How might we respond to this?

THE LIBERATION OF LISTENING....

✦   In **ORDINARY LIFE** the possibility that there are always other ways of seeing has been constantly put before us all through the 20th Century. From the vigorous campaigns of the suffragettes, through the independence struggles of former colonies, to more recent uncovering of the extent of child abuse and incest in our society and the racial justice issues given prominence by the Stephen Lawrence Enquiry, there have been repeated indicators of the importance of listening, especially listening to those whose voices had previously been ignored or dismissed. In ordinary life, society-as-a-whole in places like the UK, North America, Australia and New Zealand is having to learn to listen to voices it once refused to hear.

✦   This need to listen has huge implications for **READING THE BIBLE**. Bible Reading has to become again what I suspect it may have been in the early church - a communal event with ongoing debates and discussions WITHIN AND BETWEEN fellowships as to what God is saying. Paul's letters witness to a lively diversity of opinions on what the Bible means *(see the 'parties' with their various teachers discussed in 1 Corinthians 1:10-13. Paul calls for the church to be united with 'only one thought and one purpose' because the debates have turned into dangerous divisions, but there must have been a lot of listening and debate going on...even Paul's own letter is a part of the process as he sends in his contributions to the Corinthian debates* *from far off Ephesus.)* We cannot finally decide on our own, or even within our own like-minded fellowship, what a particular Bible passage 'means'. We have to have ways of hearing and listening to divergent voices to improve our chances of hearing God and not simply reading our own biases into God's Word. Bible Reading has to be as ecumenical as possible, as multicultural as possible, as international as possible. Even the opinions of outsiders, agnostics and sceptics may be hugely important. Of course we can still read the Bible alone and sense God speaking to us from it, but solitary Bible-reading becomes but one component in a great web of interpreting, listening, debating and understanding that spans the whole world - the decisions we make are never final, our understanding is never complete, no matter is ever finally settled in this life. For the Bible, every perceived meaning remains provisional.

✦ Once more **JESUS KNOWS US WELL**. He seems to relish his involvement in the great ongoing debates about the meanings of Scripture. This is the teacher who shockingly interjected, "You have heard that it was said…. but I say to you…" *(Matthew 5:21f)* yet he still wanted his followers to take the perceptions of the scribes and Pharisees very seriously *(Matthew 5:20)*. Again, he was clearly ready to hear and respond positively to the arguments of a Gentile Woman in the territory of Tyre *(Mark 7:24-30)*. For all his reputation as a teacher who 'spoke with authority' *(Mark 1:22)*, Jesus clearly listened to tradition, he listened to opponents, he listened to those whom others left voiceless and ignored.

✦ **THE DISTURBING THING** about this need to listen is probably (again) the way it makes finding 'the truth' more complicated and less certain. I don't think this means we have to go around in a permanent cloud of crippling doubt. I think it means we can dare to believe boldly, but always keep listening to others with the possibility that we may hear something new, challenging and important. Oliver Cromwell put it memorably in a letter to the General Assembly of the Church of Scotland in 1650, "I beseech you in the bowels of Christ, think it possible that you may be mistaken"[88].

✦ I believe that **THE SPIRIT OF GOD** is seeking to lead us ever closer to the truth, yet this rarely happens in "Damascus Road" moments of naked revelation *(Acts 9:3-6)*. Often and often, when we believe the Spirit has led us into new understanding, it is through the words of other people, or observing the predicament of other people or a coming to terms with what other people seem to believe. Listening to others is a vital part of being open to the leading of God's Spirit, a God-given means of rescuing us from the risk of endlessly doing violence by the way we interpret the Bible.

5.   *THE UBIQUITY OF VIOLENCE*

We come now to the ideas of those, such as Jacques Derrida and Michel Foucault, who have travelled furthest away from the idea of accessible objective truth and are loudest in their denunciations of the Modern World. They are known, perhaps aptly, as 'Deconstructionists'. One of their key ideas is the connection they make between INTERPRETATION, POWER and VIOLENCE. This may not be a connection you or I would easily make on our own, but I think there *is* something important here.

If we are not able easily and accurately to describe 'the truth' by applying a careful method (as was assumed by just about everyone from Calvin, through Descartes, Boyle, Wellhausen and Warfield to my primary school teachers), if our interpretations are not simply mimicking what is 'there', what *are* we doing when we make interpretations?

Interpretations (the Deconstructionists would tell us) have now to be seen as assertions; bids for 'my' views to be considered as 'true'; attempts to 'define' things for others on 'my' terms. My interpretations seek to impose the power of my 'meanings' in a way that silences or does violence to others, their ideas and their opinions. The bigger the interpretative claim, the more it seeks to 'explain', the greater the violence it is likely to do to others. 'Grand Narratives' (or *metanarratives*') that seek to explain 'everything' and thereby marginalise, silence or do violence to all whose own stories do not 'fit' are particularly dangerous. Examples of 'Grand Narratives' would include not only stories like the modern myth of progress, Fascism, Stalinism, and Maoism, but also British Imperialism and some versions of the Christian and Islamic Stories and their divergent meanings for believers and unbelievers (don't forget the Crusades, the Inquisition, the death penalty for heresy in Calvin's Geneva, Cromwell's repressive campaign in Ireland......).

Loren Wilkinson, illustrates for us the basic idea of how interpretations can be violent as they bid for power. She offers the analogy of disagreements within the church about what the Bible 'means':

> Christians who have had the experience of being involved in a battle over some specific issue of biblical interpretation - be it eschatology, economics or the role of women in the church - know the rancour which can seep in, all the more because we are convinced that the book on whose interpretation we disagree is of ultimate authority.
>
> *Loren Wilkinson,*
> *"Hermeneutics and the Postmodern Reaction Against "Truth"" p.136 89*

Although the Deconstructionists would not accept the possibility of any text having "ultimate authority", this example should help us church people remember the pain, even 'violence', we may have felt as we faced the risk of having another interpretation imposed in preference to our own. This known and felt violence is but one tiny example of the gruesome history of human violence which Deconstructionists argue is rooted in the history of imposed interpretations and imposed 'meanings'. Defining someone as a 'slave' or an 'alien', or 'insane' or a 'witch' or a 'criminal' or an 'asylum seeker' or 'Juden' or 'Tutsi' has often been a means of imposing power and effecting ostracism, a loss of humanity or violence, a way of legitimising death, even genocide. Deconstructionists point an accusing finger at every sort of Empire, at the Modern World, at the history of the Western Church. They have identified evil and a real connection to how we've kept on trying to legitimate it, explain it, excuse it, civilise it, justify it or paper it over.

Even though we decline to accept their assertions that there is no access to 'truth', that there is no limit to the number of possible interpretations of a text, that every interpretative act risks violence to the 'meaning' found by another, we still have to face this haunting connection between interpretation, power and violence. It is a recognition of 'sin' and 'fallen-ness' and the terrible collusion and complicity in all this violence of those who would be seen as civilised and cultured - a complicity that has continued through much of world and church history. It says that fallen-ness intrudes into what we're doing even when we read a text, especially, we may suppose, when we read a text that we might interpret as giving us firm authority for our actions. There will always be the temptation to interpret such texts in a way that supports our bid for power, whilst loudly maintaining to our selves (and to anyone else who'll listen) that we are being fair and objective. Beware, reader, we can do violence and never admit to it because we dare not see it for ourselves.

How might we respond to this?

THE UBIQUITY OF VIOLENCE....

✦ In **ORDINARY LIFE**, we all know the potential violence of language. I grew up with the chant "Sticks and stones may break my bones, but words will never hurt me!" ringing in my ears. If what it claimed was true then we wouldn't have needed to chant it, like a mantra, in response to the cruel taunts of playground bullies. Indeed, the words often hurt longer and did more damage to self esteem than the physical violence offered with it. Even as adults, though we learn to shrug off a lot of what we hear, we die a little every time we have to block out the unjustly judging words of another human being. And harsh words can still do deep violence to us when they come unexpected, or when we're vulnerable, or we hear them on the lips of someone we had hitherto trusted as a friend.

✦ In **READING THE BIBLE** we encounter a lot of violence. This book is dense with real struggle and cruelty. But alongside the recorded physical violence of individuals and armies is the interpretative violence evidenced in the text itself. Some violent acts, such as the enslaving of the Hebrews by the Egyptians, are clearly pronounced to be wrong *(Exodus 3:16-17)*. Yet, in other places, acts of genocidal violence are presented as cleansing acts required by God *(e.g. Joshua 8; I Samuel 15)*. Anyone who would approach the Bible as (in some sense) the authoritative Word of God has a lot of work to do to come to come to terms with the verbal violence woven into many Bible texts. But just as troubling is the way the Bible has been used down the centuries to give protection to those who would do violence to others. Arrant anti-Semitism, racism, genocide, the slave trade, the wholesale expropriation of land and resources, and the repression of women are among a long list of forms of violence that have been given an apparent legitimacy by appeal to the Bible. If we would respond with integrity to the challenge of the Deconstructionists, surely we have to admit that the Bible is not in any way 'privileged' and exempt from the risk of violence that seems to come with human use of language. We see the clear marks of verbal violence and power struggles both in parts of our authoritative text itself and, time and time again, in the history of its interpretative use by our forebears. So, we must presume, the risk that we, too, will engage in violence and coercive power play when we try to use the Bible is very real.

✦ Even in this difficult area, **JESUS KNOWS US WELL**. These are the very sorts of issues Jesus is tackling with that lawyer who wanted to know who was, and who was not to be treated as a neighbour. The story of the Good Samaritan is Jesus' attempt to jolt the lawyer out of legitimating the exclusion of Samaritans and Gentiles from his circle of care and compassion *(Luke 10:25-37)*. Indeed, by personally shouldering the legal violence of the Roman authorities, the religious violence of the Jerusalem temple establishment and the mob violence of the disappointed crowds in the city, Jesus seems to be consciously taking on our violence in all its forms. Surely the crucified Christ, more than anyone else, understands our violence and seeks to liberate us from every form of cruelty?

✦ **THE DISTURBING THING** is that two thousand years later, we still try to co-opt the Word of God to legitimise our petty power struggles and give respectability to our casual acts of violence. If the Deconstructionists can turn up and catch us at it, like Nathan challenging the guilty King David with his story of a stolen lamb *(2 Samuel 12:1-10)*, then so be it... we need all the help we can get.

✦ **THE SPIRIT OF GOD** who inspired prophets like Amos and Micah to denounce injustice, regardless of personal cost, is no respecter of persons. If we hear a challenge to what we say that accuses us of violence against others and using the Bible to legitimate our violence, then we have to listen very carefully. God's Spirit may be speaking to us.

6. THE JUDGING OF MEANINGS

This wariness of the danger of doing violence by imposing meaning on others has led Deconstructionists to abandon any idea that we can decide between meanings. For them, every meaning anyone 'finds' in a text is valid for that person or their shared community of readers. We cannot say that this reading is 'right' whilst that reading is 'wrong'. You simply cannot 'misinterpret' the text. Even the author of the text cannot resist your reading. They cannot say, "No, I didn't mean that, I meant this... You misunderstand me." Once it is written the text is anybody's to interpret how they like. And as for the idea that there might be some accessible 'truth' out there beyond our attempts to impose meaning on one another - forget it! Christian philosopher James Olthuis attempts to summarise this sort of Deconstructionist approach for us. He hears them to be saying: "Better the...... abyss of uncertainty than the totalitarian presence of meaning and its cauldron of oppression"[90]

But are there only the two alternatives? Must we accept either the neat one-on-one mapping of meaning on to truth (as is clearly expected by the Westminster Confession of Faith which talks of the true and full sense of any Scripture as being "not manifold, but one".[91]) or this radical Deconstructionist scepticism about meaning that totters on the edge of the abyss of meaninglessness?

A whole clutch of scholars[92] would argue for a middle course. They would argue that there may be more than one 'right' reading of a text (even at times meanings not intended by the author) but they would also argue that some readings will be 'wrong'. Again, they would argue that we cannot assume that finding 'the truth' is straightforward, but they would also agree that it is unduly pessimistic to assume that we cannot decide between meanings or ever receive any real communication from the author in a text they have written. Yet, even accepting this less extreme position leaves us with a problem - how do we decide which readings are 'right' and which are 'wrong'?

Paul Ricoeur deals with it, calmly, like this:

> The text presents a limited field of possible constructions... It is always possible to argue for or against an interpretation, to confront interpretations, to arbitrate between them and to seek agreement, even if this agreement remains beyond our immediate reach.
>
> Paul Ricoeur, "Interpretation Theory: Discourse and the Surplus of Meaning"
> (Fort Worth, 1976) p79 [93]

He sounds completely unfazed by the dilemma, though he has no elaborate or subtle test to apply in every case and would probably be distrustful of attempts to produce one. Still, I believe that Ricoeur is saying that there may be a number of 'good' interpretations, yet the possibilities are far from limitless. Again, I take him to mean that by careful assessment of alternatives and appropriate, thoughtful argument we should, in most cases, be able to discard the absolute 'turkeys' and agree how the rest fit together. Yet (and this is important), we may not always get 'agreement' right away - we may have to live with tension and dissonance, at least for a while. I also find implicit in what he says the idea that we may sometimes have to change our minds.

I admit I like this approach because it holds the possibility of texts actually communicating something to me and my fellow readers (not each of us deciding for ourselves what they might mean, which would leave us to have fun reading Bible texts, but no possibility of an authoritative "BIBLE", so far as I can tell). This approach also allows for the possibility of multiple meanings and an adjudication process to decide which readings seem fair. Yet, to me, it seems realistic that it does not propose some grand scheme, method or mathematical formula for deciding which readings are 'good' readings; the decision process has the atmosphere of a family meeting or a gathering of friends rather than the precision of a laboratory or the finality of a House of Lords or Supreme Court appeal ruling. We might get it wrong, but when we know more, we can admit this and agree to change our minds - like much of life, every decision is provisional.

So, am I just suiting myself (albeit in good company) in not going the whole way with the Deconstructionists' radical scepticism about meaning? Am I just kidding myself in thinking it might be possible that texts can communicate something real? Perhaps. On the other hand, once the dust has settled after the collapse of the Modern, maybe even the Deconstructionists will grow up, settle down and feel less need to reject everything. I have a strong suspicion that there is just a wee bit of radical posturing going on here. Deconstructionist ideas seem determined to shock. We'll have to wait and see. In the meantime, I feel free to continue believing in the possibility of Scripture - of God communicating with us through some sort of text - and of the Bible being that text.

How might we respond to this?

THE JUDGING OF MEANINGS....

✦ In **ORDINARY LIFE**, we expect to have to decide between meanings. Think of what happens when someone gives a public address - a sermon, a talk at a primary school assembly or a televised party political broadcast. We would not be surprised to discover that every listener heard something slightly different. Nor would it be particularly controversial to suggest that exactly what each hearer 'heard' was affected by their own 'baggage' of experience, ideas and loyalties. Yet, most of us would equally want to think that the speaker 'had something to say' and wanted us all to hear it. Moreover, if they were any good at public speaking, we would expect that what most of us 'heard' would bear some relationship to what they *intended* to say. Some might 'hear' things that the rest of us would not recognise, we would say "You _mis_heard her". Certainly, we would accept that there might be layers of meaning offered and received. "What's he really getting at?" is a fair question when listening to a preacher, a politician or a head teacher. We would be surprised if they didn't have a clear idea of 'the big picture' that affected, even controlled, what they were saying. Spotting someone's Grand Narrative ('I can see where she's coming from!') is part of the interest of listening. All in all, we are used to operating in a world where truth is subtle and elusive and meanings can be various and layered but not limitless. We are skilled at handling 'baggage', but still believe real communication of even complex ideas and perceptions is possible. It's a hermeneutical jungle out there, but, we can cope - this jungle is our home.

✦ When we come to **READING THE BIBLE**, if we are to have any possibility of 'Scripture' conveying intended meanings from God to us, then, again, we have to resist full-blown Deconstructionist ideas. Yet the very nature of the texts in the Bible and the way they often refer to or hint at other texts and stories suggests layers and strands of meaning that often operate simultaneously. Indeed, the way the New Testament quotes and refers to the Old Testament, often proposes meanings that the original human author of the quoted Old Testament passage is unlikely to have intended *(consider, for example, the 'proof' texts given in Matthew Ch.2)*. The Bible seems to operate in a world of multiple but not limitless meanings where study always seems capable of uncovering new possibilities and deeper layers of meaning. The Bible is very much at home in our world.

✦ Yet again, **JESUS KNOWS THIS WORLD WELL**. The Jesus of John's Gospel constantly plays with layers of meaning in the discourses and conversations we have recorded *(see, for example, the conversations with Nicodemus and the Samaritan woman at the well in John 3 & 4)*. Even the Jesus of the pithy sayings in the other three Gospels may be adept at re-treading a story or a saying *(compare Matthew 22:1-10 and Luke 14:15-24)* and hinting at other meanings *(see, for example, Mark 12:1-12, the parable of the tenants in the vineyard)*.

✦ **THE DISTURBING THING**, if we are looking for clear sharp truth, is the uncertainty and disagreement that multiple meanings allow. Yet, why must God speak to us with the careful clarity of an infant school teacher giving her children safety instructions before a class outing? Perhaps the uncertainty gives us room for learning and growing, the possibility of a developing relationship?

✦ According to this way of seeing, **THE SPIRIT OF GOD** is liberated by the richness of the text. It is through this poetic possibility that the Spirit is able meet with us, challenge us, elude our defences of logic and order, surprise us with newness of seeing and being, help us to find God.

7.   THE RECOVERY OF STORY

One final change that seems to be happening as the Modern World loses its absolute status in the world of ideas, is the recovery of respect for STORY. At times it seemed as if the modern world thought that stories were a bit like nuts - once you had cracked them and got the kernel of truth out of them you could simply throw the broken bits away. In a world where the objective and the universal were idolised, stories (any stories) were embarrassingly particular, specific and imprecise.

Now, in a world where every voice is to be heard, every life is to be acknowledged to have 'meaning' - story, whether your story or my story or a made-up story that says something you want to say has been re-instated as valid, beautiful, important. Yes, the Deconstructionists get all worked up about Grand Narratives, but that is because they are afraid such big stories will override other peoples own stories. Story is valued now. Story is important. Story is recognised as a quintessentially HUMAN vehicle for sharing ethics and ideas and meaning.

The Bible is a huge story largely made up of smaller stories. It never quite managed to be the neat assemblage of propositional truth that the Modern World seemed to think it should be if it was to be taken seriously. So, this recovery of respect for story could be quite significant for us.

How might we respond to this?

THE RECOVERY OF STORY....

✦ **ORDINARY LIFE** is experienced as story. This is the most human way of understanding anything or anyone – 'Just sit down and tell me exactly what happened'. We skill our children in the subtle arts of hearing and telling stories as soon as they start to use language. Indeed, the philosopher Alasdair MacIntyre makes a compelling case that we 'make sense' of the things that happen to us through a process of weaving them into the ongoing story we tell ourselves about ourselves.[94] It's hard to imagine how any human culture could operate without heavy reliance on the use of story.

✦ When we come to **READING THE BIBLE**, we find not a recipe book for life, nor a legal text for the faithful, but a vast multi-stranded story. Even the legal bits are set in the context of the story of God's people. Recovering a rich appreciation of story allows an exciting refreshment of huge tracts of the Bible. If there is truth here, it is woven into the stories; unpicking and sorting the threads risks destroying so much.

✦ Yet again, **JESUS KNOWS US WELL**. Jesus is a consummate story teller. Stories, with all the subtlety and challenge they allow, seem to be his preferred means of communication. Without an appreciation of storytelling is it possible to truly appreciate and know Jesus?

✦ The word we use of a good story is "inspiring" - meaning that it puts the Spirit into you. For many of us, it is through the *stories* in the Bible that **THE SPIRIT OF GOD** speaks with the most power and effect, touching heart and mind, even healing the soul.

3.4 Are we simply following fashion?

To some, all the ideas we have explored in this chapter will be almost boringly familiar, but to others they may sound like ideas from another planet, a desperate lurch into a strange world of gimmicks and fashion, a 'selling out' to the ways of the world - nothing here that could possibly help us 'rightly handle the Word of Truth' (2 Timothy 2:15). I think we should take that natural wariness (or 'suspicion') seriously. After all, we have been warned about being 'blown about by every wind of doctrine' (Ephesians 4:14).

So, before we go any further, let me put before you a number of arguments that persuade me that these particular ideas about how we find meaning in texts are sensible. Indeed, I would reckon them to be the most sensible ideas on how to approach a text that are currently available to us - sufficiently sensible that we should deliberately employ them as we seek to understand the Bible.

1. A REASONABLE RISK

There is always some risk in trying a new approach. Yet trying something new with your eyes wide open and a commitment to due care can still be a reasonable risk, a risk worth taking.

For example, both Luther and Calvin were real innovators in their approach to Scripture. Luther ignored the accepted layers of interpretative tradition that had been built up over hundreds of years to approach the text directly and freshly. Calvin developed a whole new approach to the business of commenting on the Scriptures, which he appears to have derived directly from the secular 'Humanist' scholarship of his day. Indeed, his own first 'Commentary' was not on a Bible book at all but on the *'De Clementia'* of Seneca, an Ancient Roman Stoic writer who was very much in vogue in Humanist circles in Calvin's time.[95] Calvin's style and approach to Scriptural commentating can be directly related to the techniques used in his Commentary on Seneca, completed whilst he was still studying in Paris. He then proceeded to apply all the latest ideas on the interpretation of secular texts, at which he considered himself particularly adept[96], directly to the interpretation of Scripture.[97]

On the other hand, clinging too strongly to the ways of the past can lead to a limiting rigidity of approach. The preservationist tendencies of the Calvinists who followed Calvin and the Lutherans who followed Luther produced baroque, systematised versions of their master's teachings that Calvin and Luther might have found hard to recognise[98]. Again, as we noted before[99], the defiant rigidity of the Princeton theologians (C. and A. A. Hodge and B. B. Warfield) became harder and harder to follow through the developing 20th Century. Resisting possible new ways of seeing no more guarantees a right grasp of 'the truth' than trusting in the latest methods.

Thus, if new ideas seem to help, bring new insight, untangle old intractable problems, yet make us wary of claiming too much, they should be seriously considered as a reasonable risk, a risk worth taking. Such ideas must not be dismissed out of hand. In the previous section of this chapter I sought to show that many of the new ideas about how we interpret texts are indeed helpful as we approach the Bible. They seem to offer more space for creative and imaginative approaches to the Bible even whilst they offer much sterner warnings about the dangers of claiming too much for our interpretations. I find that balance of more creativity with more caution and greater awareness of what we are doing to be eminently sensible. Do you?

2. A REAL PROBLEM

For me, another part of the argument in favour of using the new methods in approaching the Bible is the difficulties that now seem to attach to some of the old ideas. In particular, I would point to the ever-growing argument that the Modern World's presumption of easy objectivity simply does not fit. The decay of unquestioned optimism about inevitable human progress, allied with the richer variety of competing ways of seeing that are now available to us, make the old assumption of the objectivity of the well-meaning European gentleman-scholar look quite unsustainable now. It simply doesn't wash any more.

Granted, there is a danger of swinging the other way and accepting with the Deconstructionists that there are only individual subjective interpretations and an "abyss of uncertainty"[100]. Yet, as we have argued, this need not be so. It may be less exciting to say that the world we live in is probably somewhere in the middle, but it is hardly a surprising suggestion. To acknowledge that we all carry 'baggage' does not automatically imply that there is no 'truth' out there or that we are incapable of ever travelling closer to it. The problem with our lack of objectivity may simply mean that finding and agreeing the 'truth' is harder than we thought. All we can ever have (even in astrophysics) is our current best estimate and the suspicion that we may be getting a bit closer.

Be that as it may, to imagine that we can all carry on assuming that the truth is always clearly and dependably obvious to us is to ignore the cumulative evidence of history. Indeed, a self-suspecting caution about the distorting ideas we all bring with us is as wise now as it was when Jesus spoke of specks and planks. We, ourselves, are all 'part of the problem' when we are searching for the truth. Surely it's better to acknowledge it?

3. A HELPFUL ENDING

Even though it had clear Christian and Reformation roots, the Modern World of Science and Progress has never been an entirely satisfactory place to read the Bible. This pseudo-scientific confidently 'rational' sort of a world view has always chafed in a number of places. It never liked miracles or the supernatural; it had no respectable place to put 'faith' (because faith couldn't be faith and be entirely rational); it mistrusted spirituality and 'enthusiasm'. Whether it was the pared-down 'history' of a Wellhausen or the tightly-structured 'dogmatics' of a Warfield, the shared assumptions of the Modern World took the richness, depth, diversity and tensions in the Scriptures and reduced them to something neater and more perfectly-formed. Yet this perfection seems to have been achieved in the way that a telegraph pole is milled straight and geometrically-precise from the unique, history-laden shape of a living tree; much of the vigour, beauty and individuality is simply stripped off and discarded. I, for one, will not mourn the demise of the Modern World View as the only way of seeing.

Whilst I would admit that the new, less up-tight, relativist 'Postmodern' world brings in a whole new set of dilemmas and difficulties for people who believe they have received the Word of God, at least this new world lets People of Faith in the door without strip-searching them. So Postmoderns don't acknowledge any difference of category between Mormons, 'Moonies' or Methodists?... Then, as Christians, we'll just have to rise to the challenge and put our point of view across persuasively, personally, appropriately. Steve Moyise, writing about this new situation, puts it like this:

> If Christianity has something important to say to the world, then it will have to rely on its intrinsic persuasiveness rather than claims of infallibility (whether of Pope, Bible or synod)
>
> Steve Moyise, "Introduction to Biblical Studies". (Cassell. London. 1998). p.93

But the church has been here before. Paul the Apostle faced just such a task of persuasion in Lystra and Derbe and Thessalonica and Berea and Athens and Ephesus and Corinth and... *(Acts 14, 17, 18 & 19)*. We, too, will have to set up shop, look, listen and share. We may get booted out of some places but we might be heard in others and, like Paul, we might attract a completely different crowd from the one we thought we ought to get. We'll see.

The move out of the 'Modern' way of seeing seems to me like a sensible moving-on from increasingly unsuitable premises, not a fashion-infatuated rush to occupy the new. Moving house always brings trauma and the risk of unknown, unexpected problems and complications, but it often makes life better in the long run. Might not ending our stay in the Modern World be a real help to those of us who cherish the Bible?

4. AN ACCURATE DESCRIPTION

Another factor that helps me warm to these new ways of approaching whatever text we are trying to read, is the way they seem to echo what we all do in ordinary conversation. As we asked the question "How might we respond to this?" of each of the seven ideas we considered I began my responses with a consideration of what we do in "ordinary life". Each time, it seemed to me that these new ways of approaching texts were asking us to acknowledge that when we read, we treat texts the same way that we treat other people when we engage in conversation.

We EXPECT the various factors that have shaped someone to affect their response to what we say *(The Impossibility of Objectivity)*. We EXPECT that getting to know other people is a gradual cycling process of befriending *(The Spiral of Learning)*. We EXPECT to use our suspicion as a tool as we evaluate other people and, even though we don't like it, that their suspicions of us may, at times, be justified *(The Importance of Suspicion)*. We have come to EXPECT that there's validity to a whole range of different perspectives on life: that women have voices as well as men, that black people have points to make as well as white people... and so on *(The Liberation of Listening)*.

We EXPECT to find people using and abusing words to influence, even manipulate, other people's thinking as they struggle for power and influence *(The Ubiquity of Violence)*. We EXPECT to find different layers of meaning in what people say to us *(The Judgement of Meanings)*. We EXPECT to receive new knowledge and insight by listening to the stories people tell *(The Recovery of Story)*.

I would suggest that, without stopping to think about it, we are all highly-skilled hermeneutical operatives when it comes to everyday human interaction. We can all (in conversation): come up with theories to 'explain' other people's attitudes, warm to the other person, 'smell a rat', learn a whole new way of understanding something, be manipulative, find new layers of meaning, pass on sophisticated ideas in stories... and all before breakfast.

A significant factor in persuading me that these new theories about how we read texts are worth taking seriously is their 'common sense' quality. They seem to propose that we regularly treat texts very similarly to how we treat people (for better or for worse). Am I alone in finding this persuasive?

5.   A BELIEVABLE ACCOUNT

Intriguingly, these new ways of explaining the process of reading and understanding, give a believable account of the difficulties and tensions about reading the Bible faced by the Reformers and their successors, that we noted in Chapters One and Two. Indeed, they helpfully suggest ways we might move beyond some of the problems that caused so much anguish to earlier generations.

LUTHER and CALVIN and ENGLAND in 1646

In Chapter One, having reviewed the disputes about the Bible in the times of Luther and Calvin and again in England in 1646, when ancestral 'Congregationalism' and 'Presbyterianism' vied for ascendancy, we concluded that there were real problems with both the 'free for all' and the 'careful scholars' approach to finding the truth of the Bible. Our contemporary explanations of how we find meaning in texts give a plausible account of both failures. They suggest that the easy presumption of objectivity served all parties badly. Moreover, they imply that everyone would have been better served if they had learned to listen to one another, included everyone in the ferment and the sifting of interpretations, shared the practical insights of ordinary, ignored, poor people and the relevant knowledge and skills of scholars, all under the guidance of the Holy Spirit. That might have led not only to less violence (and there was LOTS of violence) but also to a better grasp of what the Bible was saying to everyone - even if they couldn't all agree about everything.

Of course, the whole idea would have been impossibly anachronistic in 16th Century Germany or 17th Century England, but we have contemporary parallels where we could reasonably appeal for listening, sharing and mutual humility in approaching the Bible together. There is, at times, an arid stridency in the mutual critiques of evangelical and various 'liberation' theologies. It still seems to be too easy just to find fault with the other party's argument or presuppositions or method, or accuse them of not being true to the Bible, before stomping out of the room in triumph or disgust. Yet discourse about this or that Bible passage will surely involve real co-operation in addressing the issues together. These new ways of approaching the whole business of reading and making sense give us a clear account why that should be so. By this account, our various biases and our potential for interpretative violence make a culture of mutual listening our only real chance of finding 'the truth' rather than simply inventing our own gods.

WELLHAUSEN & WARFIELD and THE CENTURY THAT FOLLOWED

In Chapter Two we considered the raging disputes about the value of critical scholarship in the 19th & 20th Centuries when both sides claimed some sort of 'higher' ground from which to look contemptuously on either the irrationality or the faithlessness of the other side. Again, the explanations of how we view texts that we are now considering give (with hindsight) a tremendously helpful account of what was happening. They identify clearly the failures of the Modern world view and its assumptions about the nature of knowing, that mean that the ground both sides chose to stand on was far less secure than they thought. Also, they suggest that the stark choice between 'rigorous rationality' and 'keeping the true faith' that seemed to split academy from church was far too simplistic. All knowing is more subtle, risky, exciting and provisional than either 'side' allowed. Both the Sceptics and the Faithful had a lot they could learn from each other, if only they could learn to listen and debate creatively, rather than defensively dispute and denounce.

Even in viewing the disputes about the Bible of previous centuries, these new ways of seeing offer us a way to interpret what was going on at the time that seems at once more imaginative and more cautious, more creative and more pragmatic than the ways of seeing that were grasped so firmly and so certainly by the various protagonists. They give a believable account of what was going on and why and what we might try to do about it now. Doesn't that sound helpful?

6.   A GREATER AWARENESS OF SIN

All this talk of suspicion, violence and struggles for power certainly makes the whole business of reading and interpreting texts (especially the ones we consider important) sound rather nasty. I consider that fair. I find it helpful. It comes considerably closer to alerting us to the selfish, manipulative, even sinful, way we humans tend to behave than the received enlightenment vision of the objective scholar selflessly seeking truth for the good of all. These new ways of reading are much more realistic about what Christians call sin. Welcome to the real world!

7.   *A MORE HONEST APPRAISAL*

For me, the most important argument for taking these ideas 'on board' as we approach the Bible is that they seem to allow the Bible to 'BE ITSELF' more successfully than the truth expectations of the Modern World. These ideas seem better able to take the Bible on its own terms, rather than tell it what it ought to be. They allow a more honest appraisal of what the Bible might be trying to do with us and for us.

The weight of this argument should be much more evident when we have reviewed BOTH the expectations we have inherited as to what the Bible should be like AND attempted a fresh overview of what we actually find when we turn and read the Bible itself. These two concerns will take up much of the next chapter (sections 4.1, 4.2 and 4.3). For now, let us simply note that there is an argument to be made that these methods can help us take the Bible more seriously on its own terms. Surely that is what we should be trying to do!

3.5 A personal journey

Another major line of argument that has persuaded me of the validity of these new ways of approaching texts has been my own personal 'voyage of discovery'. This is about as far from an 'objective' or a 'universal' argument as it's possible to get - yet it has been very powerful for me. I owe it to you to give you some account of it. My own story has been one of gradually, even painfully, discovering the sorts of ways of seeing that these new ideas represent. Bear with me as I tell something of my story....

My initial Christian nurture during my student days in St Andrews was shaped by the Christian Union movement - the evangelical student fellowships with a deep commitment to "What the Bible says". Although, in our 'C.U.' Bible study we often had a real struggle to find and agree 'the meaning' of a particular Bible passage, I and my fellow 'God Squad' members presumed that there was a unitary, clear meaning to each and every passage of Scripture. Anyone who might suggest differently was obviously 'unsound' and not to be taken seriously.

Moving to Birmingham (as a postgraduate student) I began worshipping in an inner city, evangelical, Anglican church. I began to become aware of issues of class and culture. Traditional 'Brummie' working class families and local African Caribbean families had quite distinct cultures from the broad UK middle class culture in which I had hitherto lived. If we were to share the Gospel in inner city Birmingham, did we have to 'convert' people to 'British middle class values' as well as introduce them to Jesus, the Galilean Jewish Saviour? I didn't think so, but how did one disentangle 'Christ' and 'culture'? Reading H. Richard Niebuhr's famous book "Christ and Culture"[101] didn't really help. It simply confirmed that there was a wide variety of different possible answers to this question. 'The Truth' was starting to get a little more complex - intriguing, yet unsettling.

My next move was to Nigeria, where I spent two fascinating years as a Biology lecturer at a new university. I was closely involved with 'NIFES' (Nigerian Fellowship of Evangelical Students) and worshipped with the congregation attached to a local seminary run by both indigenous Nigerian and American missionary staff. But the world looked very different from Africa. I read voraciously - including African Literature (in English) and African History. Time and again, as I 'discovered' for myself how exploitative, even evil, Western Imperialism looked from where I was now, I found myself asking "Why didn't anyone tell me this before?"

You see, in both history and geography lessons with my brave primary school teachers I had been nurtured into the shared belief in the great civilising mission of the British Empire. We had rejoiced that the fruit of British efforts had allowed colonies like the Gold Coast and Nigeria to receive from us the gift of independence and join us as 'junior brothers' in the great British Commonwealth of Nations. Now, living in Africa, with the help of African novelists like Chinua Achebe, Ngugi wa Thiong'o, Doris Lessing and Nadine Gordimer and the rich blessing of personal friendship and fellowship with uninhibited Nigerians, what had once seemed positive and obvious was now deeply suspect. What I had previously been taught and taken to be 'The Truth' read like deliberate propaganda. I was beginning to learn about the importance of suspicion and the impossibility of objectivity.

Perhaps even more disturbing to me was the discovery that missionaries could be very human and fallible. I was shocked to find blatantly racist attitudes amongst these people that God had called to serve the cause of Christ in another culture on another continent. The sensitivities of Nigerians, even of Nigerian Christians, even when they were arguably Bible-based, appeared to be of no consequence to many of the missionaries I met. I was, in truth, dis-illusioned. In the company of some of the most committed and evangelical Christians I have ever met, I was discovering a lot about the hidden baggage that my own culture kept trying to smuggle in. I was exploring the necessity of suspicion of my own people's story, the liberation of listening to people from other cultures, the near ubiquity of violence in the way my people had run the world, the complexity of the judgement of meanings, the importance of everyone's stories. Two brief years in Nigeria changed the way I saw just about everything. I thank God for that special time and for the people I met there.

Returning to Scotland, to study divinity in preparation for ministry, I couldn't fit back in. I needed the company of Africans, their perspective, their perceptions, their alternative grasp of the reality of my homeland and the ways of our shared world. But this whole justice and respect thing was bigger than I'd thought. I remember getting all heated, defensive and patronising when a woman quietly questioned my use of the phrase 'fellow men' in one of my prayers whilst I was a student on placement. I remember, also, how my reaction worried me and how the realisation gradually seeped in that I simply had to learn to hear and respect the voices of women speaking of injustice - I couldn't select some areas of injustice and silence or ignore others. I still had a lot of un-learning to do.

All the while, in Aberdeen, I was grappling with the Bible. I was helped in approaching the New Testament by the quiet rigour and careful judgements of Howard Marshall, a leading evangelical critical scholar and in approaching the Old Testament by the challenging vigour and demanding questions of William Johnstone, a thought-provoking successor of William Robertson Smith, the Professor ousted by the Free Church Assembly in 1881 for his use of the Higher Critical methods[102]. I started to hear the distinct voices of the different Gospel writers, feel the tensions between competing strands of tradition running through the Old Testament, discovered that the long history of Bible interpretation had involved a much richer variety of approaches and techniques than I'd ever suspected. Yet somehow the God I met through the pages of this complex, subtle, richly diverse book was more attractive than ever. Every time I discovered further turns and twists in the complexity of 'reality', I could go back to the Bible and find these real issues had been evidenced in its pages all along, I just hadn't seen it.

As I completed the academic part of my training for ministry, I felt I should check out for myself whether white people in apparently multiracial parts of the UK were as racist as the majority of white expatriates I had met in Nigeria. Was the UK church racist, and if it was, where did I fit, what might I be called to do? I asked what was possible and was given a placement with the United Reformed Church in Hackney, a vibrantly multicultural borough in London's East End. Indeed, I found this so exciting that, after the 10 months of placement, I accepted ordination by the United Reformed Church and remained in post as a minister in Hackney for eight years.

The processes of discovery, self-discovery and Bible-discovery continued. As well as being a minister in the United Reformed Church's Hackney Team Ministry, I was seconded to a third-time post with 'The Zebra Project'. This was a local Christian project worrying away at the interface between the developing black majority churches and the traditional UK churches that so often were their irritable landlords as well as their reluctant neighbours. Attending many conventions in black majority churches I heard, again and again, individual testimonies to the pain of black Christians who on first arrival in the UK from the Caribbean or Africa had found only rejection by their Christian brothers and sisters when they had expected a warm welcome. These and all the other apparently-intractable injustices of inner urban life gave the reading of many Bible passages a stark new edge that they had lacked in safe suburbs.

I began to find that the insights of Walter Brueggemann's writings on the Old Testament gave a powerfully relevant depth to the message of the prophets, a recognisable earthiness to the stories of David, a painful poignancy to Jeremiah's startling account of God's role in the destruction of Jerusalem that all resonated powerfully with the realities of Hackney life and Hackney faith and Hackney people. I also got excited by the work of Gerd Theissen on the social setting of the Church we meet in Paul's letters to the church in Corinth. I was not too worried by the finer points of Theissen's theories about the Corinthian Church and its divisions and whether every detail was entirely justified by the evidence. More importantly, Theissen had brought me to the exciting realisation that the same sorts of social issues (race, class, inherited taboos, mutual mistrust of the well-educated and the less-educated, social status and church status, etc., etc...) that seemed almost more important than theology to Christians in 20th Century inner London, had probably been just as vigorously and mischievously at work in the life of this Bible church in Paul's time. Why had I never seen this before? Watching the world around me, listening to other interpreters I was still proceeding on a spiral of learning, still learning to listen.

I felt truly privileged to be able to share something of the insights of Brueggemann and Theissen with a regular tutor group of black Pentecostal Christians at the New Testament Assembly's Training Institute in Tooting. Spirit, black experience, social analysis and Bible coalesced in a most exciting way as we studied first the church in Corinth, then prophets and prophecy. I found the real richness of SHARED Bible study.

Whilst in inner London I began to have visits from South African Christians who were involved in the struggle in their country and had come over for study tours to Europe. They fascinated me with their stories of trying to empower the people to stand up for justice in the face of relentless, harsh injustice. They shared *"The Kairos Document"*[103] and it's evangelical sister, *"Evangelical Witness in South Africa"*[104]. These two broad-based documents produced by hundreds of church people and theologians give voice to a sort of African liberation theology. Between them they had a profound effect on me. For they not only spoke prophetically to the harsh injustices of apartheid South Africa and the real failures of the South African churches to address them in a biblical way, but also (by implication) challenged the more-subtly-disguised injustices of my city and my world. In 1987, right at the height of the final repressive phase of the South African struggle, the Christian Fellowship Trust (who had brought many of these challenging South Africans to my door) sent me on a seven week study tour to South Africa. They wanted me, as one of a stream of ordinary British church people, to experience the interface between the Church and the political struggle in South Africa for myself.

In South Africa I did my best to stay afloat in a rich soup of experiences that was boiling with the best and the worst of human behaviour. I agonised over the question of how God and the Bible (as revered in the well-attended churches of the oppressors as in the well-attended churches of the oppressed) fitted with it all. As I read the Gospels in the light and shadow cast by the South African situation of 1987, I found a Jesus who, like Moses and Amos and Micah before him, was unafraid to take sides. I found a Jesus who never colluded with the special interest groups to which he was presumed to belong. He never made self-protective common cause with religious types against those they would condemn. He never made self-protective common cause with men against women. He never made self-protective common cause with fellow-Jews against Gentiles[105]. He never opted for divine or angelic support to rescue him from his human dangers, even when things got desperate. Confronted by the sort of brutal questions about your deepest loyalties that surrounded you every day in apartheid South Africa, Jesus looked like a quiet but determined TRAITOR to every party interest he could have claimed and every privilege he could have presumed at the expense of others. Without denying his maleness, or his Jewishness or his role as a religious teacher, or his closeness to God, he never colluded with the expectations of advantage in status and power that the world effortlessly presumed would go along with these particularities. Reading Jesus' story in South Africa in 1987, it seemed to say to me with all the stark force of Jesus' own sayings to people of privilege that he met - "don't deny who you are, but <u>learn</u> to live as a traitor to all your special interests". As a white, male, Western, university-educated, middle class, ordained minister on a steady income with pension rights, that left me with a lot of learning to do. I truly struggled with that challenge. I still do. I still do.

Apartheid South Africa in 1987 was life with the 'contrast' button turned up high. The sharpness of the choices, the clarity of the moral challenges affected everything I saw, even the Bible itself. My picture of Jesus was left with no comfortable soft focus. There was nowhere to stand and be detached or 'objective', no language that was 'neutral', no way of reading that did not either collude with injustice or begin to protest with those who suffered. The tensions and passions of the Bible came vividly alive. And when you returned home, you recognised the slightly subtler cousins of all the shameless mechanisms of injustice; you could not escape awareness of the ubiquity of violence.

Continuing in ministry in Hackney, then for the last thirteen years in inner urban Birmingham, tended to reinforce rather than unravel all these painful discoveries about how we find meaning in the Bible, in the world and in ourselves.

Clearly, these ideas of the impossibility of objectivity, the spiral of learning, the importance of suspicion, the liberation of listening, the ubiquity of violence, the judging of meanings and the recovery of story, were not something I first encountered by reading esoteric books about hermeneutics. The interaction of Bible and life during my individual journey of discovery, guided (I dare to believe) by God, has gradually introduced me to them and their powerful effects over the last thirty years.

I freely admit that, as I have journeyed on, these ideas have become more and more important to me as I try to approach and read particular passages in the Bible for the preparation of sermons and group Bible studies. I delight in the importance these ideas attach to the process of finding meaning in Bible passages. I love the way they insist that hearing God in the Bible (and not simply our own voices echoing back) is necessarily a shared task of the whole people of God. I am excited by the way they expect Bible reading to be a task involving everyone, not only scholars, yet they still allow for a broadening range of different scholarly approaches that are all free to contribute to the debate about meanings. I am intrigued at the way they seem to require a practical humility in approaching any Bible passage. I sense something right in the way they encourage us to expect challenge when we turn to a text from the Bible. I am rebuked by the way they will not allow us peace and love without justice.

I'm greatly encouraged by the way they suggest that understanding the Bible is always work in progress, that our conclusions are always provisional, that, indeed, "The Lord hath yet more light and truth to break forth from His Word."[106]

Whilst I cannot claim any objective value for it, my own personal journey with the Bible in my hand has been a key factor in persuading me why I should take these ideas about the search for meanings seriously. I offer my own story to you unashamedly in the spirit of personal testimony. I cannot read the Bible without its effects. It may include major distortions, yet I cannot remove them - only hope that, if it does, I can add new experiences that might bring a better balance.

Make what you will of my uncompleted story, but I am left wondering what your uncompleted story has been telling you!

CHAPTER FOUR

SEEING THE BIBLE WITH FRESH EYES

4.1 Two ways of Seeing the Bible

I suspect that every Christian encounters the Bible in two quite distinct ways:

✦ **THE BIBLE IN BITS** - Here we read and interact with single portions, specific 'readings' and particular passages. Probably most of our regular encounters with the Bible (through sermons, Bible studies and personal devotional reading) are of this sort - encounters with the Bible 'a bit at a time'.

✦ **THE BIBLE IN OVERVIEW** - Here we attempt to meet the teachings of the whole Bible as 'Scripture' or 'the-Bible-as-a-whole'. This is the wisdom of the whole Bible all summed up, added together, clarified, sorted and presented to us in creeds, confessions, catechisms, doctrinal statements and Church pronouncements.

Of course, these two approaches are not unrelated. As we suggested in Calvin's case[107], we surely hold our current understanding of the teachings of the Bible as a whole in the back of our minds whenever we individually or in groups approach a bit of the Bible. A clear agreement that a particular proposed interpretation of the text we are studying "goes against the Biblical doctrine of ......" will often be enough to cause most of us to swiftly discard that particular interpretation of our study passage. On the other hand, the cumulative effect of various encounters with particular passages may eventually engineer a shift in our perception of what 'the-Bible-as-a-whole' is saying.

Be that as it may, I reckon that, as church people, we all approach and use the Bible in these two distinct but related ways. What is more, I strongly suspect that we handle the Bible rather differently depending on which approach we are currently following...

I. APPROACHING THE BIBLE IN BITS

When we confront a specific bit of the Bible, in a sermon or Bible study, many of us are already broadly 'Postmodern' in our approach. We are probably open to most, even all, of the new ways of seeing that we discussed in the last chapter, even if we've never stopped to think about them before. Many of us must have absorbed important changes in attitudes and understanding from the developing general culture of the late 20th Century by a slow process of 'osmosis', by specific crises in understanding, or by a combination of both.

These ideas about how we find meaning in texts may also be operating even as you or I are seeking the meaning(s) of a particular bit of the Bible. You see, when we approach a PARTICULAR PASSAGE from the Bible we are likely to use the support of one or more commentaries on the relevant book of the Bible, reading what is written about our selected passage. If we are using any recently-published commentaries they are likely to rely heavily on the ongoing scholarly debates about that passage and its possible meanings that freely involve Roman Catholic and Protestant scholars, liberal scholars and evangelical scholars, the insights of our contemporaries and the views of scholars from previous times. They may also include, where appropriate, the views of various liberationist scholars and refer to recent studies that employ sociological or narrative approaches to the Bible. Evangelicals may prefer the fruits of all this scholarship and debate to have been carefully sieved through a 'sound' evangelical commentary, but many recent evangelical commentaries are more than happy to draw from and debate with the whole range of contemporary scholarship. Thus, when we approach individual portions of the Bible in sermon or Bible study we are ALL receiving a steady drip, drip of ideas from the shared world of Biblical scholarship - a world where these new ideas about the search for meanings are becoming more and more commonplace. So, whether we realise it or not, many of us may ALREADY be approaching both Bible study and sermon preparation with a broadly 'postmodern' sensibility and an interest in the sorts of questions this would imply. Indeed, more and more of us are finding that, when we are looking at an individual Bible passage, these new approaches offer more promise than threat, more help than hindrance, more challenge than confusion. I suspect that these ideas are increasingly shaping the way we try to read any bit of Bible. They seem to make sense and, in practice, they help.

2.   APPROACHING THE-BIBLE-AS-A-WHOLE

Yet when we (particularly in the Councils of the Church) turn to issues of guidance, doctrine and ethical authority - that all expect us to make sense of "THE-BIBLE-AS-A-WHOLE" (or the Bible in overview) - the picture is a little different. Here clarity, consistency and certainty have always been at a premium. Here, we tend to look more to the interpretative and summarising 'construction work' of theologians and ethicists rather than the verse by verse and phrase by phrase analysis of Bible commentators. Here we are under significant pressure to try to find consistent, authoritative Bible meanings, Bible doctrines, or Bible standpoints on particular issues or topics. As a result, we are more likely to depend on extracted collections of 'relevant' texts from all over the Bible, analyses of 'The Biblical Meaning' of key words used again and again in the Bible, or simply accept the opinions and arguments of respected scholars or denominational working groups who seek to affirm for us 'What the Bible says...'. We will probably be paying less attention to the specific context and theology of particular Bible authors and audiences and leave aside significant consideration of the impact of their motives, style, narrative or rhetoric. We are much less likely to be employing the new ways of reading outlined in Chapter Three[108].

As we approach the whole Bible looking for clear, unified meanings ('What the Bible says...'), these new ideas about interpretation of texts appear to be offering us complications where we are seeking clarity, caution where we want confidence, choice where we would prefer a simple certainty. As the process of generating reliable, non-contentious doctrinal and ethical statements from the Bible is already difficult (recall the endless history of Christian theological disputes), no-one wants to make it harder. So, we mostly remain stubbornly 'Modern' in our approach to the Bible as a whole.

Historically, Councils, Synods and Assemblies in almost every denomination have turned to the Bible to develop doctrine, construct creeds and confessions, make decisions on moral matters and act as the Church's final arbiter of doctrine, faith, morality and ethics. For example, the Westminster Confession of Faith of 1647 states:

> The supreme Judge, by which all controversies of religion are to be determined, and all decrees of councils, opinions of ancient writers, doctrines of men, and private spirits, are to be examined, and in whose sentence we are to rest, can be no other but the Holy Spirit speaking in the scripture.
>
> *The Westminster Confession of Faith (1647), Chapter 1, Section 10 109*

Three hundred and twenty-five years later, the Basis of Union of the United Reformed Church, formed in 1972, similarly says:

> The Word of God in the Old and New Testaments, discerned under the guidance of the Holy Spirit, [is] the supreme authority for faith and conduct of all God's people
>
> *The Basis of Union of the United Reformed Church, Schedule D, Version 1, clause 3*

Indeed, the idea that the Bible is the place to look for the authoritative Word of God must surely be as close as we can get to a shared 'Christian' understanding[110]. Other denominations and traditions may express the matter in different ways, but Protestant Christianity in general and Reformed Christianity in particular stand united in a sense of being under the 'authority' of the Word of God found in the Scriptures of the Old and New Testaments. Similarly, the Catholic and Orthodox Churches (despite a somewhat different approach to authority and variations in the accepted canon[111]) would not expect either Pope or Council to make an authoritative doctrinal statement that clearly contradicted the Bible's perceived teachings.

Through both Reformation and Modern times, Reformed Churches, in common with most other Christian denominations, have repeatedly tried to depend upon the Bible as if it were an exact legal document. It has been revered as a sort of church 'constitution' which should, in principle, be competent to decide any issues relating to doctrine, faith, morals or church order. As the old saying goes, settling any dispute should simply be a matter of "quoting Chapter and Verse". If the Bible did not, in practice, give clear guidance on a particular point, or there were texts that appeared to be in conflict with each other, then the denomination's accepted Confessional Statement (such as the Westminster Confession) could be used as a reliable guide or filter. As the Confession was taken to be a summary of the teachings of the Scriptures as a whole, its use was not seen as introducing anything new or different - the integrity of the authoritative Bible would not be seen to be breached.[112]

All through the 'Modern' period this allowed a number of other related assumptions about the way the Bible would operate to be taken as obvious facts in the churches. Even, the onslaught of 19th Century German Critical Scholarship (vividly characterised by Albert Schweitzer as "the struggle against the tyranny of dogma".[113]), largely failed to dislodge most Christians' expectations as to how their church should generate its doctrine and ethics from the Bible as a whole. More recently, the spread of new ways of handling texts that appear to be comfortably employed when we are considering individual Bible passages, have probably not made so much impact on the historic assumptions about how Churches can reasonably generate 'Biblical' teachings from the Bible.[114]

This big, bold Reformation expectation that the Bible should function as the final arbiter of all truth for the church (*'Sola scriptura'*, i.e. 'Scripture alone') brought with it a number of related expectations about Scripture and how it might operate. That first chapter of the Westminster Confession, *"Of the Holy Scripture"*, talks confidently (without any expectation of argument or disagreement) when it lists "the consent of all the parts" and the "entire perfection" of the Bible as ways in which "it doth abundantly evidence itself to be the Word of God"[115].

With the increased suspiciousness of our own times and the recent developments in our understanding of how we find meaning in texts, we need to stop here and ask to look carefully at the clutch of ideas that have so easily attached themselves to the assertion that the Bible is "THE WORD OF GOD". Do all the diverse parts of the Bible actually "consent" or agree about everything? In what ways can we consider the Bible to possess "entire perfection"? Are these inherited ideas facts borne out by what we find in the Bible itself, or assumptions smuggled in because they make things clearer and easier if they are taken to be true? Let's lay out these inherited ideas, then turn to the Bible itself and see if they 'fit' with what we find. Then we can try to decide whether they look like facts or assumptions.

Here is my summary of these inherited ideas about the-Bible-as-a-whole:

```
┌─────────────────────────────────────────────────────────────────┐
│            INHERITED IDEAS ABOUT THE-BIBLE-AS-A-WHOLE             │
```

1.   The Divine Authorship of the Bible ensures that the **ONE, CLEAR VOICE of GOD** can be heard within all the Scriptures no matter how varied the work of particular Biblical authors in style or intention. Any challenge to the univocal quality of the Bible can be seen as a challenge to Divine Authorship. Any apparent discrepancies in theology between Bible authors need to be explained away.

2.   The message of the Bible can be taken to be straightforwardly **UNIVERSAL**, that is applicable in every place, time and cultural setting, with only the simplest and most obvious of adjustments for changed cultural circumstances.

3.   Clearly, this story of God's purposes for humankind in the Bible constitutes the grandest and most complete **GRAND NARRATIVE** of them all, explaining definitively the true purpose of everything in a way that can be used to construct reliable creeds, confessions and catechisms for the church.

4.   The Bible as God's saving and necessary message for his people, once filtered through the correct Confessional Statement, is **ETHICALLY PRECISE** in the moral and practical guidance it gives.

5.   The Bible, filtered through the correct Confessional Statement, clearly distinguishes the true believers of the **ONE TRUE CHURCH** from all those misled into error and falsehood.

```
└─────────────────────────────────────────────────────────────────┘
```

I suspect that (although they wouldn't use my language!) a lot of people in various Reformed Churches, as in other denominations, would broadly accept these ideas as 'true' (with the possible exception of the fifth inherited idea about the 'true' church). I can just imagine some folk saying "Isn't that what the Bible is there for"? But how well does the Bible fit these inherited expectations of what it should be like?

4.2   What have we got in the Bible?

I invite you to join me in viewing the Bible from five distinct standpoints, each one related to one of the five inherited ideas we have listed above.

1.   *A DIVERSE LIBRARY*

I f we turn to the Bible and try to look at it with a fresh inquisitiveness, we find more of a 'library' than a 'book'.[116] The writings in the Bible are startlingly diverse.

For a start, let us consider **THE SPREAD OF TIME** taken in assembling this 'library'. These works represent an enormously-extended period of human history. Jesus of Nazareth, the key figure in the Gospels, and his ancestor King David, whose story is told in *1 and 2 Samuel*, must have lived around a thousand years apart (at least as far apart in time as we are from William the Conqueror). Beyond that, the stories of Abraham, Isaac and Jacob portray a period hundreds of years before David. Whatever the precise nature of God's involvement with this collection of books, a vast array of different people must have been involved in its telling and retelling, recording, editing, copying, preserving, collecting and recognition as 'Scripture'. Contrast this with Al Qur'an, where the Word of Allah is offered through the mediation of one Prophet who was inspired to write it all down word for word as he heard it, all during one part of his adult life. For Al Qur'an there is no editing, no periods of oral transmission, no disputes about what's in and what's out, no division of Scripture-making tasks between various people living in different times and different contexts who may never have met, most of whom remain unknown to history. It's all done and dusted through one prophet within twenty-five years (probably between about 610 CE and 632 CE)[117]. In comparison, the God who speaks in the Christians' Bible seems to have been very relaxed about involving an *enormous* team of human co-workers over many, many generations.

Between them, the books in this library speak with a huge range of **DIFFERENT** VOICES. Even when we come to works that purport to be from close colleagues who journeyed side by side for months on end in the service of the gospel we hear authors with totally distinct voices. The author of the book of *Acts* and the Paul who wrote *1 and 2 Corinthians* and *Galatians* have different literary styles, different vocabularies, even different understandings of what is important and central to the good news of Jesus. Indeed, so great is the difference between the portrayal of Paul's core theology in *Acts* and what we find in his own letters that some modern scholars find it hard to accept that the author of the book of *Acts* ever met Paul or even read his letters, despite the 'we' passages in *Acts* that seem to imply that the two authors travelled together.[118] The God whose Word is represented by this library clearly allows a lot of space for individuality to its human authors. If Calvin is right to characterise the human authors of this library as God's 'secretaries',[119] they are clearly not copy-typists or stenographers; the individuality of each author, even in their theology, shines through very clearly.

Within and between the volumes of this library we find **A WIDE VARIETY OF LITERARY** and **ORAL STYLES** and **TYPES**. There are some directly prescriptive passages in legal language giving both civil and religious law (see much of *Exodus, Leviticus, Numbers* and *Deuteronomy*). There are extensive collections of history-like stories, often rich with a pre-history of oral telling and retelling that may reach back for centuries (see *Genesis, Joshua, Judges, 1 and 2 Samuel, 1 and 2 Kings* and *1 and 2 Chronicles*). There are collections of the public sayings and actions of particular prophets (see *Amos, Hosea, Micah*, etc...). There are the texts of worship songs for use in the Jerusalem temple (see the book of *Psalms*). There are assemblages of pithy aphorisms and proverbs and extended philosophical musings by world-weary intellectuals (see *Proverbs* and *Ecclesiastes*). There are coded dreams and fantasies intended to convey concealed hopes to those who can de-code them (see parts of *Daniel* and *Revelation*). There are preserved letters from wandering pastors addressing the troubles of far-off churches (see the letters of Paul). There are carefully compiled collections of stories about Jesus each of which has an overall shape and purpose (see the four Gospels).

Such diversity of styles would not sit well with a God anxious, above all, to impart clear, precise propositions. The founding fathers of the United States of America knew the style and tone necessary for a legally-binding foundational document. The Bible simply does not read like the Constitution of the United States. Might God have been intending something rather different?

All in all, the various books and anthologies in this library evidence a rich diversity not only of literary styles but also of social settings, spirituality and theology. Intriguingly, the different books often tell and re-tell parts of their inherited tradition from quite **DISTINCT PERSPECTIVES**. Religious and civil laws given in *Exodus* and *Leviticus* re-appear in an altered context in *Deuteronomy* (see, for example, the different but related accounts of the offering of first fruits given in *Leviticus 23:10ff* and *Deuteronomy 26:1ff*). The history given in *1 and 2 Samuel* and *1 and 2 Kings* appears re-worked with a different perspective and purpose in *1 and 2 Chronicles*. Then, when we come to the central story of Jesus, we have FOUR distinct accounts of Jesus, each one using or re-using stories and incidents recounted in the other gospels. Three of them are clearly related (*Matthew, Mark* and *Luke*) but still offer their own unique perspectives on the story whilst the fourth (*John*) provides a telling of the story quite distinct in its tenor, approach and handling of the events and their significance. Surely a God intent on giving a single, definitive account of what happened and what it meant could have done so, inspiring those who closed the canon to select only one version as the 'true' Gospel? Yet this Bible seems irreducibly intent on providing us with multiple voices in the accounts it gives of crucial events and their significance.

Indeed, some of the individual books appear to be anthologies that include collected variants of the same story where both versions have been respectfully preserved alongside each other in a bigger work with its own theological purposes (see, for example, the stories of Jacob leaving home in *Genesis 27:41-45* and *28:1-9*).[120]

All this **DIVERGENT RE-TELLING**, with a refusal to reject either alternative version, underlines the literary and theological diversity of the whole collection and the complexity of the assembling process. David Carr suggests that this process of the growth of texts is typical of the Ancient Near East. He concludes:

> One might say that the ancients tended to change and supplement the very texts that they cherished the most..... Within this context, a mark of scripture was its multi-voiced character, not its alleged authorial unity.
>
> *[italics original]*
> *David Carr, "Untamable Text of an Untamable God", INTERPRETATION, October 2000, p.352*

If, as we believe, this library of diverse works is 'the Word of God', it is unlikely to be so in the obvious, simplistic way presumed by the Bible interpreters of the Modern World. For here there is remarkably little material that presents as the direct instructing Voice of God. Even Jesus, "The Word made flesh", unlike his earthly near-contemporary Paul, has not left us any directly-written or personally-dictated work. We only ever meet Jesus through the selective memories of other witnesses, we only ever see him through the eyes of other people or hear him through their edited accounts of things he said. Rather, in this Bible, God is to be heard through hundreds of voices in diverse social and historical settings in ways remembered, recounted and reassembled many times over, using a huge range of literary styles and constructs with no obvious interest in imposing a single unifying voice or viewpoint on this rich diversity of material.

Indeed, a better case can be made that there is a deliberate intent to provide us with diverse voices than any intent to impress us with a single voice. Moreover, this Bible declines to offer a clear account of how we are to balance and weigh all these different voices or decide who is 'right' when the voices are not obviously in agreement with each other.

> Looking at the Bible we have suggests that:
>
> **THE WAY GOD SPEAKS TO US IN THE BIBLE does not readily fit with our inherited ideas of how God OUGHT to speak to us.**

2.   A PARTICULAR STORY

Even though the Bible is a library-like collection of writings containing a rich diversity of styles and opinions, assembled over hundreds and hundreds of years, it is, at the same time, a very particular story. All these writings represent material gathered along the way by one particular historical strand of a particular faith group with its roots in a particular set of places and events, its imagery steeped in particular landscapes and their seasons. Indeed, the New Testament, in its reading of the Old Testament, deliberately narrows the particularity of the story even more. The writings in the New Testament take a very particular reading of much of the Old Testament, deliberately focussing it through the story of Jesus as its intended fulfilment and true meaning. For Christians, God is speaking to us through a single highly-particular historically, culturally and geographically rooted story.

Yet, we believe the Bible to be the Word of God for us and all other peoples of all times and places. Consequently, we have to take this very particular material rooted in a very particular history in a particular set of places to be God's way of communicating with all people in a limitless range of other historical and social settings and places. We have to allow this very particular material to be, in some sense, universal.

So, we have to develop some way of deciding which details of this story are specific to the original people, communities, times and places and which are directly or indirectly applicable to us and our community and any other communities and settings it might encounter. We cannot read these writings as the Word of God without some sort of extrapolation and re-interpretation from their particular settings to our own and others' settings. Yet, the Bible itself gives us little more than hints as to how we should decide such matters.

For example, the account of the Council of Jerusalem in *Acts 15* allows that the full weight of the Law given in the Pentateuch need not apply to Gentile Christians, requiring only that they "abstain from what has been sacrificed to idols and from blood and from what is strangled and from fornication" (*Acts 15:29, NRSV*). But where does this leave us? Do some of the Ten Commandments still apply? Are whole sections of the books of *Exodus, Leviticus, Numbers* and *Deuteronomy* simply to be discarded? What, specifically, is included in the ban on 'fornication'?

Intriguingly, the two items in this very short list of cross-cultural moral requirements which appear to be clear and straightforward - the injunctions to abstain from eating blood and from eating meat from animals that have been strangled - have come to be ignored by much of the church in our own time. I have never heard of a United Reformed or Presbyterian or Congregational or Anglican or Baptist or Methodist Church taking a firm line and rebuking members who ate 'black pudding' (or other blood-based foods). Nor have I heard churches insisting that their members must eat only 'kosher' meat from animals killed in the prescribed fashion. Yet these seem to be the clearest and most authoritative teachings in the New Testament about what is required of Gentile Christians.

Thus, if we are to take this very particular story to be God's Word for all times and places and peoples, we are left without any clear guidance how it is to be read out of its own setting into the setting of another community of readers.

> Looking at the Bible we have suggests that:
> **DECIDING what is 'UNIVERSAL' and what is 'PARTICULAR' in Scripture is not as easy as our inherited ideas expect.**

3. A KITCHENFUL OF INGREDIENTS BUT NO RECIPE

When we turn to the Bible to search out what it says about "the world, the universe and everything"[121], we immediately run into a problem. There are many, many passages in the Scriptures that give us clear indicators and vivid ideas as to how we might best view the world, and the great drama of God's purposes, but no one place that seems to set out a straightforward comprehensive account of God's Grand Narrative. Relevant ideas are scattered through the Bible with no clear guidance as to how they all fit together. It is as if the Bible provides us with copious supplies of ingredients for making fabulous fruit cakes, but no single, specific recipe to tell us how to combine them.

Historically, the Church has often felt the need to construct some sort of summary of the Christian Faith to aid its 'digestibility'. Time and again churches and denominations have felt the need for properly-organised officially-sanctioned accounts of God's Grand Narrative. These are presumed to be clearer accounts of what is found in the Bible, suitable for testing the orthodoxy of an individual's faith. The simplest form of such a statement is called a "CREED". Most of us have probably declared our faith in the words of 'The Apostles' Creed' or 'The Nicene Creed'[122]. They list the barest outline of "what we believe about God". More extended and elaborate accounts of the key structures of our faith (and how it explains the way the world is) are called CONFESSIONS or DECLARATIONS of FAITH. The Westminster Confession, whose drafting in 1646-7 featured in Chapter I Section 4 above, is a prime example of such a Confession. Beyond that some individual theologians have written extended multi-volume treatises intended to provide a thorough guide to the Christian Faith with helpful doctrinal neatness and systematic theological thoroughness. A classic example of this, as we noted in Chapter I Section 3, is John Calvin's famous "*Institutes of the Christian Religion*"[123] which he originally intended to serve as an introduction to Scripture.[124]

In the Modern World, Creeds, confessions and even extended treatises on dogmatics were taken to be refined and ordered essences of the truths found in the Bible. Thus, for much of the last 300 years The Reformed Tradition has been parented as much by Calvin's "*Institutes*" and the Westminster Confession as by the Bible itself. Yet, as time went by, many of the assumptions and interpretations contained in both the "Institutes" and the

Confession began to look increasingly problematic to more and more of those supposedly bound by these normative statements of the faith. Take, for example, the situation of a number of Presbyterian Churches that still retain the Westminster Confession as their official 'Subordinate Standard' of the faith. In order to retain this 350-year-old Confession as a test of whether their ministers subscribe to the true faith, they have had to allow ministers 'liberty of opinion' on such points of doctrine as do not enter into the substance of the faith'[125]. Indeed, they appear to have had to refrain from spelling out exactly which doctrines and ideas in the Westminster Confession are covered by that liberty of opinion clause and which are still fully to be applied. And why do they keep this tenuous connection to this aged confession? It would appear that writing a new binding statement in the 20th or 21st Century to properly replace the Westminster Confession is just too dangerous. It would probably risk schism. It would certainly require a lot of heated debate. So, it has seemed safer to some Reformed denominations to leave the grand old Confession sitting there like a sort of constitutional monarch - looking regal but lacking real, practical authority across the church as a whole.

Still, it is much easier to acknowledge today than it was in 1646-7 that Confession-writing is an interpretative act. Any attempt to summarise the Bible's message is going to be selective. Some things will be left out, others given greater prominence and the selections made will inevitably be influenced by the setting, assumptions and opinions of those who construct it. Even the creeds agreed by the Councils of the Early Church can now be seen to have been shaped by the theological and philosophical debates of their own age (not all of which seem comprehensible or relevant today)[126]. Again, the few that now take the trouble to read the Westminster Confession or the Savoy Declaration[127] must be struck by the extent to which they exude the ideas, attitudes and ethos of their day, age and party, including some ideas that are hard to accept today.

In giving us this Bible as our Scriptures, God has apparently declined to provide us with either an off-the-shelf pre-packed Grand Narrative Cake or even an officially-approved recipe giving clear instructions as to how to bake it ourselves. The Bible may come tantalisingly close, but it resolutely stops short of providing an official unified account of the Christian Grand Narrative that we could all sign up to, however much we all wish it would. Indeed, it is even notoriously coy about providing a clear statement of the Doctrine of the Trinity. So, we have to write the creeds, the confessions and the theological treatises; the Bible doesn't do it for us. Moreover, it provides no clear and exact rules as to how we should go about it. Thus, each 'family' has its own recipe, handed down and developed over generations. But who is to say that other recipes might not be just as good or that our existing recipe cannot be improved or developed?[128]

> Looking at the Bible we have suggests that:
> **SUMMARISING THE MESSAGE OF THE BIBLE in creeds and confessions is not as straightforward as our inherited ideas expect.**

4.   A STRANGE RULE BOOK

If we now approach the Bible seeking clear moral and ethical guidance, what do we find? Certainly, there are many rules here in direct legal language, as well as deliberate moral tales, practical aphorisms, specific instructions to churches by pastors speaking in God's name and instructive words from Jesus himself. Yet, taken as a whole, the Bible is a long way away from the consistent, ordered legal directness of a good Act of Parliament or a well-written Bill passing through Congress.

Alongside all the material that can be read in a legal way the Bible sets other sayings that seem to question, modify, subvert or even replace the whole legal approach to morality, ethics and religion. Consider these examples:

✦ **AMOS & MICAH** represent an established prophetic tradition that resists any idea that God can be bought off by compliance with the religious requirements of the Law. Amos presents a God who thunders "I hate, I despise your festivals... even though you offer me your burnt-offerings and grain-offerings, I will not accept them... but let justice roll down like waters, and righteousness like an ever-flowing stream" *(Amos 5:21-24, NRSV)*. Micah, in an equally famous passage, has God resisting elaborate, prescribed offerings, and says what the Lord truly requires is that we "do justice, and... love kindness and... walk humbly with... [our] God." *(Micah 6:6-8 NRSV)*. Yet, this is the same God who, according to *Exodus, Leviticus, Numbers* and *Deuteronomy* gave elaborate laws about required offerings and festivals.

✦ **JEREMIAH** tells of God's distress at the way his people have persisted in breaking his covenant with them. In chapter 31 God tells how he is going to make a new and different covenant. This one will be different because, God says, "I will put my law within them, I will write it on their hearts". ... then there will be no need to teach God's ways to anyone because "they shall all know me." *(Jeremiah 31:33-34, NRSV)*. Here the law is but an imperfect means of offering a covenant relationship with God; a means that could (and should) be replaced with a more direct relationship of the heart - a non-legal direct covenant of friendship.

✦ **THE SERMON ON THE MOUNT** in Matthew's Gospel has Jesus declaring that "not one letter, not one stroke of a letter, will pass from the Law" until the end of time *(Matthew 5:18)*. Yet Jesus immediately follows with a series of sayings "You have heard that it was said... but I say to you..." *(Matthew 5:21-48)*. These sayings all make the Law far more stringent and radically demanding. They also move some of its commands from the realm of outward actions that other people might see to the realm of inward thoughts and feelings that only God can observe. In a subtle but important way this prevents these central elements of the Law from operating practically as shared community rules. As Robert Tannahill puts it whilst considering part of a parallel passage in Luke's Gospel *(Luke 6:27-31)*:

Jesus' teaching uses forceful and imaginative language, which is to be clearly distinguished from legal language. Legal language must try to provide clear definitions in order to regulate external behaviour. Forceful and imaginative language is not concerned with clear definitions. ...... [It is] not concerned primarily to regulate external behaviour but serves to stimulate moral insight by challenging the ruts in which people move. ...... It can change action by working through the imagination, challenging old assumptions and suggesting a new possibility whilst trusting the hearer to work out the details.

Robert C. Tannahill, "LUKE", (Abingdon Press, Nashville, 1996), p.117.

✦ **JESUS and the TEACHERS of the LAW** are regularly reported to be engaged in serious disputes in Matthew, Mark and Luke's Gospels. It is often for those who most zealously try to keep the Law in every prescribed detail that Jesus reserves his strongest words of condemnation *(e.g. Matthew 23:1-32)*. Challenged about the failure of his disciples to observe the Law of the Sabbath, Jesus recounts a story of how David broke the Law to feed his men and concludes, "The Sabbath was made for humankind, and not humankind for the Sabbath." *(Mark 2:27)*. Jesus seems to see the Law as a pointer to a deeper truth, not the truth itself.

✦ **ACTS** tells us of a decision of a Council in Jerusalem that the full rigour of the Jewish Law simply does not apply to Gentile Christians, apart from four specific provisions that will allow Jewish Christians to share table fellowship with them *(Acts 15:29)*. As we noted above, it simply does not make clear whether any of the Ten Commandments still apply or in what ways the books of *Leviticus Numbers* and *Deuteronomy* continue to be part of 'The Word of God' for Gentile Christians.

✦ **GALATIANS** finds Paul adamant that the cultic requirements of the Jewish Law must not be made to apply in any way to Gentile Christians. Without wishing to encourage licence or self-indulgence, he radically questions the applicability of the Laws in the Old Testament, urging that Gentile believers look instead to faith in Jesus and the power of his Spirit to 'save' and sustain them.

So, the Bible has a lot of "LAW", often detailed and explicit, but it also has important passages that question the full validity of these laws or openly reject much of the legal material without giving clear indications as to exactly which laws are 'in' and which are 'out'. Quite how the balance between the legal material and the critical material should be constructed is not spelled out in the Bible. No-one can be certain that they have got this balance right, nor that others have got it wrong.

Looking at the Bible we have suggests that:
IDENTIFYING WHICH BIBLE RULES APPLY TODAY and HOW they are to be applied is not as simple as our inherited ideas expect.

5. A CHOICE OF MANY MANSIONS

Personally, the Bible has long afforded me a very real sense of belonging - a spiritual and emotional home, a place where I feel accepted with all the comfort of grace and forgiveness. For me, the Bible acts as the one crucial catalyst for individual and shared spirituality in devotions, bible study and worship. Its realism and honesty and, above all, that incredible central story of God come in Christ willingly embracing rejection, condemnation and death on behalf of us all, make life liveable. This is my "shelter from the stormy blast"[129].

Yet, should I so readily assume that I'm included in the people of God and that those whose ways shock me need to reform before they can feel at home within the community of Bible believers? The Bible itself gives conflicting messages. Janet Tollington has pointed out to me[130] that *Deuteronomy 23:1-3* gives some very precise instructions on the total exclusion of eunuchs, illegitimate children, Ammonites and Moabites (and their descendants for up to 10 generations), whilst *Isaiah 56* powerfully reassures eunuchs, outcasts and all 'foreigners' of a princely welcome if they simply keep the Sabbath. Then, in the New Testament we have Jesus saying, in one Gospel account: "Whoever is not with me, is against me" (*Matthew 12:30*) and "Whoever is not against us is for us" (*Mark 9:40*) in another.

Just look at who, in our own day and age, is comfortable here. For, no matter what your own particular theology, or the limits set by your own denomination (and the others it recognises), the Bible seems to provide just as comfortable a spiritual home for people of vastly different theologies and world views. I delighted, when I visited South Africa in 1987, to meet brave people struggling for justice sustained by the Jesus they met in the Bible and the promises of a God of justice they found there. Yet, week by week, many of those who oppressed them or for whom the whole apparatus of oppression was kept in place, turned to the same Bible, preached and studied in Dutch Reformed and other churches, to find their own strength to carry on resisting change. Such diversities of comfort could be witnessed again and again all across the world and all through Christian history.

You and I share this book with inquisitors and Quakers, slave owners and their slaves, pietists and liberals, Christian Socialists and right-wing dictators, Desert Fathers and Pentecostals. Each has taken it to be the authoritative Word of God and, we must presume, believed themselves to be living broadly within its precepts, though their understandings of what the Bible means in practice must, at times, be mutually exclusive.

I imagine that we are all selective in affirming the bits of the Bible that make us feel most at home and quietly ignoring or cleverly glossing the bits that would require us to change. The Bible seems to offer a home to a vast range of different people, without ever giving us clear guidance as to how we can decide who should be evicted.

> Looking at the Bible we have suggests that:
> **Bible guidance as to WHO THE TRUE BELIEVERS ARE is not as clear as our inherited ideas would expect.**

4.3 Why don't we get what we expect?

When we look closely at the Bible, it resolutely refuses to fit with our received expectations of what it ought to be like. It does not matter how many Christian denominations look to the Bible to be the final arbiter of dispute, the Bible simply does not present as a carefully-constructed legal reference work intended to settle once-and-for-all the theological and ethical disputes of the people of God.[131] As was argued in the previous section (5.2):

WE TEND TO EXPECT:	IN THE BIBLE WE FIND:
✦ the **ONE CLEAR VOICE OF GOD** speaking through all the Scriptures	✦ a **RICHLY DIVERSE LIBRARY** shaped by countless authors, editors and story-tellers, with many different voices and many theologies
✦ a **UNIVERSAL** story applicable to every era, place and culture.	✦ a **PARTICULAR** story with no clear guidelines as to how we might 'universalise' it for other situations.
✦ The grandest **GRAND NARRATIVE** of them all, giving in definitive form an explanation of "the world, the universe and everything".	✦ Whilst it is bursting with theological ideas, the Bible gives no single clear summary of doctrine, no single statement of the faith, **NO SINGLE ACCOUNT OF 'THE TRUTH'**.
✦ A source of **PRECISE ETHICAL GUIDANCE** that shows us clearly how we should live.	✦ The Bible leaves **AN UN-RESOLVED TENSION BETWEEN ETHICAL GUIDANCE and PROPHETIC VOICES** that challenge every attempt to read this guidance as 'law'.
✦ Clear guidance as to who are and who are not the true believers of the **ONE TRUE CHURCH**.	✦ The Bible **DOES NOT MAKE CLEAR WHO IS A TRUE BELIEVER**, and who is not one.

How are we to account for this great divide between our inherited expectations of what the Bible "should" be like and what we find when we look at the Bible we have?

In principle, there are three possible explanations of this discrepancy:

✦   There is no God. The Bible's just a collection of human writings.
✦   God is inept when it comes to writing Scripture and did a sloppy job.
✦   God is actively trying to challenge and alter the way we think, so the nature
      and structure of the Bible reflect this.

Many outside the church find considerable strength in the first of these possible explanations. For them, the Bible clearly falls short of what we would have a right to expect of a book that purported to be "The Word of God". For me, the very size of the discrepancies between our inherited expectations and the Bible we have makes both of the first two explanations implausible. Could either a lackadaisical deity or a team of human ghost writers and editors settle for a product so ill-fitting for its intended market? Could they resist the temptation to sharpen it up a bit and make it more plausible?

I am much more intrigued and attracted by the third possibility - that God is deliberately trying to challenge the way we think. The Bible may be designed to unsettle our certainties that we might be open to meeting God in a quite different way from the one we had anticipated. Perhaps the discrepancies are there because God has *gone beyond* our rather naïve expectations, providing a more subtle, complex, challenging and poetic work with a different set of purposes from what we dare to presume. This richer text may, in addition, better reflect the character and personality of God than the stereotypical picture of a sort of cosmic monarch we sometimes seem to expect. Indeed, the divergence may be due to the very existence of a God behind the text; a God who is not a projection of our expectations but a person in their own right with their own 'agenda' and purposes that the text is designed to help us to meet.

I'm going to argue that the God of the Bible is not satisfied with being confined to the roles which we often presume to be appropriately god-like - absolute monarch of creation and unchallenged king of his own people. I believe that this dissatisfaction can be seen again and again in the Bible. I see it in the intense, difficult relationship between God and people in the Old Testament. I see it in the way the church develops in the New Testament. I see it most clearly of all in the central story of Jesus, "God with us", "Word become flesh", "Christ crucified".

So I find it only fitting that the very texts of the Bible do not conform to the constitution-like clarity that our inherited expectations of Scripture seem to presume. Indeed, I would argue that they are specifically designed to help us find a much more intimate, exciting, risk-taking and demanding God than the meeting of our expectations could ever permit us to encounter.

Let's look, then, at the ways the God of the Bible seeks to meet us and how the Bible seems carefully (even creatively) designed to help us in that meeting.

4.4   What might the Bible be trying to say?

What sort of God and what sort of relationship with God are effectively offered to us in the Bible? Let me, with due trepidation, suggest six ways in which the very nature of the Bible seems to call us to an encounter with God that goes far beyond what our inherited expectations would allow.

First, I'd like to suggest two ways in which the Bible adamantly refuses to 'play our game'. I'll try to identify two strands of divine resistance to our coercive ways of reading that I find woven into the very structure of the Bible. I'll propose that the very nature of the Bible is designed to challenge both our determination to 'domesticate' God, and our desperation to find 'closure' and the comfort of certainty.

Then, I'd like to propose four ways in which the Bible offers us an alternative way to encounter God. I'll argue that the Bible is constructed in such a way that it offers us a God determined to be our friend, a God who is resolutely vulnerable in the moment of our meeting, a God who can only be rightly met if it is a shared meeting involving us and others and a God who must be freshly encountered by each new generation and each new community of the people of God. Let's look at each of these ideas in turn...

I.   DEFEATING DOMESTICATION

The Old Testament has a rich stream of stories that combine to form a long, winding narrative of the relationship between the choosing God and the chosen people. As generation succeeds generation, there's a lot of distress on both sides of this relationship. Anger, frustration and a sense of betrayal recur again and again, yet somehow the cord is never broken, the covenant is always renewed, even if only by a remnant of the people or by the persistent love of a much-maligned God.

Indeed, the whole Old Testament storyline can be read as a struggle between God and people to establish who is ultimately "in control". We read how the people (and, in particular, their kings) endlessly sought ways to get God to deliver what they wanted when they wanted it and otherwise leave them free of irritating and unwarranted divine intrusion. Again and again, they sought a well-trained, dependable, domesticated God who 'knew his place'. Sometimes they dared to believe that by careful manipulation of their God they could effect the domestication themselves. And stories of their recurring efforts are interwoven all through the Old Testament with stories of God remaining resolutely elusive, unfettered, hard to predict, endlessly surprising - even whilst deeply committed to this wayward, manipulative people.

I am particularly drawn to the complex and intriguing tale of King Ahab of the northern Kingdom of Israel and the prophet Micaiah-ben-Imlah in *I Kings* 22. The King determines to go to war against the Syrians. He invites the help of his visiting southern neighbour, Jehoshaphat, King of Judah. Prophetic advice is sought. Four hundred court prophets say "Go! God is with you!", but the King of Judah asks whether there is also a prophet of YHWH ("the LORD") available. The solitary, disliked Micaiah is summoned and after some circling playfulness between king and prophet, admits that God wants King Ahab killed in battle. The King promptly imprisons Micaiah (as a sort of insurance against his prophecy of doom) and sets off to have his war anyhow. In a further attempt to elude the will of God, King Ahab rides into battle disguised as an ordinary soldier, leaving Jehoshaphat, King of Judah, to attract the Syrian attack. Yet, Jehoshaphat survives endless ferocious attacks unscathed whilst one casual Syrian arrow finds the disguised Ahab and mortally wounds him. Who's in charge?

Yet, this struggle to determine who is ultimately in charge is played out between God and people all the way from Eden to Exile. Let's review some well-known stories…

'In the beginning', Eve and Adam are fascinated by only one thing. They cannot resist the tempter's beguiling promise of god-like control (*"You* will be like gods" *Genesis 3:5*); they risk all they have to achieve this goal. Later, outside Eden, their son Cain becomes murderously aggrieved when brought face to face with God's total freedom; he simply cannot accept that God is free to reject his offering whilst accepting his brother's, without providing any explanation (*Genesis 4:5*). He cannot control or domesticate God, so, with displaced anger, he kills his brother.

Later in Genesis, both Abraham (the father of the nation) and Joseph (the one with the Amazing Technicolor Dreamcoat) face fearsome trials in order that they may learn the central importance of trusting God come-what-may. They leave us impressive examples of how costly it can be to take the road to the right acceptance of the God-ness of God (*Genesis 22:1-14, Genesis 37 and 39-45*).

Through the rest of the Pentateuch the Children of Israel are endlessly at logger-heads with God. "Is the Lord with us or not?" (*Exodus 17:7*) sums up their attitude to the God who has rescued them from slavery, kept them alive in the wilderness, commits to them in solemn covenant, but never seems to do exactly what they want just when they want it. Threats of mob violence against Moses when there's no water in the desert (*Exodus 17:3f*) and the peevish decision to make a golden calf to worship whilst Moses is up God's mountain (*Exodus 32:1-6*) are but two examples of their repeated attempts to have their way and declare themselves to be the real masters.

Later, when Solomon in all his glory reigned over imperial Israel, did he build a grand temple in Jerusalem simply out of respect for his God? Or did he calculate that such a temple (with its own god) would impress both his subjects and his royal neighbours and, at the same time, help to ensure that the cult of YHWH was not an uncontrolled breeding ground for opposition and dissent? Who stood to gain most out of this juxtaposition of grand temple and imperial palace?

Later still, prophets like Amos and Micah object (on God's behalf) to the casual assumption made by wealthy people in Israel and in Judah that God can be bought off. They denounce any idea that giving generous offerings and sustaining elaborate temple worship will divert God's attention from injustice and the exploitation of the poor (*Amos 5:21-24 & Micah 6:6-8*). Even the forced exile to Babylon, the unthinkable event that appears to break God's covenants with Abraham and David, is explained by Jeremiah as God's only possible response to a people who had come to rely on the totemic powers of the Jerusalem temple to protect them - turning God's designated place of worship into yet another idol (*Jeremiah 7:1-15*).

Besides this, the many stories of apparent apostasy, of the people turning to other gods - to Baal, to Asherah, to worship at 'the high places' - can be seen as but further attempts to find a more manageable God who will deliver what they want when they want it. Hence the significance of Elijah's three year drought and public showdown on Mount Carmel - it counteracts and destroys Baal's credentials as a-god-who-delivers-on-demand (*I Kings 17 & 18*); it shows that YHWH, not Baal, is the one who controls the coming of the rains.

Thus, the narrative line of the Old Testament plays out in successive generations this constant dispute between God and people. Is God simply a service-provider answerable to the people for contract compliance (which leaves the people in control as they can at any time decide to award their 'contract' to another more amenable god)? Or is God a free agent who chooses to offer a real relationship of lovingkindness, yet who is ultimately 'in charge'? Each generation seems to have to re-discover the answer for themselves.

When we turn to the Gospels, we find Jesus engaged in analogous disputes with the Pharisees and with his own disciples. The offensiveness Jesus clearly finds in the meticulously-careful religion of the Pharisees seems to lie in the effective sidelining of God through exact legal observance. Jesus denounces the way this permits the believers to continue unchecked on their own chosen paths, even when this is contrary to the very spirit of God's Law (*Matthew 23:23-24*)[132]. In other words, he is objecting to the use of scrupulous observance of the Law as a strategy that avoids the challenge and costs of a real relationship with God.

On another level, Peter's objection near Caesarea Philippi to Jesus' first prediction of the way of the cross (*Mark 8:31-33 & parallels*) and James and John's joint request for thrones in glory on Jesus' right and left (*Mark 10:35-45*) both betray a sense among Jesus' own disciples that he must fit in with their expectations rather than they be challenged and changed by knowing him. This can be seen as yet another expression of the persistent human determination to try to domesticate God. Yet Peter, James and John display no guile or calculation and no awareness of what could possibly be inappropriate about their attitudes. The urge to keep control and make God fit into our world seems as natural and unselfconscious as breathing.

Thus in both Testaments we find recurring engagement with the ceaseless human urge to make God safe and manageable. Yet we also find this human ploy constantly being wrecked on the shore of God's refusal to be co-opted, presumed upon, controlled, used, or domesticated. So, the Bible seems to be developing the case that there is a well-nigh universal human desire to "be like gods" and fit even faith and religion into our world, rather than risk the dangers of relationship with the God who is there. In such circumstances, the awkward refusal of the Bible to fit our expectations can be seen as a strength rather than a weakness.

A neat, legal, precisely-ordered foundational book giving all the laws of God could be treated as no more than a service contract. God in person would become almost irrelevant and the would-be religious could concentrate their efforts on careful compliance. The most important issue would be identifying the boundaries between sinful evasion and permissible avoidance of God's Laws. The church's ministers and priests would be no more than the religious equivalent of good tax lawyers - professionals who soothingly help us to minimise the disruption to normal life and personal freedom that might be caused by God's somewhat-intrusive requirements.

Instead, the very awkwardness of the Bible levers open space for encounter with a wild personality-rich God. This sort of book, full of stories with multiple meanings, unresolved tensions and partially-answered questions endlessly challenges our desire for a cool, law-giving philosopher-God whose ordinances we can attempt to keep whilst we remain in charge. This is the gloriously free and undomesticated book of a free and undomesticated God, or, as David Carr puts it, the "Untamable Text of an Untamable God".[133]

The Modern World, with its emphasis on the power of autonomous human reason, was always at odds with the untameable nature of the Bible and the untameable nature of its God. With hindsight, the elaborate systems of the 'Federal Calvinism' that helped to shape the Westminster Confession, the 'historical' analysis of the 19th Century German critics[134] and even the arid 'common sense' approach of Warfield and the Hodges in Princeton[135] all look suspiciously like attempts to domesticate both the Bible and its God. Clearly, we must be wary of our motives when we use the whole force of human reason and human logic to impose a 'sensible' structure on the Bible. Rather than successfully taming God or Bible, we may simply be constructing a cage for ourselves.

How might we respond to this?

DO <u>WE</u> TRY TO DOMESTICATE GOD?

If the Bible itself tells a long stream of stories of God's people attempting, in each successive generation, to domesticate God, are we any different? ...I strongly suspect not.

In all sorts of ways your average United Reformed, Congregational or Presbyterian Church is as much at risk of quietly but determinedly attempting to domesticate God as anyone...

If we rely on the power of precedent (*"but we've always done it this way..."*), if we keep church going by a rich reliance on routine (*"but Margaret always draws up the flower rota..."*), if we feel safest with the familiar (*"I really don't like that new way of..."*), if Church or Elders' Meetings are more to do with organisational issues than with vision (*"we spent half an hour trying to decide whether we should have an artificial Christmas tree next year..."*), then we are "AT RISK!" All these attitudes suggest that we may have settled into a rather domesticated understanding of God. And remember, a successfully domesticated god is not God at all, it's an idol - something we have devised and made ourselves for our own comfort.

Let me ask two questions:

"If God wanted our church to do something daring, imaginative, different or risky, would there be any chance of it getting through Church Meeting or Kirk Session - or would *we* know better?"

"If God wanted *me* to do something daring, imaginative, different or risky, would there be any chance I would hear and respond?"

2.   CHALLENGING CLOSURE

Consistency may not be a pre-eminent human virtue. Though, at times, we may devote ourselves wholeheartedly to the vain struggle to keep God under our control, at other times we may be just as anxious to seek out a God who can ease the pressure of threatening possibilities and dilemmas by deciding things for us. At moments of crisis and in times of change, order, clarity and certainty about the truth can seem deeply reassuring and vitally necessary. As we observed earlier in our discussion, many of us "have a deep need for 'closure', for some sort of parental figure who gives us a clear ruling on what the truth of the matter must be"[136]. Ideally, we want that to be God.

I imagine it is when the comfort of God-given certainty is at the top of our wish-lists that Reformed Christians sense the enduring attraction of the work of John Calvin. The wider culture may be content to stereotype him as some sort of nasty, draconian kill-joy. We remember (and secretly admire) his apparent success in sorting the Bible into a neat system of timeless, obvious truth. We may not agree with all of his 'system' (if we even know what it contains), but we are reassured that he was able to produce it. For us, Calvin embodies Christian certainty. Calvin and the Reformed Tradition that followed reassure us that our felt need for 'closure' is both legitimate and respectable. Indeed, 'closure', or the availability of a reassuringly neat answer to any of the big questions, feels like an important part of our Reformed birthright. Our thinking seems to go something like this…"Calvin wouldn't have left us in any doubt, would he? Calvin's God may have been stern, but he was definite."

But look again at the lasting effects of such apparent certainty. It brings enormous risks. It doesn't take long for the eagerly-sought comfort to evolve into a settled complacency, even an unattractive smugness. Outright arrogance may not be far behind and forgiveness, understanding and kindliness become harder and harder to find. Eventually, even grace can become a hard-bitten, mechanical and joyless business in the hands of God's cruelly-certain people. It's sad, it's ugly and, at its worst, it's unrecognisable as the faith of the followers of Jesus. Indeed, I suspect it is these very effects of closed certainty that have most damaged the reputation of Reformed Christians in the wider world. Where else, for example, did the enduring image of Puritans as profoundly-unattractive people arise? Why else is the picture of Scotland's John Knox (a preacher of grace with many a positive passion) still so forbidding, so chilling?

For me, these dangers provide some explanation why the Bible we have makes no attempt to allow consistently for the closure, clarity and certainty we often crave. On the contrary, the Bible again and again seeks to open our minds to new possibilities rather than close our minds with old certainties. Jesus, most especially, when handling 'the Law' (*Matthew 5:17-48*), or arguing with legal experts and Pharisees (*Matthew 23:1-36*), or preaching in parables like 'the Good Samaritan' (*Luke 10:25-37*) and 'the Prodigal Son' (*Luke 15:11-32*), or even in deliberately taking the way of the cross (*Mark 8:31-38 & 10:35-45*) seems much more interested in 'opening' us to new ways of seeing than offering us any sort of 'closure'.

In Walter Brueggemann's apt phrase, "There are no answers at the back of the book."[137] The God of the Bible resolutely refuses to provide them. When we try to interpret the Bible there is nowhere to check if we got it 'right'. Whenever we think we've found certainty in the Bible there always seems to be another voice that questions or undercuts what we think we have established or another way of reading the very words we have read that supports different conclusions. We are always left 'at risk' in the process of knowing. Our knowledge of the God of the Bible is always interpretative, always provisional, always open to challenge by others and, most importantly, challenge by God. The very nature of the Bible announces God's intention to do something far more risky and dangerous than offer us the comfort of closure.

Always, the Bible leaves us holding on by faith. We may not always want that, but, it could be far healthier for us in the long run. It could be an important part of what the Bible is intended to offer us.

How might we respond to this?

DO WE SEEK CLOSURE?

Once more I'm deeply suspicious of you, but also, I must add, of me....

"Cherished beliefs" are the key issue this time. How secure are our unquestioned certainties?

How justifiable is that security? Do people with different opinions simply annoy or infuriate us, or do we retain the ability to listen, to respond, to debate, to change our minds in part or altogether, if there is weight to the other person's argument?

If God wanted to give us a fresh understanding of a particular issue, what chance would we have of hearing, how likely is it that we would respond positively?

3.   *FINDING FRIENDSHIP*

I have argued that the Bible, both in its contents and by its very structure, presents a God who is determined to unsettle our expectations of a divine king, resist our efforts to keep ultimate control and refuse us the false comfort of closure. But what sort of God does the Bible present as an alternative? What sort of relationship with God do the contents and structure of the Bible positively promote?

My simplest answer is the word 'FRIENDSHIP'. For me, the Bible presents as a collection of writings that give us access to a God who persistently seeks our friendship.

I certainly can't claim this as an original idea. Indeed, it is probably a pre-supposition of every sermon on grace ever preached and the dazzling wonder at the centre of the faith of many a Bible believer down through the centuries. Even 20th Century Bible scholarship could recognise the centrality of this theme; Walther Eichrodt's epic post-war account of the theology of the Old Testament[138] was organised around the 'big idea' that God was a God of covenant, or, as Walter Brueggemann summarises it, "that the God of Israel is characteristically a God *in relation*"[139].

Let's, once more, review some familiar Old Testament stories...

Whilst God's interest in people is evident in the very act of their creation and in the intimate personal enquiries made of Adam and Eve (*Genesis 3:8-19*), it is the Covenant made with Noah after the Flood that establishes God's willingness to make clear commitments in order to build relationships with people (and, indeed, with all creation, *Genesis 9:8-17*). The covenant of blessing made with Abraham (*Genesis 15:4f & 22:15-18*), the personal wrestling with the renegade Jacob (*Genesis 32:22-31*) and the long story of the trials of Joseph that deepened his trust in God (*Genesis 37 & 39-47*) all underline God's interest in deep and appropriate friendship with particular individuals and their families.

The account of the Exodus from Egypt, the wilderness journeying and the covenant made between God and people at Sinai, that fill the rest of the Pentateuch, show a God who is intent on friendship and commitment (sealed in a solemn covenant), even with a people who regularly fail to respond to impressive quantities of divine help and protection. All the laws and regulations given in *Exodus, Leviticus, Numbers* and *Deuteronomy* are given in the context of this covenant-making between God and people. Both the giving and the keeping of the Law are presented as expressions of relationship, of deep mutual regard and commitment between God and people; they are expressions of mutual commitment to a profound friendship.

Further on in the Old Testament, the personal story that most fully shows God's interest in friendship is that of David, the shepherd boy who became king and, despite real and catastrophic failures, was promised a permanence of favour for his family for ever (*I Samuel 16 to I Kings 2:11*). Thereafter, much of the rest of the Old Testament, from the Psalms through all of the prophets, evidences a God open to intimacy, personally involved with people, so concerned about friendship that the fate of peoples and nations hangs on it. Think, for example, of the impassioned words in *Hosea 11* where, having poignantly recounted God's love for the people of Israel, the people's fickleness and the judgement they are due, the prophet presents God saying:

> "How can I give you up, Ephraim?
> How can I hand you over, O Israel?...
> My heart recoils within me;
> my compassion grows warm and tender.
> I will not execute my fierce anger;
> I will not again destroy Ephraim;
> for I am God and no mortal,
> the Holy One in your midst,
> and I will not come in wrath."
>
> *Hosea 11:8f (New Revised Standard Version)*

The central distinguishing feature of God, according to this prophecy, is the persisting commitment to friendship and love that goes far beyond both natural justice and human reason.

But, for the Christian, it is the New Testament that takes the presentation of God as our friend to new heights. The whole story of Jesus can surely be understood as God risking everything in offering us friendship and ensuring that the offer is not restricted in any way - 'Israel' is now to include *anyone* who will hear and receive. Indeed, both the key theological ideas of the New Testament - incarnation and atonement - speak powerfully of a God who will go the whole way to relate to us creatively, appropriately and effectively in friendship and love. Incarnation is, at heart, the idea of God laying aside the status and trappings of 'god-ness' to draw close alongside us regardless of cost. Atonement is, as the very Anglo-Saxon word we use tells us, a self-surrender in death to win for us an AT-ONE-MENT with God.

Gospel story after Gospel story presents a Jesus who, in these ways, seeks to be our truest friend. When Matthew tells us that Jesus is to be called Emmanuel, which means "God is with us" (*Matthew 1:23*), when Mark tells of Jesus outraged that the children have been kept from him (*Mark 10:14*), when Luke shows the risen Jesus quietly joining two distraught confused disciples on the Emmaus Road (*Luke 24:13-32*), when John says "God so loved the world that he gave..." (*John 3:16*), they are all weaving important threads into a picture of God-in-Christ that has far more to do with gracious, sacrificial friendship than any right to lordship over us. And these are only samples of many, many Gospel stories that all tend in the same direction.

Thus, taken together, the whole story told by both the Old and New Testaments presents a God intent on seeking our friendship. Yes, a God who is still intent on being God (not an adjunct of our life-style), but a God who wishes us to be the very friends of God.

However, it is not only the contents of the Bible that seem intent on presenting the friendship of God. The very structure of the Bible, that seemed so inappropriate for a divine king's foundational document for order and control, is more than appropriate as the key text of a God intent on friendship.

✦ Friendship is inherently **DIVERSE AND VARIED** with no two friendships exactly alike. This is echoed by the richly diverse quality of the Hebrew and Christian Scriptures.

✦ Friendship is inherently **DEVELOPMENTAL** (you *grow* in mutual understanding as friendship matures). Again, this is echoed by the developments in mutual understanding evidenced by these stories of a people and their God that run from Abraham to the interpreters of the risen Jesus.

✦ Friendship is inherently **POETIC AND PERSONAL** rather than coldly logical. Once more, the Bible is often richly poetic, powerfully personal and unashamedly emotional rather than limited to the legal, the logical and the exact.

✦ Friendship is an attempt to live out a **SHARED STORY**. Supremely, the Bible presents as an overlapping patchwork of shared stories that somehow combine to tell a bigger story, the story of the vast friendship of God.

So, it is my case that inviting us to respond to the friendship of God is central to both the content and the structure of the Bible. That is why, I would argue, it singularly fails to fit our expectations as to what it should be like. Many of our inherited expectations of the-Bible-as-a-whole were predicated on our search for a handbook to help us to do our duty to a superior. If God is seeking to help us do something far more daring than careful obedience, then the foundational document for relationship with God MUST confound our expectations and MUST challenge us to open up to the bigger more exciting, more demanding possibilities we are invited to experience. For, I suspect, God has always intended a way of knowing that is more relational than rational, more about befriending than dissecting, more connecting than objective. Both the Bible and the very nature of human knowing seem adapted to allow for this.

4.   VALUING VULNERABILITY

The Bible paints a picture of the friendship of God that is darkly profound in its insight. This insight is present all through the Old Testament, but comes into sharpest focus in the heart of the New Testament, in the accounts of the death of Jesus. Quite simply, you cannot love without the risk of hurt, rejection and disappointment. To offer friendship is to be **VULNERABLE**.

Again and again, through the Old Testament, our God is challenged by the cost of love. We read of a God who experiences anger, disappointment, determination to be faithful, a rage for retribution, even powerful jealousy. In ways that some find offensively 'anthropomorphic' or 'human', the whole gamut of the pain of love is ascribed to God, even whilst other Bible authors remind us how different God is from us.

Add together the transcendent pictures of God's otherness, like Isaiah's vision in the temple (*Isaiah 6:1-5*) or God's final rebuttal to Job (*Job 38 & 39*), and those vigorous accounts of God's involved agony (like God's pain in *Hosea 11:8f*, quoted above) and we are left with a picture of a God who is assuredly and actively God, yet who CHOOSES, for friendship's sake, to be 'at risk' in our world. This, I would suggest, is the God we are invited to watch in the solitary, agonising Christ of Gethsemane and mocked, abused and rejected on the cross at Golgotha. This is the shocking wonder that John seeks to express at the start of the fourth gospel when he waxes lyrical about the pre-existent, divine Word, then says abruptly "and the Word became flesh... and lived among us" (*John 1:14*). This is the outrageous message that Paul the apostle has come to preach that is "a stumbling block" and "a foolishness" (*1 Corinthians 1:23*). The very heart of the message we find in our Bible is about the redemptive vulnerability of our God, who came to be beaten, spat upon, abused and cruelly killed, all to win us back as friends.

So, it should not be such a surprise to us that the Bible, the vehicle for this staggering message, is itself 'at risk' in our world. It is only fitting that the Bible is vulnerable to our interpretative use and abuse. A God who accepted our torture and rejection "like a lamb that is led to the slaughter" (*Isaiah 53:7*) may well have constructed the whole of reality in such a way that even "the Word of God" is always at the mercy of our competing interpretations. It makes sense that this sort of God should leave our understanding of Scripture always interpretative, always provisional, always open to challenge by others. It even makes sense that this sort of God should leave us space to misinterpret, abuse and subvert the written Word of God, just as our spiritual ancestors shouted "Crucify Him!" when the Word of God stood before them in the flesh.

The Bible tells us that when Jesus himself walked our earth people who met him face-to-face made their own widely divergent interpretations of the one they were encountering. They often failed completely in their efforts to make sense of who they were meeting and how they might respond. Their responses were often controlled by self-interest or limited by the cynical stereotypes of the world they knew. It should not surprise us, then, that the Bible itself is just as vulnerable to our interpretative violence. Surely this fits well with the startling God we meet in the pages of our Bible?

5.   CREATING COMMUNITY

Another aspect of God's availability for true friendship with you and me also seems to find an echo in the nature of the Bible itself. The God of the Bible shows an endless desire to create **COMMUNITY**, to build a people, not just rescue individuals from a failing world.

Certainly, as the Bible tells it, God has often had to be content with a small band of faithful followers - 'a remnant'. Yet, from the extravagant promises made to Abraham (*Genesis 17:4-8*) to the first effects of the outpoured Spirit on the day of Pentecost when untutored Galileans found they could, by the Spirit's prompting, speak every human language (*Acts 2*), the Bible presents a God who seems intent on gathering a people. The Bible also invites us to be part of a people who will find friendship with each other even as they find friendship with their God.

It is only in keeping with this central purpose of God that:

✦   the search for divine truth in the Bible itself should be a shared task not a solitary one

✦   the truth of the Bible has to be sought by bringing together the diverse insights of a diverse people

✦   the Bible cannot rightly be read alone, that each new generation should continue and extend the conversation that seeks for God's meaning

✦   the whole process should be endlessly fraught with passion and disagreement and persuasion and change.

It is my argument that the Bible does not present as "the answers at the back of the book"[140], because that would save us the risk of involvement with God and with others. If the answers were all there in black and white we wouldn't need to work through the 'problems', engage in friendships, help each other face up to our prejudices, share in creating and sustaining community with God and with each other.

Instead, the Bible and the wider nature of human knowing both seem to require us to share in the widest possible communities of learning. The elusiveness of truth in general (and Biblical Truth in particular) seem designed to make us dependent on each other as well as on God.

6.   ALWAYS ANEW

The Bible presents us with significant, unchanging memories of the acts of God, around which our faith is to be built. The Jewish Festivals celebrate remembered aspects of the Exodus for each generation. Similarly, the Christian Festivals of Christmas and Easter annually re-present remembered accounts of the life, death and resurrection of Jesus. Yet, the very nature of the texts of the Bible make it clear that we are not simply invited to slot into and assume the unalterable faith of our forebears. Rather, each new generation, each new community and each individual is invited to meet God **ANEW**. We are invited to find a grasp of the faith that re-balances and re-appraises the faith for our own setting and context.

Sometimes there will be a huge dissonance between the remembered faith and the lived experience. Many of the Psalms bear witness to the sense of 'disorientation'[141] that this brings. For example, the personal experience recounted in *Psalm 73:2-14* is starkly at odds with the inherited and recited memory of the dependability of God in the opening verse of the psalm (*Psalm 73:1*). The tension is real and the psalmist has to go on and make their own re-appropriation of the faith at the far side of a maze of doubt and self pity (*Psalm 73:15-28*). Again, *Psalm 137* captures a furious moment of anger and betrayal felt by those taken into exile in Babylon. "How could we sing the Lord's song in a foreign land?" (*Psalm 137:4*). Somehow, the exiles have to find an answer to their question if the faith is to continue with them.

But it is not only at stark moments of personal or community distress that the process of re-balancing and re-engaging needs to take place. Each new generation and each new context or community must rediscover and reappraise the faith in their own context. Each generation must integrate what they find in the Bible with their own community experience and story. Of course, it is possible to be a victim of the fashions and fads of one's day and age. But, whoever we are, hugely significant parts of identities and how we make sense of our world are shaped by that world and the particular influences and experiences that have shaped us along the way. If I am to grasp the truth, it must be me that does the grasping and I can only grasp it as who I am.

I watched American missionaries in Nigeria fretting and worrying over the way Nigerian believers would grasp the Gospel from within their own cultural context. Yet strenuous efforts to ensure that Nigerians received the 'true' faith of the apostles seemed largely to result in an insistence that the Good News had to be permanently encased in the culture and mores of the American Mid West. This was often puzzling to Nigerians brothers and sisters as aspects of Nigerian life were often closer to the social world of Jesus' Galilee than was the social world of middle America. Yet, as some of the missionaries saw it, that did not count.

The reason for considering this now is that the very structure of the Bible seems to be designed to encourage and enable this process of re-configuring and re-grasping the faith in each new context and generation. Every encounter with God in the Bible seems to be in the midst of the context and story of a people or a person, even where the details of the context have not been explicitly recorded. The generation by generation accounts of the faith of Israel from Abraham to the return from Exile, that in repeat versions take up much of the Old Testament, and the recounting of the Gospel in four discrete ways for four divergent communities all signal the rightness of re-appropriating the story in our own context and encountering God afresh. The challenging words of Old Testament prophets inviting the people to re-view their faith in the context of their own failure or of other contemporary events and the diverse contexts of the various epistles to young churches in the New Testament again suggest that this message must be forever re-appropriated by each new community, generation and context.

The 'feel' of the faith and the balancing of its message changes even with the move from the Jerusalem Jewish church to Antioch in Syria and on to the cities of Asia Minor and Greece, even though it is still the death and resurrection of Jesus that is being proclaimed. Even within the Book of Acts, the Faith is an interaction between the God of the Gospel and real people in real settings; and in each setting both Bible and people affect the resulting theology and ethos of the church.

As the old saying goes, "God has no grandchildren". We all have to do theology, and do it in the context both of the Bible and of our own situation – our inheritance, our experience, our world. The Bible unashamedly presents a God who is always to be encountered anew.

4.5 Where does this leave us?

I confess I find a certain beauty in the picture of the Bible that has been emerging through Chapter Four:

✦ these wild, untameable Scriptures that defy our every effort to make them neat or ordered or tidy so that they may offer us a God whom we cannot co-opt, coerce or control *(defeating domestication)*

✦ these open, unresolved Scriptures that deny us the safety of closure so that they may open us to a God who is infinitely bigger than our imagining *(challenging closure)*

✦ these diverse, intriguing Scriptures that take a lifetime and more to befriend so that they may introduce a God who surrendered his life out of love for us *(finding friendship)*

✦ these unprotected, vulnerable Scriptures that risk being mercilessly misconstrued so that they may also offer us saving encounters with the vulnerable, crucified God *(valuing vulnerability)*

✦ these shared, multi-voiced Scriptures that must be interpreted with wide, diverse conversations so that they may bring us all together as the people of God *(creating community)*

✦ these story-rich Scriptures where God is always met in context so that we are forced to meet God anew for ourselves in our own situation, in our own story, in our own way *(always anew)*

Going further back in our argument, I also find something profound in the ideas about how we make sense of texts that we considered in Chapter Three. I am particularly struck by their implications for reading the Bible. I find a deep appropriateness about the way they invite us to:

✦ own up to the influences that have shaped us and affect what we may or may not see *(the impossibility of objectivity)*

✦ go on and on building new and deeper relationships with all the texts of the Bible *(the spiral of learning)*

✦ be at least as suspicious of our own motives as we are of others who read differently *(the importance of suspicion)*

✦ listen to diverse voices to help us distinguish God's truth from our own prejudices *(the liberation of listening)*

✦ face up to our own potential to use Scripture to do violence to others *(the ubiquity of violence)*

✦ be open to new meanings in Scripture we had previously ignored or dismissed *(the judgement of meanings)*

✦ value the richness of the Biblical narratives and the stories they tell *(the recovery of story)*

Again, I think there is something that feels authentically 'Reformed' about this whole approach to the Word of God. It seems to sit well with two of the most famous Reformation rallying cries - *"Sola Scriptura!"* (Scripture alone) and *"Semper reformanda!"* (always being reformed). *Sola scriptura* is a cry to step out from behind inherited ideas and look at what we actually have in the Bible itself, using all the gifts, ideas and insights of everyone who is prepared to contribute.   is a declaration that the process of reforming is never complete and each new generation has more work to do, new insights to bring, fresh challenges to face, unheard voices to take into account - especially as we seek to sit together under the Word of God.

We honour our forebears more if we push on with the same determination to seek God's truth that they showed, than if we refuse to believe or do anything they did not believe or do.

That concludes our overview of what we find when we try to encounter the Bible today. We're now (in PART THREE) going to look at the particular issue of using this Bible in the construction of Christian Ethical responses to the issues we face today.

BEING BIBLICAL

PART THREE

BIBLICAL ETHICS FOR TODAY

CHAPTER FIVE

HOW DO WE DECIDE WHAT GOD WANTS US TO DO?

5.1 Biblical Ethics

At the beginning of this book we set out to address the issue of how we rightly use the Bible to generate Christian Ethics for today. It was argued that we needed to 'take three steps back' to get a reasonable perspective for the task. Part One went right back to look at the history of how the Bible has been viewed and handled since the Reformation. Part Two then looked at how we might view the Bible today, in the light of the developing perceptions of how we read any and every 'text'. Now, in Part Three, we turn to an investigation of how we may use the Bible to fashion the Christian Ethics by which we seek to live. But we will do so by building on what has been investigated and uncovered in the previous two parts of the book.

In this chapter (Chapter Five) we will be investigating how we might try to answer the "How?" question. We will be helped by the fresh ways of viewing texts in general that were developed in Chapter Three and the picture of the Bible itself that was developed in Chapter Four. By the second half of the chapter we will be trying to answer the question "How do we use the Bible to discover God's will for us in a Reformed Church at the start of the 21st Century?" However, before we engage directly with that question (in sections 5.4, & 5.5) we have some preliminary matters to address.

Firstly, we need to pick up a couple of issues to do with BIBLICAL AUTHORITY. Living in a setting where both the Modern and the Postmodern worlds seem to share a deep distrust of anything like Biblical Authority, how do we justify claiming that the Bible has 'supreme authority' over us? Then again, what is the precise nature of the authority that the Bible seeks to have over us? We'll consider both these matters in section 5.2 – "By what AUTHORITY?"

Secondly, we need to start considering what is involved in using the Bible in generating CHRISTIAN ETHICS. We'll begin by reviewing the complex of diverse materials the Bible puts before the would-be Christian Ethicist. Then we'll take a very quick overview of the use of the Bible in Christian Ethics in the second half of the twentieth century before concentrating on the recent work of Richard B Hays. Hays has made a particular point of trying to produce a careful methodology for the use of the Bible in generating Christian Ethics – how well does he succeed? We'll look at all these issues in section 5.3 – "Trying to answer the "HOW?" question".

Then, and only then, will we proceed - in section 5.4 - "Entering God's conversation" - to pick up on our own analyses of the nature of texts in general and the Bible in particular. We will try to see how the understanding of the Bible developed in PART TWO might offer us a simple model that could help shape the way we use the Bible to generate our Christian Ethics. Following that, in section 5.5 – "Seven proposals for conversationalists", I'll put to you seven underlying ideas that form the basis of my current understanding of how we can 'do' Christian ethics today.

5.2 By what AUTHORITY?

As we began to look at the Bible at the beginning of the previous chapter we noted that right through Reformation and Modern times Reformed Churches have kept insisting that the Bible (interpreted by the Holy Spirit) is the final arbiter of what Christians should believe and do. As examples, we looked at the Westminster Confession of 1647 and the Basis of Union of the United Reformed Church of 1972. Remember that even the 1972 confessional statement says:

> The Word of God in the Old and New Testaments, discerned under the guidance of the Holy Spirit, [is] the supreme authority for faith and conduct of all God's people
>
> *The Basis of Union of the United Reformed Church, Schedule D, Version 1, clause 3*

Yet, later in Chapter Four, I tried to demonstrate that the Bible, in many and various ways, fails to conform comfortably with our expectations. So, before we proceed to look at how the Bible can be used to guide us, we need to look closely at the nature of **BIBLICAL AUTHORITY** as we may reasonably view it at the start of the 21st Century. I propose that we do this in two parts. Firstly, I think we have to take some account of the underlying resistance to any and all ideas of authority that now pervades the secular society of the West. Secondly, I will invite you to consider the sort of Authority over the Church that the Bible still seems to be seeking.

I.   RESISTANCE TO AUTHORITY

A deep and settled distrust of authority has become one of the commonest core values in much of secular society all across the Western world today. Richard Bauckham suggests "we have got to the stage in the western cultural context where for many people authority is indistinguishable from authoritarianism".[142] In other words, any person or text that seeks to tell you what you ought to believe or do is just being bossy or patronising and should be ignored or resisted with the sort of fixed look that adolescents reserve for parents who are exhibiting embarrassing levels of inappropriateness.

Intriguingly, this distrust of all attempts to impose authority is probably the only core value shared by the otherwise divergent world views of the Modern and the Postmodern.

The Modern World View recognises some sorts of authority; indeed, it is centred on a deep respect for the authority of the scientific expert. But the Modern World has always been resistant to any source of authority that cannot be "checked, tested and criticised"[143]. The embarrassing, untestable particularity of the Bible needed sorting; hence the rise of 'the science of historical theology'[144] and its historical critical method as the Modern World's primary tool for dealing with the Bible.[145] This distrust of all untestable sources of authority led, also, to efforts to relate the ethical teaching of the Bible to the universal moral values that were presumed to lie behind them, moral values that could (surely?) be deduced by the application of human reason. Indeed, it may only have been the central place of the Bible at the heart of European culture that saved it from dismissal as mere superstition. Such easy dismissal as superstition was regularly used to deny any value to the traditions, beliefs and moral codes of the various subject peoples of the empires Europeans were scrambling to acquire across the world.[146]

The emerging Postmodern World View is, if anything, far *more* distrustful of 'authority'. Even the efforts of the Modern World to find 'universal' values are now to be viewed as a distressing piece of authoritarianism – "part and parcel of the West's attempt to dominate the world".[147] Individual freedom of choice is not to be restricted in any way. Right and wrong can be considered matters of consumer preference. Groups of people may agree a particular moral code, but that is simply their shared choice. Hence the Postmodern distaste for any sort of Grand Narrative that seeks to impose its own explanations on others.

So, in this transitional world where elements of the declining Modern world still seem to be co-existing with the emerging Postmodern world, anything like 'Biblical Authority' has a thoroughly bad name. The Bible is all too easily caricatured as a mean-spirited book of "thou shalt nots…" Its authority out on the streets of our towns and cities is eroding from day to day.

This, I suspect, has **three** significant effects on those of us in Churches who try to find in the Bible our 'supreme authority for faith and conduct'. **Firstly**, it makes meaningful mission to our neighbours somewhat harder. The crucial patch of shared understanding where we might reasonably stand side by side with a non-Christian neighbour whilst we each attempt to understand our differing world views is getting very small. Still, that might be the spur we need to be more creative and more relevant in our efforts to share our faith. Recently, I found myself quickening my step as I passed a street preacher brandishing his Bible and bellowing Bible-based certainties at shoppers in the Market Square in Cambridge. Even whilst I respected his courage, I ached with embarrassment at the yawning, unbridged gap between his world view and the likely world views of his intended audience. Back in the days of the Apostles, some Athenians may have scoffed at the Apostle Paul as he raised his voice in their public square, but at least (as the Book of Acts tells it) he made subtle and sustained efforts to relate his message to the way Athenians saw things (*Acts 17:16-34*).

Secondly, the widespread erosion of any recognition of Bible authority amongst our neighbours may be directly affecting many within the church. Those who have struggled to retain some sensitivity for the way our neighbours see things may well have developed for themselves some level of anti-authoritarian suspicion of the Bible, or the Old Testament or the idea of Divine Law. I suspect there are many who are deeply sincere in their faith in God and the message of Jesus, yet who feel a real uneasiness with talk of a 'supreme authority for faith and conduct' because (like their non-Christian neighbours) they have come to equate authority with authoritarianism. As I see it, this is to misconstrue the nature of Biblical authority. I suspect that the sort of 'authority' the Bible seeks to have over the Church may be much more anti-authoritarian in nature than they allow. We need to keep talking.

Thirdly, others within the church may be over-reacting against the world's woeful waywardness and its refusal to recognise the authority of the Word of God. Some, I fear, turn confidently to the Bible seeking an aggressively authoritarian authority to which they may whole-heartedly submit. They are looking for a definitive, dependable list of God-given regulations to govern all their life and living. Again, I would counsel caution and urge a fresh and careful look at the nature of the authority the Bible seeks.

So, exactly HOW does the Bible seek to have authority over the church?

2.   *WHAT SORT OF AUTHORITY?*

We noted in Chapter Four that even where the Bible gives extended lists of moral and religious laws, these are set in the context of the story of the Choosing God's relationship with the chosen people.[148] Those of us who carefully memorised the Ten Commandments in our youth can, of course, quickly remind the rest of us that even these ten direct instructions (mainly straight "thou shalt nots...") are pre-fixed with an explicit reminder of the story that gives a basis and purpose for all this law-giving...

> "I am the LORD your God, who brought you out of the land of Egypt, out of the house of slavery; you shall have no other gods before me......"
>
> *Exodus 20:2 & 3 (NRSV)*

Here, at what is probably one of the most awesome moments of encounter with the Authority of God in the whole Bible (*read through Exodus 19 and 20 to get a vivid flavour of this*), the authoritative words of instruction are set in the context of developing RELATIONSHIP and God-given RESCUE. God and people have travelled far together, through many dangers and disagreements; they have an established relationship, a ground for trust, a context for ongoing faithfulness. More than this, the bedrock of their relationship has been the rescuing intervention of God in the people's hour of need; they are called to respond to what God has already done for them.

So, the basis of their commitment to God is not to be fear of God's unlimited coercive power, or reluctantly-offered obedience but free choice growing out of gratitude.[149]

The prior gracious act of God, powerfully recalled and re-enacted in each annual celebration of the Passover, stands before all the subsequent story of God's people and every call to accept God's authority throughout the rest of the Old Testament. Yes, there are some staggeringly frank passages (*especially some Psalms and the Book of Job*) that take God to task for an apparent lapse of faithfulness, but even the bleakest of such passages presume that this God is a God with a track record of relationship and rescue. The unremitting gloom of *Psalm 88* (some 18 verses of relentless complaint hurled directly in the face of an apparently unresponsive God) still begins by invoking God as "O Lord, God of my salvation…".

This central theme of the Hebrew Scriptures is more than underscored by the New Testament as it puts before us the story of Jesus and how his death and resurrection affected his first followers. Here the characterisation of God as a God of relationship and rescue is gloriously re-presented as the very crux of the Christian Scriptures. Here there is both a practical resistance to legalism by Jesus (*see Matthew 5*), by Paul (*see Galatians 3*) and by the Council of Jerusalem (*see Acts 15*) and a massive re-focussing on relationship rooted in the costly rescue effected at Calvary. This is what makes the Good News good news. In the Christian Bible, Authority is the authority of the slain yet living 'Lamb of God', to whom (in John's apocalyptic vision) those rescued and made friends of God fervently sing "Worthy is the Lamb!" (*Revelation 5:12 NRSV*). This sort of 'authority' is far, far away from arrant authoritarianism.

The clear centrality of relationship and rescue (at awesome cost to God) that is the basis of authority in the Christian Bible is underlined by the differing interpretative histories of the Christian and Jewish Scriptures. Even in the time of Jesus, the Jewish Scriptures, which were a rich interweaving of 'story' and 'instruction', were viewed pre-eminently as *'Torah'* (Law). After the fall of Jerusalem in 70 CE, this three-fold collection of Law, Prophets and Writings came to be surrounded in a growing interpretative collar of legal explication and detailed practical applications in the *Mishnah* (early 3rd century CE), the *Tosephta* (4th century CE) and the Babylonian and Jerusalem *Talmuds* (4th to 9th centuries CE).[150] Whilst this is clearly still the story-rich Law of the God of relationship and rescue, Judaism uses *'Torah'* as its central model of Scripture and the surrounding collar of 'oral' law[151] requires endless hours of careful study by every devout, orthodox Jewish believer[152]. (A roughly parallel collar of writings that seek to explain and apply the Scriptures with greater practical detail is also a feature of Islam, where Al Qur'an is accompanied by extensive circles of *'hadith'* or traditions about the prophet Mohammed that present him as a practical example for every detail of right living[153]).

The Christian Bible, with its central story of Jesus, 'the Word made flesh', seems to take the whole notion of Scripture off in a distinctly different direction, right away from the idea of a holy book of authoritative law. Instead, the New Testament seems to offer the cross as the defining moment of rescue in an ongoing relationship between God and people and Jesus himself, the LIVING WORD, as the living embodiment of what the Bible is all about. This AUTHORITY is not some innate, inevitable authority of the all-powerful Creator God but the winsome authority of the one who 'emptied himself, taking the form of a slave' and 'humbled himself and became obedient to the point of death, even death on a cross'(*Philippians 2:7,8 NRSV*). Certainly, God is still the creator of the universe, the Old Testament retains all the passages of legal material that tell us what to do and Jesus and Paul and the other New Testament writers add some very explicit instructions for right Christian behaviour. Yet, in contrast to the Jewish and Islamic Scriptures, the addition of the New Testament writings means that the Christian Scriptures move decisively away from any overall classification as 'God's Law'. Instead, they offer us a vast unfinished story of relationship between God and people, with its pivotal point in the story of Jesus, that invites us to freely offer our own stories as part of its living continuation[154].

Although, as we argued in Chapter Four[155], the Bible never gives a single unified, definitive version of its overall story, these Scriptures are to all intents and purposes offering us a sort of self-assembly Grand Narrative[156]. As Richard Bauckham puts it:

> "The Bible is not primarily a book of timeless doctrines or a book of moral laws.
> It is primarily a story".
>
> *Richard Bauckham, "Scripture & Authority Today", Grove Books, Cambridge, 1999, p.10*

Yet just as I would argue that the Bible's authority is very different from the outside world's caricature-like understanding of intrusive divine bossiness, I would argue that this Grand Narrative is a very strange Grand Narrative – a Grand Narrative that can work against the sort of coercive violence that is typical of the world's Grand Narratives, a Grand Narrative that seeks not to enslave but to free those who accept it as their 'sacred canopy'.[157]

So, as Christians, we are indeed a people under authority - not by the coercive bending of our embattled wills, but by the winning of our hearts and minds, of all that we are and do, by the extravagance of God's grace. We need to be quietly yet firmly unashamed of that in the face of the deep distrust of any external authority that seems so pervasive in secular circles of the Western world. For, I would argue, it is only in the acceptance of this amazing authority that authentic freedom can be found. We are called to show by our lives in community with God and each other that the freedom of the 'parentless' autonomous agent so revered by the Modern World[158] and the freedom of the self-reinventing, 'pick 'n mix' Postmodern[159] are both gross self-deceptions. Yet, if we are to have any chance of making our case, we surely need to be deeply aware of the special nature of the authority the Bible seeks to have over us and the unique quality of the subversive, liberating Grand Narrative it puts before us.

✦ I view the Bible's authority as authority over God's people that is won rather than imposed – the authority of **GRACE, the grace of the Lord Jesus Christ**.

✦ I see the Bible's authority as a matter of hard-won friendship and developing devotion rather than exacted obedience – the authority of **LOVE, the love of God**.

✦ I find in the Bible's authority the promise of authentic life we can live joyously together rather than the isolating imposition of a cold unchanging list of "thou shalt nots…" – the authority of **FELLOWSHIP, the fellowship of the Holy Spirit**. *(2 Corinthians 13:13)*.

To put this in the language of Chapter Four, I see the Bible's authority as the authority of friendship, the vulnerable risk-all friendship of a God who seeks truly to meet and be deeply known by each and all of us. I invite you to hold the nature of that authority in mind as we seek to investigate HOW we decide what God wants us to do.

5.3   Trying to answer the 'HOW?' Question

It's taken quite a long and winding route to get here, but answering this particular 'How?' question is the stated goal of our shared quest. In the light of all the matters we have already considered, we now need to consider directly the key question that we set ourselves - "How do we, in a Reformed Church at the start of the 21st Century, go about finding God's truth in the Bible to help us construct Christian ethical responses to the issues we face?".[160] I am proposing to take the following three preparatory steps:

1. Looking at what the Bible itself is offering us.

2. Asking how the Bible has, in practice, been used for the task of ethical construction.

3. Seeing if we can we agree a single unified method for ethical construction.

So, let's go…

I. WHAT HAVE WE GOT TO INTERPRET?

We have already considered, in the previous chapter[161], an argument that the Bible offers us a very strange rule book with a whole host of unresolved problems and challenges for the would-be Christian Ethicist. Indeed, it was further argued that this awkwardness could be a deliberate part of God's way of interacting with us.[162] But at this point it would probably be helpful to stop and remind ourselves of some of the ways in which the Bible remains resolutely 'awkward' from the point of view of any Christian community trying to live in the light of God's truth in the Bible.

✦ **'BIBLE TRUTH' SEEMS TO COME IN MANY DIFFERENT FORMS**
– besides quantities of 'law-like' instructions and commands *(e.g. 'Thou shalt not kill' (Exodus 20:13); 'Husbands love your wives' (Colossians 5:25))* the Bible contains many aphorisms and proverbs that provide moral guidance in a distinctly different way from a command *(e.g. 'A cheerful heart is a good medicine' (Proverbs 17:22))*. Again, there are parables, made-up tales with moral meanings and ethical import *(e.g. Nathan's powerful story of a stolen lamb when confronting King David in 2 Samuel 12 and the many famous parables of Jesus, such as the Good Samaritan in Luke 10:29-37)*. There is a vast patchwork of narratives of people and events told to convey truth and give us guidance and example from which we can learn. There are inspired prophetic utterances that seek to challenge us with the direct voice of God. There are visions and apocalypses with hidden layers of meaning that still seek to guide and direct God's people. There are Psalms and Songs addressed to God that seek to teach us by example the wide diversity of acceptable spirituality. Often these different literary forms are woven closely together...... most of the law is set in the midst of extended narratives about God's people; we hear Jesus telling parables within some of the stories narrated about him; Deborah's, Hannah's and Mary's songs of praise are woven into their stories; a telling of a prophet's prophetic deeds is often interwoven with records of their inspired utterances. The recognising, weighing and valuing of all this diverse material with moral meaning packaged in distinct literary forms is always going to be a major challenge to any and every Christian enquirer.

✦ **MANY BIBLE COMMANDS HAVE FALLEN INTO ABEYANCE** – A debate rages through the New Testament as to how much of Moses' Law in the Pentateuch still applies to Gentile Christians. It is clear that the ceremonial and religious elements of the law no longer apply directly (Acts 15 & Galatians 3) but a wide variety of opinions have been expressed ever since as to how much of the 'moral' law in the Pentateuch still applies. For example, the Ten Commandments, including the command to 'Honour your father and your mother' (Exodus 20:12), seem to still have weight.[163] But are we expected, as a result of this, to take a 'stubborn and rebellious son who will not obey his father and mother' to the elders at the town gate so that all the men of the town can stone him to death (Deuteronomy 21:18-21)[164]? Other commands in the Bible, including many in the New Testament are also now widely ignored. Richard Bauckham offers the following illustrative selection[165]:

A VARIED SELECTION OF WIDELY IGNORED BIBLE COMMANDS

1.   You shall not eat flesh with its blood (Genesis 9:4)

2.   Do not be too righteous and do not act too wisely (Ecclesiastes 7:16)

3.   You shall not sow your field with two kinds of seed, nor shall you put on a garment made of two different materials (Leviticus 19:19)

4.   Greet one another with a holy kiss (1 Thessalonians 5:26)

5.   [Women], do not adorn yourselves outwardly by braiding your hair (1 Peter 3:3)

6.   Let a widow be put on the list [for church support] if she is not less than sixty years old and has married only once (1 Timothy 5:9)

7.   Anyone who is unwilling to work should not eat (2 Thessalonians 3:10)

8.   Slaves, obey your earthly masters with fear and trembling (Ephesians 6:5)

9.   If anyone will not welcome you or listen to your words, shake off the dust from your feet as you leave that house or town (Matthew 10:4)

10.   Give to everyone who begs from you (Luke 6:30)

Listed by RICHARD BAUCKHAM "Scripture and Authority Today", pp16&17

As one further example we might note the non-observance, in many Reformed Churches, of Paul's apparent instruction to the Corinthian Christians that 'women should be silent in the churches' *(1 Corinthians 14:34)*. On what basis can we justify our common practice[166] that some Biblical commands are to be obeyed as they stand, some 'spiritualised', some turned into de-coded cross-cultural 'examples' and some ignored altogether? Who decides? How should they do the deciding? The Bible itself does not make this clear nor, by and large, do we!

✦ **MANY PRESSING ETHICAL ISSUES SEEM TO BE IGNORED BY THE BIBLE** – It is understandable that a book completed nearly 2000 years ago would not necessarily address in detail all the ethical issues of our own day and age. Nevertheless, there are real problems deciding HOW we assemble and extrapolate Biblical guidance to apply it to issues that are entirely new or have taken on a distinctly different moral profile from Bible times. Genetic engineering, collective bargaining, geriatric care, democratic governance, immigration controls, and a whole diverse host of other moral issues rely on improvised lines of argument based on extracted and refined Bible 'norms'. By the time we have a specific proposal as to what 'the Christian stance' should be on many of the moral dilemmas of our day we've travelled a long, long way from the richly dense text of the Bible. All that bridging work that carries us from texts to ethical proposals is the work of fallible human beings who are all lugging around a lot of baggage, so all their proposals must be open to challenge, debate and change and all their conclusions must be provisional.

✦ **BIBLE ETHICS ARE EMBEDDED IN CULTURES UNLIKE OUR OWN**
– From the memories of the life setting of desert nomads in the stories of
Abraham, Isaac and Jacob through to the life of fledgling Christian communities
in the Graeco-Roman cities of the Eastern Mediterranean in the 1st Century CE,
all the cultural settings of the Bible are far different from any 21st Century setting.
Yet every story, every proverb, every commandment in the Bible is embedded
in one or more of these ancient cultural settings. We never get ethical material
in a 'pure' culture-free form. Ideas of honour and shame, sickness and health,
selfhood and community, the spiritual and the corporeal that may underlie and
significantly shape an ethical command or appeal or story in the Bible may have
been so obvious to its first hearers or readers that they are never articulated or
explained. Yet, our ability, at this distance, to re-enter that 'world' and understand
its meanings and values is strictly limited. When we view recent work by scholars
like Gerd Theissen[167] and Wayne Meeks[168] (and those who have followed after
them[169]) we see impressive efforts at cultural detective work and our chances
of avoiding serious misunderstanding of the world that Paul and the Church
in Corinth shared seem to be significantly improved. But there's always the
chance that we have entirely missed a key aspect of the shared culture, with the
result that our reading of something Paul said is far removed from what he was
intending... and we might never know. Cultural distance sets us a real challenge
when we seek to connect ethical guidance from previous millennia to the ethical
needs of our own day and age.

✦ **THE BIBLE IS A BOOK OF TWO TESTAMENTS** – There are real issues
about how the two testaments of the Christian Bible relate to each other. To what
extent and in what ways does the New Testament supersede or 're-read' the Old
Testament? Can Christians approach the Old Testament directly or only via the
New Testament when they are seeking ethical guidance? Which parts of the Old
Testament, if any, are 'abrogated' by the injunctions of the New Testament? As in
so many of these issues, the Bible does not appear to speak with a single clear voice
and Christian history displays a rich variety of strategies, including, it must be said,
the deeply suspect yet commonly-used strategy of 'select what you like from the
Old Testament and ignore the rest'.[170]

✦ **JESUS SEEMS TO BE AT THE HEART OF A BIBLE DEBATE ON ETHICS**
– As we noted before, there is an established prophetic tradition that challenges the
people's approach to both the religious and moral laws of Israel. Amos, Micah and
Jeremiah, amongst others, object forcefully and passionately to people hiding behind
the Law's demands in an effort to hoodwink God and get away with injustice.
Jesus, in his own way, whilst affirming the Law as God's Law, also works powerfully
to challenge strategies of defensive compliance amongst the religious observers
of his day.[171] Paul (once a strong exemplar of the very tradition Jesus challenges)
goes on, in his letter to the Christian Church in Rome, to develop the idea of
how even God's Law can be a stimulus to sin *(Romans 7)*. All of this material
unsettles any attempt to produce a calm, rational, ordered legal code for Christians;
it scuppers any expectation that careful compliance will be enough to please God.

Moreover, it leaves us with unanswered questions as to how or where we strike a balance between the 'law-like' materials that invite compliance and these prophetic challenges that seek passionate commitment. Perhaps the intention is that the debate continue all through the life of the church.

Thus, with particular regard to developing Bible-based Christian ethics, our earlier ideas about the nature of the Bible as a whole are sharply evident once more. The Bible sets us a complex and subtle interpretative task yet gives us little or no guidance as to the right and wrong ways of doing it. There is no bluffer's guide. There are no 'assured results'. There are no 'answers at the back of the book'. We have to work on this together, wholeheartedly, without ceasing and without any prospect that the job will ever be definitively completed this side of glory. Is that hard enough for you?

2.   HOW HAS THIS BEEN DONE IN PRACTICE?

By the second half of the Twentieth Century the ways of the Modern World had had significant effects on Christian Ethics and how and where the serious thinking was being done. Now, there were professional academics who could be called "Christian Ethicists" – philosophers and theologians who had specialised in applying all the relevant techniques, methods and assumptions of the Modern university to the issues of Christian Ethics. With the Modern emphasis on specialists and experts the implicit expectation was that Old Testament and New Testament scholars would quarry their respective bits of the Bible for definitive accounts of what it was saying, then theologians would develop a richly relevant theological understanding for us today based on the work of the Bible scholars, then the ethicists would move in and develop the implications for Christian life and witness, then the popularisers would write it up in an accessible form for church people to read and then (I suppose) it was up to church people to put it all into practice.

Of course, it never really worked like that. For a start, the work of the various Biblical scholars was always developing and changing and never got sufficiently settled to allow it to be used as a firm foundation for theologians and ethicists.[172] Also, in practice, Bible scholars, theologians, ethicists, all turned their hands to the whole task of using the Bible to try to generate Christian ethics, but because of the way theological training is arranged, just about nobody had had a full training in the whole range of skills – Old Testament, New Testament, Theology, Philosophy, Ethics.

So, what sort of a job have the academic ethicists been doing for us all? Two recent books by Jeffrey S Siker[173] and Richard B Hays[174] have each sought to answer that question. Between them they have looked closely and carefully at the way about a dozen prominent Christian ethicists used the Bible in their work. Two findings strike me as important. Firstly, between them, Siker and Hays were able to challenge aspects of the way every single one of these ethicists used the Bible (some challenges were more serious and worrying than others). Secondly, the approaches, methods and pre-suppositions of the various ethicists turned out to be tremendously varied and seemed to lead, in their turn, to equally varied ethical conclusions.

Is that the way it has to be, or is it possible to establish some sort of clear, objective guidelines for the process of using the Bible to generate 21st Century Christian Ethics? Richard B Hays has given it a try. In his recent book, "The Moral Vision of the New Testament"[175] he has set out a careful methodology for using the New Testament to generate ethical guidelines for Twenty-first Century Churches and Christians. We'll look at what he proposes in our next section and see just how far it takes us…

3.   CAN WE DEVISE A RELIABLE METHOD?

Richard Hays openly acknowledges many of the difficulties with generating ethics from the Bible which we have been piling up. He summarises them in these terms:

> "Despite the time-honoured Christian claim that Scripture is the foundation of the church's faith and practice, appeals to Scripture are suspect for at least two reasons: the Bible itself contains diverse points of view, and diverse interpretative methods can yield diverse readings of any text."
>
> *Richard B. Hays 176*

He clearly recognises that 'the possibilities for misreading, abuse, serving one's own interests, and premature closure are ever present'.[177] He is well aware that not only in Presidential elections in the United States of America but also in ethical debates within the Churches 'everybody wants to claim the Bible'.[178] He acknowledges the irony that careful critical study of the text 'exacerbates the … problem rather than solving it'[179], for careful study makes us more aware of 'the ideological diversity within Scripture and our historical distance from the original communities'.[180]

Yet, as an established New Testament Scholar with a real commitment to the need to discern the Will of God 'in and for the community of faith'[181], he seeks to contribute his skills as a scholar and interpreter of the text to provide 'provisional discernments'[182] that might help the Church do the Will of God. But, perhaps more importantly, he wants to investigate and develop a coherent and defensible method for the journey from the text of the New Testament to the 'normative ethical judgements'[183] by which the people of God will seek to live their lives with God and with each other in the 21st Century. Watch carefully, for following what Hays does should enable us to see just how far careful method can take us. Will he be able to build us a safe, broad, dependable highway that will avoid the swamps of confusion and disagreement? Will we all be able to use his route confidently and safely to make this important journey from Bible text to clear ethical decisions for today? Let us see.

Hays divides this journey from the text of the New Testament to lived 21st Century ethic into four overlapping tasks:

✦ **THE DESCRIPTIVE TASK** – reading the text carefully

✦ **THE SYNTHETIC TASK** – placing the text in the context of the whole Bible

✦ **THE HERMENEUTICAL TASK** – relating the text to our situation

✦ **THE PRAGMATIC TASK** – living the text

He then considers the first three of these in some detail.

THE DESCRIPTIVE TASK: With care, balance and insight he provides an elegant summation of the ethos and message of each of the New Testament authors in turn, drawing on his considerable skills as a reader and interpreter of these texts and his wide awareness of the whole range of current New Testament scholarship. He provides a succinct, high quality, summarising description that seeks to respect the distinct voices and insights of the various authors.

THE SYNTHETIC TASK: Hays then looks for a method of drawing together these diverse New Testament writings into some sort of overall 'canonical' coherence (a whole-Bible way of seeing). He despairs of finding one unifying principle (such as 'love') that can act as a single lens to focus and draw out the similarity of the various texts. Instead, he proposes that we need a group of several 'focal images'. In trying to find potential 'focal images' he devises three basic tests. He is looking for: (1) the 'focal images' that are used right across the New Testament in as many books as possible, yet (2) display minimal tension with the insights of the various canonical books and (3) are of maximal importance to the message of the books in which they occur. On this basis, he identifies and determines to use the three 'focal images' that he believes best fit his criteria. These are COMMUNITY, CROSS and NEW CREATION. He rejects both 'love' and 'liberation' as possible focal images as they do not come out as well as his chosen three from all of his chosen tests. He then sets out with his three selected images to generate a synthesis of New Testament ethics.

THE HERMENEUTICAL TASK: After reviewing the work of five other 20th Century Christian Ethicists[184], he uses his three focal images as a basis from which to complete the hermeneutical journey from the insights and attitudes of the New Testament to a selection of diverse ethical problems and issues that confront the churches today. In each case he gives us a detailed, lucid argument how he has derived his ethical conclusions from his reading of the New Testament texts with the help of his three 'focal images'.

Obviously, as the author of a book, he is obliged to leave the **PRAGMATIC** task (putting all of this into practice in our daily lives) to you, me and the rest of the church.

As a contribution to ongoing ethical debate this is a fine, brave, thoughtful book from a wise scholar. As a call for due care in the way we handle the Bible in ethical debate and a plea that our method should always be coherent and defensible, this is a timely contribution that we ignore at our peril. But has Hays cracked the big problem and provided us all with 'THE RIGHT METHOD'? Can he provide us all with that dependable highway for our journey from Biblical text to Ethics for Today? I fear not – let me explain why…

For all his carefulness, as Hays himself is only too aware[185], his ordered, calm, studied approach still involves significant leaps of faith and personal judgement at *every* stage.

✦ Even the **DESCRIPTIVE TASK** involves summarising the ethos and message of each book in the New Testament on the basis of current scholarship (endlessly shifting sands of insight and opinion) and personal judgement (never objective, always shaped by time, place and cultural baggage).

✦ Then as we move to the **SYNTHETIC TASK** Hays notes that we cannot escape acknowledging significant difficulties – "any synthetic account of the unity of the New Testament's moral vision will be a product of our artifice, an imaginative construct of … the interpretative community … analogous to a director's reading of a Shakespeare play … there is no methodologically airtight way to derive proposals".[186] Indeed, when he comes to the crucial task of selecting his three 'focal images' (why three?), he acknowledges – "no-one should suppose that these images have been derived in some strictly scientific way"[187]

✦ Finally, when we consider the **HERMENEUTICAL TASK**, Hays once more acknowledges significant difficulties. He describes the process of re-applying the moral world of the New Testament to our own day, age and community as "an integrative act of imagination".[188] He talks of "Moral Judgement as Metaphor-Making"[189] and concludes that "the great difficulty, of course, lies in knowing how to judge the validity of proposed metaphorical appropriations of the New Testament. There are no foolproof procedures."[190] He also acknowledges there are real difficulties with deciding how, in practice, we balance the competing claims of Scripture, 'Reason' and 'Experience' – the three forms of significant input to our moral decision-making.[191]

Despite deliberately simplifying the whole process by declining to address the thorny issues of how the Old Testament is to fit into the Christian Moral Vision,[192] Hays has still had to rely heavily (at every step of his process) on his own skills, his own perceptions and his own interpretations. His work is personally and culturally rooted to a significant extent. All his ethical conclusions are his ethical conclusions – as much the product of his creative insight, his cultural setting and his core passions as of his careful method.[193]

Clearly, he has not been able to build a methodological 'highway' that we can all use to travel safely and easily from New Testament text to useable 21st Century ethical judgements. Indeed, to my satisfaction, he has demonstrated that it simply is not possible to build such a highway. There is no secure, 'scientific' way of doing Biblical ethics. Richard Bauckham's 1989 comment about the process of generating normative ethics from the Bible still stands – it's "more of an art than a science".[194]

For me, this inability of even such a careful scholar as Hays to establish a dependable 'scientific' sort of method to make the journey from Bible text to 21st Century Church Ethics is deeply significant. Hays has demonstrated once again the fallacy of the Modern World's expectation that the wise scholar, by maximising his or her scholarly care, could reasonably solve a problem like this for us all.

Part of the problem seems to lie with the construction of the 'reality' we inhabit and our inability to break through to sustainable objectivity (see Chapter Three). Even for the Bible, even when we're trying to agree the moral code by which we might live, there is no guaranteed route to objectivity and agreement; we all have baggage and it always comes into play.

But equally important would seem to be the nature of the Bible itself (see Chapter Four). Our church formulations implicitly expect the Bible to put an END to all our debates on contentious issues, but the Bible seems to be better suited to START up and sustain serious debate on the issues that matter. Can we use this Bible to construct Christian Ethics for the 21st Century?

5.4   Entering God's conversation

So far in this Chapter just about everything we have considered seems to be making it less likely that there is any reasonable way of using the Bible to construct ethical responses to the issues we face today. Let's look back at the route we have taken:

In section 5.2 –

✦   we distanced ourselves from the common caricature that the Bible offers us a bossy God who simply tries to impose a horrible list of "Thou shalt nots...".

✦   we noted how the New Testament takes the entire Christian Scriptures right away from the parallel Jewish and Islamic models of Scripture as 'Law', anchoring our Bible, instead, in the long, developing story of God met in relationship and rescue.

✦   we identified the heart of the authority of the Bible as the winsome authority of grace which invites a heartfelt response, rather than the imposed authority of power which demands obedience.

In section 5.3 –

✦ we listed six ways in which the Bible makes a very challenging starting point for any attempt to 'do' ethics. These were:

    1.   'Bible Truth' seems to come in many different forms

    2.   Many Bible Commands have fallen into abeyance

    3.   Many pressing ethical issues seem to be ignored by the Bible

    4.   Bible Ethics are embedded in cultures unlike our own

    5.   The Bible is a book of Two Testaments – how do they relate?

    6.   Jesus seems to be at the heart of a Bible debate about ethics

✦ we noted that in the Twentieth Century Christian Ethicists working with the Bible used a wide variety of approaches, methods and pre-suppositions and produced equally varied sets of ethical conclusions.

✦ we concluded (after watching the careful work of Richard B Hays) that an ordered 'scientific' method of deriving 21st Century Christian Ethics from the texts of the Bible is simply not possible.

So, what do we do now? In a world where any sort of objective basis for a shared morality seems hard to come by, is the Bible just a particularly bad place to begin? Are those of us who claim we have started with the Bible nothing more than a sad set of self-serving Postmoderns believing what we will, and blaming it on God?

I am far from persuaded that this is our only conclusion. I remain committed to the idea that the Bible is God's way of giving us guidance for life and living. But I think that we do have to accept some change in what we have all too easily assumed. I think it would only be honest to admit that many of our inherited ideas as to how the Bible may offer us ethical guidance have to be laid aside. Quite simply, they share too much of the misplaced, self-deceptive confidence of the Modern World. Instead, we need a way of understanding the Bible that allows for all the diversity of interpretation it seems to enable and encourage. We need a way of understanding the Bible that allows it to be an exciting means of encountering God, rather than a sort of free-standing ethical code that is an end in itself. We need a way of understanding the Bible that invites us to wrestle daily with ethical issues as a vital part of living, learning and growing in our relationship with God, rather than the freeze-dried, vacuum-packed instructions of "He who must be obeyed". Can we find another 'model' or way of seeing the Bible that helps?

Let's recall the challenging aspects of the Bible that we left resonating at the end of Chapter Four:

✦ wild, untameable Scriptures that defy our every effort to make them neat or ordered or tidy so that they may offer us a God whom we cannot co-opt, coerce or control *(defeating domestication)*

✦ open, unresolved Scriptures that deny us the safety of closure so that they may open us to a God who is infinitely bigger than our imagining *(challenging closure)*

✦ diverse, intriguing Scriptures that take a lifetime and more to befriend so that they may introduce a God who surrendered his life out of love for us *(finding friendship)*

✦ unprotected, vulnerable Scriptures that risk being mercilessly misconstrued so that they may also offer us saving encounter with the vulnerable, crucified God *(valuing vulnerability)*

✦ shared, multi-voiced Scriptures that must be interpreted with wide, diverse conversations so that they may bring us all together as the people of God *(creating community)*

✦ story-rich Scriptures where God is always met in context so that we are forced to meet God anew for ourselves in our own situation, in our own story, in our own way *(always anew)*

This Bible seems to be laden with freshness, vitality and exuberance. We are far from the worlds of constitutions, legal codes, recipe books, scholarly monographs, last wills and testaments, even of autobiographies. This book seems much closer to the vital worlds of vigorous argument and trenchant debate, lively dialogue and unending conversation. So, holding those ideas about the Bible in our heads, let's take a look at the nature of conversation...

Conversation is at the very heart of being human. It's the way we share ideas, information, insights and meanings. It's not a skill confined to any particular culture, nor constrained by any particular method; indeed it is at least as vibrant and alive in purely oral cultures as in cultures that use writing, printing, word processors and e-mail. It works just as effectively in an African village or an urban squatter camp as it does in a Harvard or Oxford tutorial. Conversation is also interactive, allowing response and then a response to the response. Conversation is the basis of all relationships, our main vehicle for understanding and befriending. Conversation is versatile, allowing its participants to interact and engage in a huge variety of ways. Conversation has no permanent rule book but it has thousands of constantly-changing codes of conduct that we have to learn and employ in each context, out of respect for those with whom we converse. Conversation can be dense, layered with subtle meanings on many different levels in a way that legal language tries to avoid. Conversation is the very home of story, for no story fulfils its potential until it is told. Conversation can challenge and confuse as well as instruct and comfort. To engage in conversation is to take risks, for there is always the possibility of being mocked, misunderstood, exploited or abused, as well as the chance to find wonders you never knew existed, relationships you later cannot imagine being without.

All these subtle, rich, vibrant and dangerous characteristics of conversation seem appropriate to the Bible we have encountered and what it seems to offer its readers. Indeed, it seems reasonable to suggest that the Bible is a sort of conversation in itself, centred on lived and experienced stories of God. But it is also possible to see it as an invitation to an ongoing conversation where God can be met afresh in each new generation and context. Arguably, anyone can join the ongoing conversation with the Bible, but the church consists of those who believe that they have met God in this conversation and are trying, together, to let that God shape and direct their lives.

Yes, this is a special sort of conversation, that took place over hundreds and hundreds of years and still allows an ongoing conversational interaction two thousand years later. It's a special sort of conversation in that it seems to involve living what you're saying as well as saying it. It's a hugely special sort of conversation in that it invites those who join in to meet and be befriended by God. Yet, I can't think of a better model of what the Bible seems to be about and how we might reasonably use it to shape our lives than 'a lived conversation with God'.

At the very heart of my proposals as to how we need to see the journey from the text of the Bible to our efforts to construct ethics today is the idea that the Bible is designed to enable us to enter God's conversation with us and with others. The Bible is an open, ongoing conversation with God and with God's people and it is in this conversation that all our debates about ethics and morals are to take place.

Amongst the implications of what I'm saying, is the frank acknowledgement that the Bible is centrally about relationship and not about rules. It does not co-operate in our efforts to construct careful moral codes that will remain unchanged in every culture through all of history. Rather, the Bible invites us to a conversation where we may meet and interact with God and with God's people in a way that enables us to find ourselves and discover how we ought to live. Yes, we may approach this conversation so defensively that we never truly meet those the conversation seeks to introduce to us. Yes, we may seek to monopolise, dominate and bore. Yes, we may try to keep hidden behind those who have entered the conversation before us. But I would suggest that the Bible is most helpfully seen as an offering of conversation with God and with his people. God has risked so much to make this conversation possible, but we must risk much too if we would enter its relationships and learn their truths.

It does not surprise me that the God of Incarnation, who gave up everything to meet and talk with the ordinary and the ignored at the mundane corners of our world, should offer us such open, interactive Scriptures. It seems to be an inevitable part of being human to be endlessly engaged in ethical debate in ordinary conversations. How many times in a week do you hear people "putting the world to rights" in pubs, clubs, hairdressers, offices, at school gates, in the church kitchen, or wherever? Regular conversation informed or misinformed by newspapers, soap operas, and the recounted experiences of participants and their friends is how we all wrestle with what is right and what is wrong. Conversation is where we 'do' ethics. So, why can't the God of incarnation use analogous settings rich in dialogue and story to engage us in ethical debate? Why must we presume that God is only interested in ending the debate, rather than encouraging us to keep thinking, keep agonising, keep trying and keep learning through our mistakes?

Look again at the four Gospels. Jesus occupies a world rich in conversation and debate. He offers very few answers, he provides plenty of provocation to think again. He is a skilled and subtle storyteller for moral purposes endlessly taking the familiar and giving it an unsettling twist that must have started many a discussion that lasted long after he'd moved on to the next village or town. Moreover, Jesus is the key actor in his own disturbing drama. Jesus is at the centre of God's conversation with us and the prompt and example for all our responses and replies.

Painfully, this conversation brings significant risk. God's invitation in the Bible to interact and respond, to listen and to speak is made to each and all of us. This conversation allows no spectators. To remain unresponsive and uninvolved is to exclude yourself, to leave the conversation, to miss out on the God whom others meet here. Yet, to respond is to let God loose in your life, allow the limitlessness of God to search for a limitless response from each and all of us. There is no casual conversation here.

5.5 Seven proposals for conversationalists

This idea that the Bible is best viewed as an invitation to join the shared conversation between God and people, allows us to give some shape to the process of developing Christian Ethics for 21st Century Christians from the Bible. But we have moved a long way from any idea of an agreed 'methodology' or a fixed set of rules. To pick up on our earlier analogy of highways and forest tracks, this conversation model helps us to get some idea of the territory we have to cross rather make any attempt to offer us a highly-engineered highway that we can all use. It's more of a map for orienteering than some sort of vast project of concrete steel and tarmac cutting right across the country. It still leaves us to develop our own routes; sometimes following others down well-beaten tracks for quite long stretches; sometimes by hacking a new path through a particular thicket for ourselves. In that spirit, let me put before you seven proposals for those who would enter this conversation. Some are presuppositions necessary to this way of seeing, others are implications drawn from it and from the nature of the Bible itself. Together they map out a way of generating 21st Century Ethics from the Bible that takes seriously both the rich texture of the Bible itself and the rich diversity of 21st century church people. What is more, you will quickly find that all these propositions have their roots in matters we have already discussed and investigated in this and earlier chapters. See what you think...

I. ALLOW FOR REAL ARGUMENT

When we were considering the new ways of approaching texts (in Chapter Three) I argued for a broad acceptance of a whole range of uncomfortable ideas. These ideas challenged the Modern World's casual assumptions about our ability to be objective and our easy access to 'the truth'. Yet, when it came to the Postmodern alternative, I followed a sizeable clutch of scholars[195] in urging you to say "NO!" at one crucial point. We declined to follow the Deconstructionists over the edge of the cliff of knowing into "the abyss of uncertainty".[196] We maintained that whilst there may be more than one possible reading of a text, some readings will always be 'wrong'. We insisted that, in principle, it is possible for us to judge a proposed meaning to be valid or invalid and to argue for other people's agreement with our decision. Yet we recognised that there will always be some disputed meanings and even extended and entrenched disagreements that will run on and on. This is of foundational importance. Without the possibility that we can argue about meanings and that the argument means something and is 'going somewhere', the whole enterprise of seeking truth in the Bible is lost. If I alone am responsible for deciding what the text of the Bible means for me, then I can never get beyond myself and meet a meaningful God in the Bible; I'll only be using the text to construct my own chosen idol. And when it comes to deciding what is right, I'll also be selecting and constructing my own personal ethics, or agreeing a shared ethic with a select group of friends with whom I happen to agree. To enter God's conversation, we must be able to argue with God and with each other and overhear the arguments that have already taken place in the Bible.

Yet I'm not too worried. If there was no possibility of arguments being persuasive and about something real what would be the point of Deconstructionist authors getting all upset when their readers 'misunderstand them'[197]. On this point, John Rogerson quotes the argument of Jurgen Habermas that all relativists engage in a "performative contradiction"[198], relying on the universal validity of argument to argue with the rest of us that universal arguments are invalid and impossible.

This possibility of real argument is the foundation layer of my case that we can construct meaningful Christian Ethics for the 21st Century from the text of the Bible. Nosing between the misplaced certainty of the Modern World and the false fatalism of the Postmodern, we have to **ALLOW FOR REAL ARGUMENT**. Meaningful, persuasive argument must be possible and debate about ethics must involve the possibility of persuasion. Without the reality of argument there would be no conversation with God, no chance to share it with others.

What am I saying here?

ALLOW FOR REAL ARGUMENT....

✦ Among the **IMPLICATIONS** of what I'm saying, I would emphasise the core determination that the Bible is able to introduce us to a GOD-who-is-there out beyond ourselves who seeks to affect and direct our ethical decisions. I am far less confident than many of the scholars of the Modern World about the ease with which you and I can identify exactly what this God is saying to us. Yet I am equally wary of the Deconstructionists' rejection of *any* possibility of communicating meaning and truth through texts. Somewhere in between, I would find a complex and risky world littered with both truth and distortions. In this world (which I take to be the one we inhabit) the Bible *can* lead you and me to a real encounter with a God whom we have not invented nor imposed upon ourselves who does offer us guidance as to how we should live.

✦ The ministry of **JESUS**, rich in words and deeds of challenge, would make no sense at all if it were not possible for him to persuade people to change the way they saw the world and the way they ought to live. Jesus, by healings, in parables, though deliberate actions and in tightly wrought arguments with his opponents, demonstrated his total reliance on the possibility of meaningful, 'real' argument. Indeed, the Jesus we meet in the pages of the Bible is himself a rich, complex and challenging argument about the nature of God, and how, therefore, we should seek to live. It is this Jesus, the central argument of life, that holds out the promise of a real, deepening encounter between us and the 'Father' of everything.

✦ To accept the possibility of 'real' argument is to be thoroughly **BIBLICAL**. For, as we have already acknowledged, the Bible itself is a forum for richly subtle argument and debate. Almost every book in the Bible relies on the reality of argument as it seeks to position itself in relation to the earlier writings that it takes to be already 'Scripture'. Almost every book in the Bible seeks to readjust or reapply to some extent the ethical implications of the Scriptures in whose shadow it has been written.

✦ This commitment to real argument is faithful to the **REFORMED** tradition, because exposing ourselves to the Bible and its arguments and expecting them to change not just our minds but who we are and what we do is the very heart of the Reformed strategy for tackling life, the universe and everything. The Reformation was a conscious acceptance of the power of Biblical persuasion as a mighty force unleashed on the politics and practicalities of church, state and people.

✦ The **PAINFUL** part of this it the way it leaves us standing out from the crowd. To accept the real power of argument is to find ourselves in stark opposition to the Western World's latest fashion for unrestricted individual choice. To proclaim openly a commitment to the existence of an objective God-who-is-there, met through the pages of the Bible, is to risk ridicule from the style gurus of the Postmodern world. It is to argue that at the heart of the carnival of life there *is* a central circus that others simply refuse to accept. It is to insist that there is a focal point for ethical decisions and a shared basis for morality, even if we are endlessly debating its exact nature and import. It is to join Paul in proclaiming for our day and age a 'stumbling block' and a 'foolishness'. It is to walk with Jesus on the road that invites rejection, to seek to win over others by taking the way of the cross.

2. ADMIT OUR NEED OF OTHERS

All through Chapters One, Two and Three we talked a lot about everybody's 'baggage' and our complete inability to be obviously objective. Surely this Postmodern critique of Modern assumptions about the reliability of the solitary, 'unparented' scholar bites deep. None of us can be trusted on our own; we all require the insightful suspicion of others.[199] Indeed, our only defence against subjective self-serving when we read the text of the Bible is to engage in dialogue, even argument, with other people. In Chapter Three I also put to you the further argument that it's not enough to engage in cosy discussion with the people with whom we are comfortable, for it is when we share an important presupposition that we are most likely to blithely ignore both its presence and its effects.[200]

So, everyone is to be involved.[201] Of course, we will need all the insights and information assiduously collected by careful scholars and experts. But the experience of the untutored who seek to understand must be valued too. Gerald West, a white theologian on the staff of the University of Natal in South Africa, writes movingly in a recent article[202], of important new insights into the Joseph story in Genesis that he gained from joining in Bible study with Zulu groups (whose members had received only a fraction of his extensive education). Their studies were based on a vivid series of woodcuts of the story made by Azaria Mbatha, a local Zulu artist. Through these pictures West 'saw' dimensions in the story, obvious to the artist, that he would otherwise never have considered at all. How many others, one wonders, have cut themselves off from new insight because they would not hear or see, because they thought they knew better?

The insights of past generations are important too (Yes, even when they exasperate us - for our very exasperation may help us in our struggle to see differently and see clearer), though not only those of our own particular tradition, nor in ways that limit the freedom of present day readers to argue against their positions.

No-one is privileged, nor is any particular voice guaranteed the first or last word, but the marginalised need to be sought out and their silenced voices encouraged to speak[203]. Who knows where a significant insight or critique may be found? By way of illustration, consider the brief appearance of the Rechabites in *Jeremiah 35*, where God and Jeremiah used their faithfulness to challenge the people of Jerusalem. This 'sect' would not buy land, grow crops, drink wine or live in houses, but insisted on retaining the tent life of desert wandering with the Lord, effectively never "entering the land". Their harsh life was a costly act of "resistance to the comfortable accommodations of settled, urban society"[204] lived in faithful obedience to the command of their ancestor. Yet these strange, marginal people (Brueggemann calls them "a religious curiosity"[205]) are held up by God and Jeremiah as examples of a community who listened to their ancestor's clear instructions and obeyed – in stark contrast with the people of Judah and Jerusalem who ignored God's persistent words of advice. God proceeds to curse the people of Judah, whilst offering beautiful words of blessing to the Rechabites (*Jeremiah 35:17-19*). These easily-ridiculed folk from the very fringes of Judean society with an absurd moral code of their own had, in the crisis, a real truth to share. Yet, Jeremiah's God is not advocating that all the people of Jerusalem should abandon city life for the nomadic life of the Rechabites. Indeed, he elsewhere insists that those taken away into exile try harder at making the most of life in Babylon (*Jeremiah 29:4-7*).

Respect for cultural diversity and the valuing of the potential insights and voices of other peoples is of endless importance for our ability to hear the God of the Bible. If the Modern 'project' of seeking a unified, singular way for everyone to see everything had succeeded, it would have been a disaster. The richest possible variety in world views and ways of seeing (provided we can find a just and gentle way to share insights and influence each other) would seem to be as important to our search for God and truth as the need for rich stores of genetic diversity is to the physical maintenance of life on our planet.

Also, according to this way of seeing, ecumenism, interfaith dialogue and apologetic debate with the faith's detractors are not optional extras for those inclined that way, but central necessities of an honest search for God's truth and any genuine attempt to read the Bible aright as a way of meeting God and as a source of ethical guidance.

As I see it, the second vital component of the process of finding our way between Bible text and valid 21st Century ethical constructs is to **ADMIT OUR NEED OF OTHERS**. A clamour of diverse voices is a necessity if we are to hear God's voice rather than the echoes of our own. To share in God's conversation is, of necessity, to share in conversation with others.

What am I saying here?

ADMIT OUR NEED OF OTHERS....

✦ Amongst the **IMPLICATIONS** of what I'm saying, I particularly
appreciate the clear emphasis on the value of diversity and difference. I
live in a multi-racial inner-city part of Birmingham, with neighbours who
daily remind me that there is more than one way of seeing and being.
Yet my immediate neighbours represent only a tiny fraction of the human
diversity God has created and nurtured on this planet. In this context
I find it very hard to imagine that almost everybody is either 'wrong' or
'very wrong' and a very few of us are blessed with getting it just about
all 'right'. Who knows where a God who is interested in all of us may
have scattered shards of the truth?

✦ **JESUS** seems to be an endless enemy of self-centred certainty, always
challenging the settled moral beliefs of those he meets. Indeed, the Jesus
we meet in Mark's Gospel finds himself learning important truth about
the porous limits and boundaries of his own ministry from a Gentile
woman from the region of Tyre and Sidon *(Mark 7:24-30)*; he seems to
need others himself as he seeks to enlarge his understanding.

✦ This understanding of our endless need for others is powerfully **BIBLICAL**
because the Bible seems to be a forum in itself, a debating place for
competing and mutually-challenging voices seeking to adjust the ethical
implications of what they have themselves received, observed and heard.
Indeed, the whole idea of prophecy in the Bible is one of God-inspired
challenge to the settled ethical understandings of God's people. The Bible
is a rich clamour of diverse voices through which the ethically challenging
voice of God may be heard and re-heard.

✦ This is a truly **REFORMED** idea because the Reformed understanding of
church governance was built on seeking God's will *together*, in Council.
Be it church meeting, elders' meeting, presbytery, synod or assembly, the
Reformed ideal is that we seek God's guidance together, that the voice of
God emerges from the clamour of our prayerful but lively debate around
the meaning of Scripture, in the face of the situation in which we find
ourselves. Only together can we ascertain how we should live as the
people of God.

✦ The **PAINFUL** part of this is that the route to a clearer grasp of God's
truth will often require us to admit we've been wrong, repent of past
certainties, own up to the distorting effect of dark forces in our own
lives. Finding the truth may confront us with our own racism, or male
chauvinism, or selfishness, or pride. It may mean being 'caught out'

and 'exposed' in the act of employing suspect arguments. Indeed, there may be a process a bit like peeling an onion in which we have to shed layer upon layer of cherished distortions as we seek to be faithful to the God-who-is-there and move away from the known comforts of our own household idol or local deity. Seeking the truth as part of the richly-varied company of the whole people of God can be deeply painful – a sort of cross-carrying in the footsteps of the Jesus we seek to follow. Should that surprise us?

3. ACCEPT THE BIBLE AS IT IS

The Reformed tradition has always prided itself in its commitment to the Bible and to the supreme authority of the Bible over the life of the church. Yet, the scrutiny of scholars over the last two hundred years has cumulatively uncovered a rich diversity in the material in our Bible, and on a scale that Reformed churches have often been reluctant to admit. The Bible that has emerged simply does not evidence 'the consent of all the parts'[206] of which the Westminster Confession had spoken so confidently in 1647. As well as being in some sense 'a particular story', the Bible is quite clearly 'a [very] diverse library'[207], pregnant with a rich variety of ethical possibilities.

Two strategies have often been employed to resist, paper over or avoid the awkwardness, dissonance and multi-voiced qualities in the Bible. On the one hand, some have proclaimed the unity and cohesion of the Bible with an unrestrained fervour that smacks of outright denial. They refuse to allow any weight to the evidence to the contrary that we considered earlier (Chapter Four, Section Two). At the same time, others (probably most of us) have effectively filleted the Bible producing a canon-within-the-canon - a more comfortable set of Scriptures that are used regularly whilst the troubling bits are silenced by being ignored. To me, both strategies are a betrayal of the Reformed ideal that the Bible should have authority over the church.

Surely the time is overdue for us to take seriously all the density, diversity and wildness in the Bible, even if we find it awkward, troubling and demanding? We need to accept the multi-voiced and multi-layered qualities of our Scriptures, as well as that deep sense that there really is some sort of unity here (though, like the presence of God in many of the Psalms, that unity may not always be immediately and obviously evident). We need to celebrate and embrace the-Bible-we-have, accepting that this is how God has chosen to speak to us. If our Bible is more like a debate than a monologue, so be it. If it is riddled with arguments and counter-arguments, propaganda and subversion (as Rex Mason has powerfully maintained in the case of the Old Testament [208]), let us dare to believe that this is how God has chosen to speak to us. Whatever our settled beliefs, there are always voices raised in the Bible that continue to question and challenge them. Might that be part of God's purpose - a deliberately built-in risk of unsettling each and all of us so that we may hear something new, thereby deepening our ethical understanding? If we are to respect the texts of the Bible and use them to construct the ethics by which we shall try to live, then we are obliged to **ACCEPT THE BIBLE AS IT IS**. The rich diversity of Bible voices must not be stifled, ignored or avoided.

What am I saying here?

ACCEPT THE BIBLE AS IT IS....

+ Amongst the **IMPLICATIONS** of what I'm saying, is a strong challenge to us all. In one way or another, it is probable that most of us operate with some sort of a "canon within the canon"; a safer selection of Scriptures that seem to give us the sort of God with which we are more comfortable. Again, we are prone to concentrate unashamedly on a favoured clutch of Scriptures that offer us a more coherent set of ethical demands and instructions. Alongside this, many of us employ the other main strategy of ducking the issue; many of us downplay the diversity in our Scriptures and claim a principled unity for the Bible that rather overstates the case. Accepting the Bible as it is will test, extend and challenge us all.

+ The **JESUS** of the Sermon on the Mount challenges and openly disputes with the very Scriptures he claims to revere *(Matthew 5:17-48* with the repeated 'You have heard that it was said... but I say to you...'). He is more than comfortable with debating and dissenting, with the voice of God heard in the midst of diverse readings, with the endless possibility of prophetic challenge to hear again and hear differently and change what you do as a result.

+ Obviously, this approach attempts to be seriously and thoroughly **BIBLICAL**. It is all about accepting the Bible we have, rather than trying to crimp and squeeze it into a more acceptable shape or form.

+ This approach also seeks to be thoroughly **REFORMED** because it addresses the Reformation's central commitment to take Scripture seriously. It challenges us all to treat the Scriptures with even greater respect.

+ The **PAINFUL** part of this is the way it leaves so much that is provisional, unresolved, open to challenge and 'at risk'. We are denied the comfort of neatness and closure. We are kept from reducing God to something containable, safe and domesticated. We live with a permanent risk of painful new discoveries about the ethical implications of the text as we humbly listen together for the voice of God to speak to us from the midst of the Bible's mixture of clashing and harmonising voices.

4.   *ALLOW THE BIBLE'S OWN METHODS*

The Churches of the Western World have just lived through an extended period where a neat, 'scientific' methodology was an absolute requirement for any area of study to be deemed serious and respectable. Yet, the Bible is not only a stubbornly-awkward collection of writings bursting with diversity; throughout its various component parts the Bible remains resolutely silent on important questions of method. All through Chapter Four and the earlier parts of this chapter we noted such silences. The Bible does not give the sort of neat guidance on methodology (or 'how to go about it') that we would wish on many questions of method. We have already noted its silence about:

+   how we ought to read the Bible out of its own time, place and culture into our own

+   how we can rightly summarise its message into creeds or confessions

+   how we can tell which Bible commands to obey, which to treat as examples from another culture, which to spiritualise and which to ignore altogether

+   how we can tell who the true believers are

+   how we ought to balance competing accounts and differing theologies

+   how we read and balance the ethical contents of commands, stories, aphorisms, etc.

+   how we ought to construct ethical responses to issues not mentioned in the Bible

+   how we ought to relate the Old Testament to the New Testament.

It would be easy to assume that the Bible's silence (or in some cases conflicting suggestions) about method leave an opening for us to supply a careful method of our own. Many such clear methods and interpretative maxims, 'patterns' and 'schemes' exist, including Richard Hay's 'focal images' (see above 5.3, subsection 3). However, it is noticeable that they often seem helpfully to reinforce the conclusions that their designers had in mind and just happen to preclude the conclusions of those with whom they disagree.[209] That, in itself, should arouse our suspicion.

I can see no particular problem in any group of interpreters of the Bible deciding that they are going to proceed by devising and employing their own clear and careful method for what they are doing.[210] Great, but we shouldn't be surprised if others come along and challenge us to produce arguments in its defence, offering a competing method of their own that allows a whole different set of conclusions. And don't be at all surprised if it turns out that it's impossible to find any acceptably objective means of deciding between the different competing methods.

No, what is indefensible is simply assuming that our method has the full authority of Scripture and that no other method is going to be valid. Where the Bible declines to offer a clear interpretative methodology, no scheme or pattern or method can be considered the "right" scheme. Where the Bible declines to offer a clear interpretative methodology, any method we provide is simply a part of our interpretation; it is not privileged in any way. There always exists the possibility that someone will come along with a different method that may be equally valid. For, if the Bible offers no method, how are we to decide?

With a logic that feels almost as audacious as Warfield's, let me dare to propose that to object to the Bible's lack of clear method and neat rules for interpretation is to object to what God has given us. Rather than seeking to supply a perceived 'shortcoming' in the Bible by devising a foolproof interpretative method to derive dependable ethics, would it not be better to ask what purpose might lie behind the Bible's lack of a clear method in so many interpretative situations? I suspect it may have something to do with a divine intention that the Bible should be better suited to starting up and sustaining serious debate than neatly ending it. As we noted earlier, our church formulations implicitly expect the Bible to put an end to all our debates on contentious doctrinal and ethical issues, but the-Bible-we-have seems to be carefully designed to do otherwise.

The most defensible approach would seem to be to allow the Bible's own methods of interpretation to be used, even when that means living with an apparent absence of prescribed method and room for each interpreter to devise and develop their own. We have to **ALLOW THE BIBLE'S OWN METHODS**. We must beware of imposing on the Bible the methods of interpretation that we find most comfortable and claiming that they must apply always and everywhere. Let me say this again... The ethics that the Bible invites us to uncover and own are not scientifically or philosophically derived. They are the products of the on-going conversation begun so creatively and challengingly in the Bible. We are invited to share in ethical conversation where we only discover each other's presuppositions and whether or not we can accept them as the conversation unfolds.

What am I saying here?

ALLOW THE BIBLE'S OWN METHODS....

+ Amongst the **IMPLICATIONS** of what I'm saying, is a clear recognition that any 'pattern', 'scheme' or 'interpretive maxim' we employ is part of our INTERPRETATION rather than something neatly objective or something inherently Scriptural. The Bible shows no awareness of our careful methods. The Bible has landed us in a place where ethical matters are always open to debate and even the most settled ethical conclusions can always be levered open from a new angle.

+ **JESUS** was a particular master at jemmying open other people's certainties. He was especially skilled at dextrously removing the very foundations of other people's complex ethical pyramids. Even the beatitudes *(Matthew 5:3-12* and even more obviously in the version of

---

Luke 6.20-26) present a Jesus playing breath-taking games with the basic truths that 'everyone' could accept. He posits a succession of clearly ludicrous propositions *(no-one* considers poverty a blessing, or hunger an advantage or that it's cool to be insulted and rejected) but then, in each case, he provides his absurd claim with the transforming effects of the purposes of God (because of *God,* the poor will inherit God's kingdom, the hungry will be satisfied, and so on…). Jesus is very much at home in this world rich with debate, dissent and new discovery.

✦ Truly, this is being committedly **BIBLICAL** because it declines to take the Bible and put it through our own interpretive sawmills, seeking instead to allow what the Bible itself allows. It takes the Bible's interpretive methods seriously as well as accepting its ethical assertions and interpretations. That is more thoroughly 'Biblical' than much of Western Biblical interpretation has been prepared to be.

✦ This is also, in a real sense, being **REFORMED**. This approach challenges our methodological arrogance, undoing the assumptions of the Modern World that our ways are always improvements and that the most scientific method is always right. It restores to the Bible a part of its authority that we all to easily tried to tame, remove or ignore. It leaves us relating to the Bible with all the vulnerability, open-endedness and imprecision of friendship and the developing ethics of developing relationship.

✦ The **PAINFUL** part of this is where it leaves us. To deny us all the comforts of neatness and closure and leave us in the midst of an ongoing debate on Bible meanings and their ethical implications is to increase our pain. No matter what our stance in the debate, we are likely to hear a lot said by others that aggravates, upsets, even distresses us. Indeed, it may even be through such exposure to attitudes and arguments that profoundly unsettle us that God may help us to grow (though, clearly, this is not to say that we have to swallow the other unsettling arguments whole!). Perhaps, even in Biblical Ethics, it's a case of "No pain – no gain!"

5.   *KEEP TALKING ABOUT ETHICS*

When it comes to ethics, I think we have to take very seriously the possibility that God's intention was not to end moral debate but start it and sustain it. We have to consider whether the internal tensions, divisions and debates evident within the Bible are meant to be some sort of example for us, rather than an unfortunate embarrassment. If the Bible itself is a sort of conversation, it would seem to imply that the intended mode of life of the people of God was always to include enlivening argument and debate about what is right and what is wrong.

Indeed, the Bible is not interested in 'Resolving the rules' – for, as Paul says, the letter kills. Rather, the Bible is intent on stimulating serious consideration of what knowing God implies for each person in each community in each generation in each setting. Unending debate is far more likely to challenge, stimulate and invite lived response than resolved rules. The Bible is an invitation to consider harder and deeper and more painfully the implications of friendship with Jesus in the situation in which we find ourselves. That is why the debate itself has so few rules, so little prescribed in the way of permitted method, so much opportunity for impassioned disagreement. WE are the ones who presume some ethical issues effectively resolved, when they may only be temporarily quiescent. The Bible leaves every practical ethical conclusion provisional; a new setting or context can always re-set the question in a new way and send us scurrying back to debate with the Bible and with one another about the right thing to do... and we may then have to go on debating that issue for generations.

I would propose that, like the arrival of Jesus in a Galilean village or town (*Matthew 10:34-36*), the Bible's intention is not to resolve all our ethical dilemmas but rather to deepen our debates and sharpen our challenges in ways that keep us talking about ethics and struggling to decide how we should live. How else are we to grapple with what is 'right' and develop our own conclusions? How else do we become involved, learn, develop, 'own' and live out our ethics with shared personal passion? We need to **KEEP TALKING ABOUT ETHICS**. The Bible seems to be designed to make ethical decisions difficult and endlessly debated with all our conclusions provisional. The conversation seems to be as valuable as the conclusions.

What am I saying here?

KEEP TALKING ABOUT ETHICS....

✦ Amongst the **IMPLICATIONS** of what I'm saying, I would particularly emphasise the way the debate about ethics passes on from generation to generation. We are always inducted into the debate by our 'spiritual parents'. In some areas of ethics we take on their opinions and perceptions without even realising, in other areas we may find ourselves reacting strongly against their ideas. Yet, it is their contribution to the ongoing debate and their readings of the Bible and its ethical messages (shaped by their own inheritance and their own life setting and experiences) that forms our ethical inheritance. The Bible always bears the impression of the hands that pass it on to us and we, in our turn, leave our own impress on it as we pass it to our successors. There is no place for any of us to read the Bible without the effects of tradition, reason and experience being involved in the ethical readings we make. Even Martin Luther, who seemed to overthrow the whole tradition he inherited, is stamped with a deeply Mediaeval and Augustinian German mindset. It did not altogether control him, but it did shape him and affected even the style and nature of his rebellion. And so, from generation to generation, the rich, evolving conversation goes on.

+ As we noted before, **JESUS** seems regularly to stir up debate and introduce moral challenge rather than offer simple solutions to ethical problems. He is expert at entering into the existing ethical debate and taking it to a new level that keeps it going and going.

+ This endless debating is clearly **BIBLICAL** because in various ways, notably in the tensions between the two Testaments, the Bible itself witnesses to an ongoing ethical debate on many issues.

+ There is a real **REFORMED** feel to all this debating. The Reformers and the Westminster divines may have felt they were making the unitary truth clear for all time, yet they were often offering but one strand in a complex debate. Luther and Zwingli both believed that God's truth should be clear and obvious, yet they strongly disagreed even about the meaning of an apparently simple saying of Jesus – "This is my body!". The Reformers, even the magisterial Reformers like Luther, Zwingli and Calvin, were always engaged in debates about doctrine, ethics and Bible meaning, even when they thought they were simply putting each other right. These debates raged all through the Reformation and continued in the Reformed tradition generation after generation right down to our own day.

+ The **PAINFUL** part of this is the refusal of resolution. Even if some ethical issues seem sorted, or at least temporarily settled, there will always be others that leave us with tensions and fracturing of fellowship and little prospect of resolution. The challenge of the moral maze is real for Christians, even Christians with the same Bible in their hands. It seems to be an important part of 'the fight'; central to the ongoing struggle of those who would be faithful to Jesus in this troubling and unsettling world.

6. AFFIRM GOD'S UNDERLYING PURPOSES

A conversation can be a long meandering sort of an affair that gets nowhere in particular. Does the conversation that flows through the two testaments of our Bible and on out through the church down to today have any sense of direction?

Based on the arguments I have already put to you in Chapter Four, Section Four ("What might the Bible be trying to say?"), I would argue that there are two key motive forces giving some direction to the ongoing conversation which God and people continue to share, centred in the Bible. At their simplest I would see these as GOD and NEIGHBOUR, the one who befriends us and those we, in our turn, are sent to befriend. Certainly, these twin foci of attention sit side by side in Jesus' famous summation of "all the Law and the Prophets" in *Matthew 22:37-40*:

> [Jesus] said to him, "You shall love the Lord your God with all your heart, and with all your soul, and with all your mind. This is the greatest and first commandment, and a second is like it – You shall love your neighbour as yourself."
>
> *Matthew 22:37-39, (NRSV)*

They are also, as we will consider at greater length in the next chapter, the twin motivating factors in the ministry of the Apostle Paul that he seems to think should be the power and purpose of all Christians. For now, let us note how he sums it up:

> ...All this is done by God, who through Christ changed us from enemies to friends and gave us the task of making others his friends also.
>
> *2nd CORINTHIANS 5:18 (TEV)*

I believe a case could be made that offering us the friendship of God as revealed to us in Christ Jesus and the summons to share that friendship with those around us are the twin motives or purposes of the whole New Testament.

If there is any guidance to keep some direction in the ongoing conversation that the Bible sets up, then (I suggest), it is the need to affirm the importance of these two acts of befriending – the befriending we have put before us by God in Christ and our mission to share that same friendship with those around us. The revealed nature of the God who befriends us, and the need to share that friendship with others seem to shape the conversation God is inviting us to join.

What am I saying here?

AFFIRM GOD'S UNDERLYING PURPOSES

✦ One particular **IMPLICATION** of this is the inherent tension between the two halves of the idea. We shall deal with this at greater length when we look at our case study of Paul engaging in ethical debate in *I Corinthians* (in Chapter 6). However, for now, we can note how the need to keep some sort of bridging contact with the perceptions of the non-Christians we seek to befriend may pull us in the opposite direction to the pull of God's befriending. God may be calling us to such radical discipleship that it might alienate us from our non-Christian neighbours, yet we are also called to reach them with the friendship of God. A real tension ensues.

✦   This tension between the call to love God and the call to love the people of this world is the tension that crucified **JESUS**. He came to be winsome and welcoming in the name of God, yet his commitment to living with Godly love, come what may, meant that, in the end, the crowds of those he sought to reach and touch with God's love gathered around him only to shout "Crucify!".

✦   This tension between the direct call of God's friendship to us and the call to befriend others in God's name is bound to be **PAINFUL** for us too. How are _we_ to balance God's call to be different with not being out of touch with those around us?

7.   ALLOW FOR THE ROLE OF GOD'S SPIRIT

Both the Westminster Confession (1647) and 'Schedule D' of the United Reformed Church's Basis of Union (1972) expect there to be a central role for the Holy Spirit in the process of hearing God speak to us from the words of the Bible. The Westminster Confession talks of the "supreme Judge" for all controversies being "the Holy Spirit speaking in the scripture". The United Reformed Church 'Schedule D' talks of the Word of God being "discerned under the guidance of the Holy Spirit". These two statements span much of the history of the Reformed faith. Formally, they both proclaim the Holy Spirit to be God's way of setting the limits to reasonable and reliable interpretation of Bible meaning, including Bible ethics. Yet, in practice, our trust in God's Spirit to guide us into God's truth has often worn a little thin.

You see, the Reformed faith has always been a particularly rational, even cerebral, 'take' on Christianity. It's a thinking faith, an argued faith, a precise and ordered faith ready to define and delineate, legislate and limit. It has rarely been altogether relaxed about the liberating work of the Holy Spirit. Calvin (perhaps with some relief?) thought that the ecstatic and miraculous manifestations of God's Spirit evident in the Corinthian Church and in the Book of Acts were phenomena confined to the Apostolic age. Both he and his spiritual descendants have often seemed happier to be the ones who, by the power of their own minds grappling with the words of Scripture, decide what is right and what is wrong. Indeed, the Reformed preference for a careful, controlling "subordinate standard" may even be a form of retreat from full trust in the work of God's Spirit in the church.

Yes, as we quoted John Ross saying in Chapter One:

> The Bible contains such [a] variety of attitudes and implications that it can be used in support of almost any doctrine.
>
> John M. Ross, 'The Westminster Confession in the Presbyterian Church of England', in A. I. C. Heron (ed.) p.89

But where are we to turn? If every creed and confession, every commentary and treatise is already an act of interpretation of the meanings found in the Bible, then which ones are to be relied upon? In our search for God's truth, we are thrown back on to our dependence on the Holy Spirit.

The Bible itself (even Paul, the former Pharisee, see *Philippians 3:5*) trusts God, most particularly God's Spirit, to lead, guide, protect and direct the people of God and their interpretation of Scripture. The Holy Spirit is seen as God's means of responding to each new turn in events, each new pressure, each new dilemma and of making relevant sense of the Bible in each new setting. If the Bible offers anything in the way of limits, controls and correctives for the ongoing conversation of God and people, it must surely be the lively, creative presence of God's own Spirit. It is the Spirit using these words written thousands of years ago who makes God present, alive and relevant to the people of God in each generation, context and predicament. It is the Spirit of God that makes our conversation with God possible.

Of course, it's not simply a matter of sitting back and trusting God. There are a whole range of contributory factors involved in how we hear God. We need to hear the interpretative wisdom of past and present generations captured and proclaimed in creeds and confessions. In addition, the power of reason is always going to be a significant tool. Again, inherited traditions will continue to form and shape us and our interpretations and new insights from careful scholars may powerfully refresh our grasp of what the Bible is saying. Also, shared experience of our contemporary events and pressures will inevitably affect our readings and the sense we make of the Bible. Yet, weaving all these influences and possibilities together and both holding us steady and opening us to new ways of hearing is the presence of the Spirit of God. We must always allow for new understanding, and the possibility that God's Spirit is leading us there. In summary, it ought to be God's Spirit leading and developing communities of believers that we should trust to constrain our readings, not some artfully devised method or legislated code of practice.

What am I saying here?

ALLOW FOR THE ROLE OF GOD'S SPIRIT....

✦ Amongst the **IMPLICATIONS** of what I'm saying is the expectation that the Bible is not simply a record of ancient faith frozen in its own time. The presence and power of God's Spirit mean that this Bible can always (in each generation) be read as God's word to us TODAY. The metaphorical leap from ancient world and ancient text to our world and our predicament becomes not only permissible, but the very purpose of reading. It is by the power of God's Spirit that these words become God's Word to us. It is through the work of God's Spirit that the debates and conversations in the pages of Scripture become <u>our</u> invitation to enter God's conversation.

✦ The freedom and constraint **JESUS** himself shows in his handling of the ancient Scriptures he quotes, echoes and re-interprets give us a graphic illustration of the Spirit's presence in the process of interpretation. He offers no clear rules that limit or define his approach, yet he interprets confidently and powerfully. Our own re-interpretations must surely be less inherently dependable and more open to question by others, but the lesson is clear – God's Spirit is there to help us make sense of God's Word for our own time, place and experience.

✦ This is being **BIBLICAL** because without trust in the clarifying role of the one Spirit of God in the whole process, these diverse books woven from diverse materials by countless authors, re-tellers and editors could never be considered to be one 'Bible' at all. Again, without trust in the ongoing role of the one Spirit of God the conversation would have to be considered as having ended with the closure of the canon. A living Spirit of God is our sole guarantor of the living Word.

✦ If this is being **REFORMED** it is because trusting in the ongoing work of God's Spirit means taking the Bible seriously. It risks a level of reformation that the likes of Calvin and the Westminster divines seem to have shied away from. It is in some ways closer to the lively worlds of Anabaptists and English Independents, but that sort of variegated vigour may be more winsome in our own day and age. God's Spirit is too important and too central to the faith to leave to 'Spiritual' churches and Pentecostals.

✦ Again, the **PAINFUL** part of this is our lack of control. We are invited to trust. We are, once again, at risk.

We are now in a position to look at how well this 'model' of handling the "HOW?" question of Biblical Ethics fits with both the Bible itself and with subsequent Christian experience. These will be the tasks of the next two chapters. As a sort of case study of how well these approaches fit with one of the parts of the New Testament that is most concerned with Christian Ethics, Chapter Six will look at the ethical debates that run all through Paul's First Letter to the Church in Corinth. Then, in Chapter Seven, we'll look at how the process of ethical debate and decision-making has worked out in practice in the course of Christian History, by sampling particular ethical debates that raged through the Churches at different times in the last two thousand years. But before we proceed, let's lay out in one place the seven proposals that make up my argument:

DEVELOPING BIBLICAL ETHICS FOR TODAY:

A SUMMARY OF OUR SEVEN PROPOSALS FOR CONVERSATIONALISTS

1:   ALLOW FOR REAL ARGUMENT
Meaningful, persuasive argument must be possible and debate about ethics must involve the possibility of persuasion.

2:   ADMIT OUR NEED OF OTHERS
A clamour of diverse voices is a necessity, if we are to hear God's voice rather than the echoes of our own.

3:   ACCEPT THE BIBLE AS IT IS
The rich diversity of Bible voices must not be stifled, ignored or avoided.

4:   ALLOW THE BIBLE'S OWN METHODS
We must beware of imposing our preferred methods of interpretation on the Bible and claiming that they must always apply.

5:   KEEP TALKING ABOUT ETHICS
The Bible intends ethical decisions to be difficult and endlessly debated with all our conclusions provisional.

6:   AFFIRM GOD'S UNDERLYING PURPOSES
The revealed nature of the God who befriends us and the need to share that friendship with others broadly shape and direct our ongoing conversation.

7:   ALLOW FOR THE ROLE OF GOD'S SPIRIT
It is God's Spirit leading and developing communities of believers that constrains our readings, not some artfully devised method or legislated code of practice.

Some may be smarting at the very vagueness of my seven proposals. All this writing, writing, writing… and this is all we get? But I would argue that **this** vagueness is out of respect for the Bible we have and the God it reveals. More explicit and incisive guidelines would simply seek to re-impose the distorting fastidiousness of the Modern Western mind and silence some of the voices that need to be part of the ongoing debate.

In his 1984 book "New Testament Social Ethics for Today"[211], Richard N Longenecker reviewed four ways of using the New Testament for the construction of Christian Ethics, all of which have significant followings in the churches of the late 20th and early 21st Centuries. In summary, he suggests these four diverse approaches view the New Testament in the following ways:

✦   A book of laws or codes for human conduct
✦   A source for universal ethical principles
✦   A place to encounter exhortation administered by God's Spirit
✦   Tactical suggestions for the individual's autonomous ethical decision-making
He is able to produce substantial criticisms of **ALL** of these positions, concluding:

> "It may be that each of these approaches is more wrong in what it denies than in what it proposes, and that each in its own way is setting forth a necessary aspect of truth for a Christian ethic.
>
> *Richard N. Longenecker, 'New Testament Social Ethics for Today', p9.* [212]

I can't help thinking that Longenecker is telling us that we will always need each other as we approach the Bible and seek to enter God's Conversation. The truth, he seems to be saying, lies in the unresolved tensions between our various understandings. We need to keep listening and keep talking. Only together can we truly become a part of God's ongoing, Bible-based conversation.

CHAPTER SIX

CONFLICT IN CORINTH – A CASE STUDY

6.1 Church Conflict in Corinth

Probably the nearest the Bible comes to offering us manuals on "How To Be a Church" or "How To Be A Christian", is the ethical advice in the Letters of Paul. Yet there is clearly a wide difference between the content and style of these letters and the sort of document we would expect to receive if we asked a 21st Century church committee or working group to provide a manual for the regulation of church life with guidance notes for individual believers.

Viewed as manuals for church life today, Paul's letters are endlessly frustrating both in what they say and in what they fail to say. If this is what we are being offered as Scriptural guidance about church life, then God has clearly got something other than a neat manual or guide in mind. So, I'd like us to explore how well they fit with our idea of an ongoing 'conversation' between God and church.

Let's look at one of Paul's ethically-rich letters to see what is going on. For us, the challenge is to see whether the 'Seven Proposals for Conversationalists' that we reviewed in the previous chapter relate *in any way* to Paul's own practice when he is 'doing' ethics with his churches.

I offer *I Corinthians* as a particular case study. You might find it helpful to have the text of this letter to hand as I will be making repeated reference to various parts of it all through this chapter.

I have chosen *I Corinthians* for three reasons. Firstly, the work of Gerd Theissen[213], Wayne Meeks[214] and others[215], using the clues already present in the text of *I Corinthians*, the account of the founding of the Church in Corinth in *Acts 18* and the final chapter of *Romans* that is filled with greetings from members of the Church in Corinth, have assembled a vivid picture of the setting and background of this letter. By the time we add in the picture of Corinth in the time of Paul assembled from classical authors and archaeology[216] we probably have a richer understanding of the destination and recipients of this letter than we do for any of the other churches to which Paul writes. Secondly, this particular letter to the Church in Corinth is probably richer in discussions of divers ethical issues and how they may best be treated by the church than any other letter of Paul. Thirdly, I've found myself coming back and back to this intriguing letter (always finding fresh and surprising things) all through my own urban ministries.

In the introduction to his recent commentary on *I Corinthians*, Anthony Thiselton[217] summarises our present state of knowledge about the ancient city of Corinth and the church to which Paul was writing. Drawing on the work of a whole variety of Biblical scholars and related work on other ancient texts and on archaeology he sketches the background and setting of I Corinthians in something like the following terms:

CORINTH AND ITS CHURCH IN PAUL'S TIME

1.   THE CITY OF CORINTH & ITS CULTURE

Situated on an isthmus where the main trade route between Italy and Asia Minor crossed Greece, Corinth had two harbours, Cenchreae facing east and Lechaeum facing west. It had been refounded by Julius Caesar in 44BC as a ROMAN colony in Greece. It was a self-confident, competitive and very prosperous trading centre with a multi-racial population but with a markedly Roman character to its civic and higher-society life.

Corinth seems to have been a city with a highly stratified community which attracted a stream of new immigrants with the possibility that astute self-promotion and trading success could enable a significant improvement in social status – i.e. lots of upward mobility (for some). Yet the emphasis on the appearance of success seems to have left many with the tensions of "status-inconsistency". A number of scholars argue that there are major connections between the pushy, success-driven culture of ancient Corinth and many of the attitudes of 21st century Postmodernism (see Chapter Three, Section Two, above).

2.   THE CHURCH IN CORINTH & ITS PEOPLE

Defying the normal approach of those who sought to make an impact in a city like Corinth by the power of their rhetoric, Paul had set up shop with friends and paid his own way in the low-status, menial trade of tent-making. Still, sewing leather and canvas in an open-fronted shop, he made contact with a wide variety of customers. As a result, he had attracted people of a wide variety of social backgrounds to the church. Although most of them were of low standing (slaves, artisans, etc. see 1 Corinthians 1:26) some were of high social standing within the Jewish, Roman and Greek communities of the city. Thus the Christian fellowships of Corinth must have been highly unusual in the sorts of social mixing they afforded in what was otherwise a highly stratified city of distinct communities.

CONDENSED FROM PAGES 1-29 OF ANTHONY THISELTON'S
"The New International Greek Testament Commentary – THE FIRST EPISTLE TO THE CORINTHIANS" (Paternoster, Carlisle, 2000)

When we come to look at the letter itself, we find evidence of a church in danger of falling apart along a number of social and theological fissures. We may suspect that when the church first began there was a truly exciting sense of togetherness generated by their shared defiance of all the social conventions of their stratified city. But, by the time Paul writes this letter from Ephesus, that exuberant closeness of fellowship is collapsing under the weight of increasingly acrimonious disagreements.

It is only three or four years since Paul had left the new-born Church in Corinth to continue his travels, so where have these disagreements come from? Gerd Theissen[218] is able to make a believable case that the divisions and differences of city life which they had so eagerly abandoned are relentlessly reasserting themselves within the life of the church. For example, Paul complains bitterly about the problem of some believers having a feast of a time at the Lord's supper whilst others are left to go hungry (*11:20-22*). Theissen argues that this reads like a practical reassertion of a yawning social class divide. Perhaps the wealthy owner of the large house where the church meets for worship has got into the habit of entertaining church friends of equal social status to a sizeable feast on worship nights, whilst slaves who have to serve dinner in other households may regularly have to forego any chance of an evening meal of their own if they are to join the worship at all. Again, Theissen argues persuasively that the acrimonious divisions over whether it is right to eat meat that has been offered in a pagan temple (*Chs. 8, 9 & 10*) may be best explained as the competing perspectives of the poor (who never see meat except at special temple feasts) and the wealthy (who have at least a smattering of philosophy that lets them argue for the irrelevance of idols and who also need to offer meat at their tables when they are entertaining business associates, if they are to have any chance of impressing them).

Whether or not Theissen has got all the details exactly right, he makes us aware that the ethical dilemmas faced in Corinth are not detached, theoretical problems designed as a neat, educational tool. These are the awkward and messy ethical problems of a real community embedded in a rich matrix of personality, economics, social status, cultural history and church politics. People are aggrieved. Tension is building. And everyone, including Paul, has their own baggage. In *I Corinthians* we can watch Paul attempt to engage in ethical First Aid in a hurting church.

It is important to remember that, like all of the letters from Paul which we have in the Bible, *I Corinthians* shows absolutely no awareness of being "Scripture". This letter was written as a passionate pastor's concerned response to a now distant church which he had previously founded and for which he still cares deeply. He is responding to information that has reached him in two forms. He has had disturbing word-of-mouth reports from Christian travellers returning to Ephesus who have just visited the church in Corinth (*I Corinthians 1:11 & 5:1*). He has also received written enquiries from the church itself on a number of matters of concern to them (*I Corinthians 7:1, 8:1, 12:1 & 16:1*). Paul shows no interest in the possibility of any other readers or listeners. This is all written as part of his pastoral relationship with particular people at a particular time and place.

So, for us, making sense of this letter is a little like overhearing one end of a telephone conversation or, as Richard Hays puts it, "reading someone else's mail"[219]. We are left trying to reconstruct the other voices and what they might have said and written to provoke the responses we find in Paul's letter. The quality of our shared detective work will affect the depth of our understanding of what Paul is saying and why he says it.

But for most of the last two thousand years we have been offered this one-sided part of a tense and difficult conversation between Paul and the Church in Corinth as "Scripture". This is a tiny fragment from a long relationship, a few words added from a distance to the mountains of teaching, exhortation and dialogue that Paul must have shared face-to-face when he was resident with the church in Corinth. Yet this letter and *2 Corinthians* are the only bits of the whole relationship that we have and, for us, these bits are 'Scripture'. So, how are they to work for us?

I don't doubt that God could have arranged for Paul to write and his churches to preserve for us something quite different. It's even possible we *could* have been left "*The Official, Practical and Comprehensive Handbook of Do's and Don'ts for All Churches Anywhere and Every Individual Christian for All Time*". Yet, instead, we have this part-fragment of ethical debate between a particular pastor and a particular church, giving arguments that only fully make sense in that particular context. This leaves me suspicious that it is not simply the ethical advice of *I Corinthians* that is offered to us to be authoritative and inspiring, but the very nature of the conversation and how it works is meant to be a creative example for us. Let me put to you that the ethical approaches and arguments that this persistent pastor uses with this aggravating fellowship are intended to illustrate for us how any fellowship of the People of God, in their own time and place, ought to be grappling with the ethical issues they face. That, I suspect, is why this letter and nearly twenty other pastoral letters form such a significant part of the Christian Scriptures.

6.2 **Paul in conversation**

So, what sort of a picture of the process of 'doing' ethics does this letter give us? HOW does Paul 'do' ethics in *I Corinthians*? Does Paul's approach relate in any way to the 'Seven Proposals for Conversationalists' that we considered in Chapter Five?

Reading and re-reading *I Corinthians* over many years has left me with the firm impression that Paul does indeed 'do' his ethics in the midst of a community conversation, consciously carried out in the continuing presence of the God he had met on the Damascus Road. Indeed, I would largely blame Paul for my own acceptance of the idea that doing ethics the Christian way involves entering God's conversation. Trying to understand what was going on in I Corinthians has been central to my own journey of understanding about the nature of Christian Ethics. So, at least some of my 'Seven Proposals for Conversationalists' have their roots in my reading of Paul's writings in general, but especially in my reading of *I Corinthians*.

That being the case, I'd like to invite you to take a look at what seems to be happening in *I Corinthians* in relation to each of our 'Seven Proposals for Conversationalists'. Will *you* be persuaded by my arguments?

I. PAUL AND THE POWER OF PERSUASION

The first of our "Seven Proposals for Conversationalists" was the idea that we had to accept the possibility of persuasive argument. Paul certainly seems to enjoy a good argument! Much of his letter is clearly responding to strong arguments on ethics in the letter he has just received from some or all of the church in Corinth. His own letter is equally about argument. From end to end *I Corinthians* is about passionate persuasion and feisty argument, using just about every technique and approach that you can imagine. Whilst he radically questions the wisdom of the world (*1:18-25*), Paul is unafraid to use any line of argument that he thinks might carry weight with the Corinthian Christians. He uses arguments from Scriptural texts (*e.g. 3:19f*), arguments based on commands of Jesus (*7:10*), arguments from the example of his own behaviour (*4:16 & 9:1-27*) and arguments based on what he and his readers consider to be 'natural' (*11:14f*). To these he adds a whole variety of persuasive skills, including irony (*2:6-16*), richly metaphorical re-application of (Old Testament) Scriptural ideas (*5:6-8 & 10:1-14*) and creative ideas of his own developed from standard images of Greek rhetoric (*12:12*). Every verse of I Corinthians seems to depend upon the persuasive power of argument. Here Paul presents as a master of ethical dialogue, an exponent of moral conversation with power and purpose. For him ethical instruction is endlessly a matter of lively argument, of winning hearts and minds, not of coolly handing down lists of do's and don'ts.

2. CHERISHING COMPETING CONTRIBUTIONS

Our second proposal for conversationalists was that a clamour of diverse voices is necessary for us to hear the voice of God. Paul seems much more aware of this than his reputation in some quarters as a bit of a religious bully would allow. In *I Corinthians* he is confronting a situation where the church seems to be falling apart into various separate groups each of which reveres a particular Christian teacher as their true leader and guide (*1:10-17*). Yet Paul resists the cheap and easy solution of proclaiming himself "right" and Apollos and Cephas "wrong". Whilst he does appeal to the church to be "united in the same mind and the same purpose" (*1:10 NRSV*), he also offers an imaginative way of seeing in which both his own teaching and that of Apollos are viewed as contributory parts of a bigger picture – "I planted, Apollos watered, but God gave the growth" (*3:6 NRSV*). This suggests a unity of purpose that still has room for a diversity of approach and understanding. Paul is allowing that his is not the only voice to be heard.

Again, when he is arguing against some of the positions that the Corinthian Christians appear to have cited in their letter to him he is wary of condemning them outright. He often says "Yes, but..." to what they've said, rather than a straight "No!". For example, he quotes their letter as saying "It is well for a man not to touch a woman" (*7:1 NRSV*) in a way that clearly allows this assertion some validity. But then he responds with a major qualification of his own - "but because of cases of sexual immorality, each man should have [sexual relations with] his own wife and each woman her own husband." (*7:2 NRSV*). This all suggests that Paul would make carefully-crafted, considerate contributions to any debate at a church meeting – considerably more courteous and careful than some of the things we say to each other today when a contentious issue is being hotly disputed.

Paul is also very careful to distinguish his own opinions from the known commands of Jesus. Before citing Jesus' prohibition of divorce he says, "I give this command – not I but the Lord -" (*7:10 NRSV*). Then, in the process of addressing the specific situation of believers married to unbelievers, he says what he thinks but starts with the tag, "I say – I and not the Lord" (*7:12 NRSV*). A little later, in a related section, he says, "Now concerning virgins, I have no command of the Lord, but I give my opinion as one who by the Lord's mercy is trustworthy..." (*7:25 NRSV*). Thus, commenting on the whole of Paul's discussion of sexual matters that fills Chapter 7, Richard Hays describes Paul's approach to ethical reflection as "firm but open-textured"[220]. He also notes that:

> "[Paul] models a welcome alternative to much contemporary debate in the church, which often seems to be characterised by strident dogmatism on one side and shrugging relativism on the other."
>
> Richard B. Hays, "Interpretation Commentary on First Corinthians" p. 130

So, for Hays, Paul's approach to ethical debate with these confused Christians in ancient Corinth is still a valid and helpful model of how to engage in ethical debate today – a model that the 21st Century church would be foolish to ignore.

In three further chapters of this letter (Chapters 8-10) Paul engages in a long and complex argument[221] about whether the church should be concerned about the issue of Christians eating meat that had been sacrificed to an idol in a pagan temple. Woven into all the complexity of his argument is a clear determination to get as close as he can to a sort of "win-win" outcome – where both those who object to the practice and those who see no problem with it can be affirmed and both can be spared having their lifestyle seriously disrupted by the opinions of their fellow believers. But, most importantly, he undergirds all his efforts with a powerful plea for everyone to show a far greater respect and understanding for those who see things differently. He builds to a point where he says, "Do not seek your own advantage, but that of the other" (*10:24*). And it is clear that that "other" can be other believers who find different ethical implications in the Gospel and Scriptures or non-believers whom we wish to win for the faith. "Give no offence," he says, "to Jews or to Greeks or to the Church of God." (*10:32*). So, although the issue of eating meat that has been sacrificed to idols is not one of pressing importance to many of us in the West today, Paul's approach to ethical debate is, once again, immensely instructive and challenging.

As well as all these ins and outs of his own thoughtful approach to ethical reflection and debate, Paul also elaborates (*in Chapter 12*) a powerful model of how we are meant to relate to each other in the church. He seems to have been driven by the levels of arrogant intolerance that have developed in this church in Corinth (in the three or four brief years since he moved away!). In particular, he responds to the claims of some of the most arrogant that they are the only truly-gifted, spiritual ones in the church. Paul takes up the common Greek or Roman rhetorician's picture of how the city works[222] – LIKE A BODY – and develops it, with one crucial difference, as a model of how the church should work. The resulting picture of "The Body of Christ" is so rich in creative implications that it is worth quoting in full:

THE BODY OF CHRIST (1 Corinthians 12:12-27 NRSV)

For just as the body is one and has many members, and all the members of the body, though many, are one body, so it is with Christ. For in the one Spirit we were all baptised into one body – Jews or Greeks, slaves or free – and we were all made to drink one Spirit.

Indeed, the body does not consist of one member but of many. If the foot would say, "Because I'm not a hand, I don't belong to the body," that would not make it any less a part of the body. And if the ear would say, "Because I'm not an eye, I do not belong to the body," that would not make it any less a part of the body. If the whole body were an eye, where would the hearing be? If the whole body were hearing, where would the sense of smell be? But as it is, God arranged the members in the body, each one of them, as he chose. If all were a single member, where would the body be? As it is, there are many members, yet one body.

The eye cannot say to the hand, "I have no need of you," nor again the head to the feet, "I have no need of you." On the contrary, the members of the body that seem to be weaker are indispensable, and those members of the body that we think less honourable we clothe with greater honour, and our less respectable members are treated with greater respect; whereas our more respectable members do not need this. But God has so arranged the body, giving the greater honour to the inferior member, that there may be no dissension within the body, but the members may have the same care for one another. If one member suffers, all suffer together with it; if one member is honoured, all rejoice together with it.

Now you are the body of Christ and individually members of it.

The picture of the body was normally used by Greek orators to prove that not everyone in the city could be part of the elite – that all the diverse roles of city life were necessary to the balanced health of the whole. Beyond that, the analogy was used to urge members of the subordinate classes to "stay in their places in the social order and not to upset the natural equilibrium of the body by rebelling against their superiors".[223] As we can see from *1 Corinthians 12:12-27*, as quoted above, Paul uses the idea to a rather different effect. He applies the analogy of a body (Christ's body) to the Christian church rather than the whole city. Moreover, whilst he does use it to underline the need to accept diversity, he then argues from the body's need for interdependence between its parts to a markedly different conclusion. His point is that the various parts of the body must show mutual respect and that *particular* respect must be shown to those who might most easily be denied it. Paul seems to be arguing for some sort of "affirmative action" - a compensatory equalising of valuing - but in a way that allows for a rich diversity in the people of God. The one Body of Christ is the place where we all must work together at living out the radical equality implied by the death of Jesus, and central to that 'living out' is a mutual acceptance of our rich diversity.

Now, to this day, we all tend to operate with a sort of hierarchy of value where those whose theology, ethics, social status or background are most similar to our own count as especially close brothers and sisters whilst others are less valued, or even made to feel that they are not properly in fellowship with us ("Because I'm not a hand, I don't belong to the body."). Indeed, all down the centuries we have devised a thousand subtle and not-so-subtle ways to signal distance and distrust to some of our sisters and brothers whilst loudly protesting our commitment to the ideals of fellowship, unity and equality. Yet these are *exactly* the sorts of practices and attitudes that Paul seems to be vigorously opposing in Corinth (The eye cannot say to the hand, "I have no need of you.") The harder we find it to value another Christian or their theology or ethical ideas or spirituality or ethnic or class background, the harder we must try to value them, hear them, understand them, accept them. And if, on the other hand, we have internalised the subtle but savage signals of other Christians that seem to say we are not truly worthy, we have to find in the affirmation of Jesus the strength to stay, believe and contribute. We all have to work against our natures. Paul is saying that this is central to being part of the Body of Christ.

Add all these diverse indicators of Paul's approach to the business of 'doing' ethics together and, I believe, *1 Corinthians* gives us a picture of a Paul who expects Christian ethics to be developed in the cut and thrust of ongoing debate and discussion between diverse Christians who all bring their own insights and their own blind spots. Paul sees ethics as a lively community task that the whole church debates and develops together. Paul *expects* ethics to be part of God's Conversation with us all, even if he would never have thought to put it that way.

3. HEARING ALL GOD'S WORD?

The third proposal for those who would enter God's conversation that we considered in Chapter Five was the need to accept the rich diversity of Bible voices without attempting to stifle them or ignore some of them. I must admit I didn't get this idea directly from Paul, so much as from the diverse nature of the Bible as a whole. Indeed, it's quite hard to identify clearly what is Paul's position on this one, for two reasons. Firstly, it's rather difficult to judge Paul's use of Scripture on such a small sample as *I Corinthians*, or even his entire list of preserved letters. Secondly, Paul's situation is rather different from ours in that for him "the Scriptures" were what we call "The Old Testament", for in his day the Gospel was still something told rather than something written. So far as we can tell *I Corinthians* pre-dates even the earliest written Gospel.

However, we can say that Paul quotes extensively from the Law, the Prophets and the Psalms and that his whole approach to doing ethics is rooted in the Jewish Scriptures. Yet he does seem to quote some Bible books far more often than others. Taking all his letters together, his four most frequently-quoted books are Isaiah (28 quotes), Psalms (20 quotes), Deuteronomy (15 quotes) and Genesis (15 quotes), with no other book directly quoted more than five times.[224] In his perceptive study *"Echoes of Scripture in the Letters of Paul"* Richard Hays observes Paul working with both his inherited Jewish Scriptures and his new-found Christian Gospel in a way that allows mutual illumination. For Paul, Hays says, "Gospel interprets Scripture; Scripture interprets Gospel"[225] Thus, as far as the limited evidence allows, we can affirm that Paul is intent on hearing God speak all across both our Testaments and letting them contribute freely and interactively to his developing understanding of his God. Even so, like all the rest of us, Paul does show a tendency to use some Bible books far more frequently than others to support his arguments.

4. MASTER OF MANY METHODS

The fourth of our 'Seven Proposals for Conversationalists' urged us to allow the Bible's own methods of Biblical interpretation to apply in all their rich diversity. Richard Hays[226] has clearly established that Paul was wonderfully inconsistent in his methods of interpreting his inherited Scriptures. Hays concludes that Paul "offers helter-skelter intuitive readings, unpredictable, ungeneralizable ... he adheres neither to any single exegetical procedure, nor even to a readily specifiable inventory of procedures".[227] Even so, Hays is able to identify five broad governing principles that seem to drive Paul's approach to the interpretation of Scripture and three key ideas that act as real constraints on his glorious interpretive freedom.

For Paul (according to Hays[228]), Scripture is to be handled in the following exciting, even dangerous, ways:

PAUL'S APPROACH TO READING SCRIPTURE

read it as pre-eminently the story of God choosing and sustaining a people

read it as God's direct word for living, active communities of believers

read it as something that has to be preached and shared, something always relevant

read it from the viewpoint of people who are living at the end of time

read it as always open to fresh, imaginative interpretations that let God speak directly to us now

Yet, Hays would also identify three key constraining factors in Paul's approach[229]. He suggests that, for Paul, a reading of Scripture **cannot** be a true reading if it fails in one of the following ways:

PAUL'S LIST OF FAILED READINGS of SCRIPTURE

any reading that denies that Israel's God remains faithful to his covenant promises

any reading that fails to acknowledge the death and resurrection of Jesus as the climactic demonstration of who God is

any reading that fails to shape its readers into a community that embodies the love of God as shown forth in Christ

Certainly, these passions and expectations seem to be in evidence in Paul's free and varied interactions with Scripture in *I Corinthians*. Paul has no single method in his approach to Scripture, but he clearly expects it to speak to him and those who hear his words, and to speak directly, freshly, excitingly, with the voice of God.

5.   CONVERSATIONS CONCLUDED OR COMMENCED?

The fifth conversational proposal we considered in Chapter Five was the possibility that the Bible intends to start and sustain ethical debate, rather than seek to stop it. To some extent Paul might have been rather surprised by this idea. He was so certain that the end times were going to be very short that his primary consideration was not keeping ethical debate going, but the urgent need to concentrate on mission before the imminent return of Jesus made it an impossibility. This, for example, is the basis of his argument that single church members would be best to stay single and not risk being distracted by the encumbrances and obligations that marriage would bring (7:29).

Yet, this whole letter shows Paul plunging headlong into ongoing debate. Even his promise of a future visit (16:5-7) seems to imply that his letter is only the first part of his response to the issues facing the Church people of Corinth. He shows no sign that he expects his letter to have ended the discussion once and for all. He is far too realistic for that. Indeed, as we noted before, he mixes some arguments where he is all but certain with others where he is remarkably tentative. And when he uses Scripture he is happy to find new meanings and offer freshly-improvised interpretations. Scripture does not have a single once-and-for-all meaning for him. Indeed, when in *1 Corinthians 9:9* he quotes from *Deuteronomy 25:4* "You shall not muzzle an ox while it is treading out the grain" he not only re-applies it to the case of Christian preachers and pastors like himself, he boldly says, "Is it for oxen that God is concerned? Or does he not speak entirely for our sake?" He delights to wrench Scripture from the setting in which it was written to make it speak in new ways to the specific issues and dilemmas of his own age and setting. This is not how you end discussion. This is more like picking an argument. This is how you keep ethical debate going.

6.   PAUL'S TWIN IMPERATIVES

The sixth of our "Proposals for conversationalists" was the idea that the twin driving forces of the Church's ethical conversation are our friendship with God and our calling to share that friendship with our neighbours. After his life-changing encounter with the risen Jesus on the Damascus road (*Acts 9:1-22*), the whole thrust of Paul's life (as evidenced both by the Book of Acts and by his own letters) is clearly his response to the friendship of God in Christ – every waking moment seems to be committed to sharing that friendship with everyone he can possibly meet – with "neighbours" in the widest sense. Paul's wholehearted commitment to the twin imperatives of receiving and sharing the friendship of God in Christ is evident in two of the most poignant and powerful sections of *1 Corinthians*.

Firstly, near the start of the letter Paul says this:

"For Jews demand signs and Greeks desire wisdom, but we proclaim CHRIST CRUCIFIED, a stumbling block to Jews and foolishness to Greeks, but to those who are the called, both Jews and Greeks, Christ the power of God and the wisdom of God. For God's foolishness in wiser than human wisdom, and God's weakness is stronger than human strength."

1st Corinthians 1:22-25 NRSV

Clearly the gift of friendship with God in Christ is so important to Paul that he is prepared to risk alienating his own Jewish people and look profoundly foolish in the eyes of the world's Greek thinkers. This foolishness is, for him, the only true wisdom; this friendship with God is the very basis of who he is. For Paul, it is the outworking of the meaning of "Christ crucified" that is the driving force of all Christian life and living and, therefore, of all the church's efforts to establish shared Christian ethics. So it comes as no surprise to see this idea clearly sculpting and shaping Paul's detailed ethical advice all through *I Corinthians*. Indeed, it is the nature of our relationship with Christ that seems to underlie most of Paul's ethical arguments and decisions. If we are united to the crucified and risen Christ, then we shouldn't be quarrelling (*3:4*), or engaging in "sexual immorality" (*5:1-13*), or taking disputes to the law courts (*6:7f*), or eating food offered to idols (*10:14-22*) or getting drunk at communion (*11:17-34*). In all these cases Paul argues directly from the spiritual and bodily implications of being united to Christ. That is why all these behaviours are deemed to be entirely inappropriate for Christians.

But, secondly, the need to share the Good News about Jesus with others is also of huge importance to Paul. In the midst of a complex argument about food offered to idols, he sums up his own personal strategy and its underlying motivation in these terms:

> "For though I am free with respect to all, I have made myself a slave to all, so that I might win more of them. To the Jews I became a Jew, in order to win Jews. To those under the law I became as one under the law (though I myself am not under the law) so that I might win those under the law. To those outside the law I became as one outside the law (though I am not free from God's law but am under Christ's law) so that I might win those outside the law. To the weak I became weak, so that I might win the weak. I have become all things to all people, that I might by all means save some. I do it all for the sake of the gospel, so that I might share in its blessings."
>
> *1st Corinthians 9:19-23 NRSV*

For Paul, in this letter, the need to win others to the cause is also a hugely important factor in shaping his ethical decisions and deciding on right behaviour. Paul is adamant that true believers "endure *anything* rather than put an obstacle in the way of the gospel of Christ" (*9:12*). They also have a self-sacrificial sense of togetherness with their fellow believers, because they know that "if one member suffers, all suffer together with it" (*12:26*). Winsome, gracious, sympathetic behaviour with those around us, both believers and searching, well-meaning non-believers (or not-yet-believers) is of crucial importance to Paul. That is why he reckons the gift of prophecy (which can encourage and challenge) to be a more valuable gift than the gift of tongues (which requires interpretation to be understood) (*14:3f*). That is why he is determined that worship should always be conducted "decently and in order" (*14:40*). That is why he frets about what those outside the church would consider shockingly unnatural (*11:14*). The only offence the church should offer to interested non-believers and enquirers is the offence of the cross.

For me, these twin engines of responding to GOD and reaching out to NEIGHBOUR are the key motive forces in Paul's understanding of how the Church should 'do' ethics. But notice that these ideas operate rather differently from each other and can, at times, be in real tension with each other. "Christ crucified" is a once-and-for-all event. For Paul, and for every generation of Christians since his time, it is a defining moment in our relationship with God that has already happened. Whilst its implications are so vast and profound that we are still struggling to explore them and live them out, the underlying event of the coming, dying and rising of Jesus is fixed in the flow of history.

Relating winsomely to our neighbours (both within and beyond the church) is, however, a rather more variable imperative. As cultures come and go or develop and change, exactly what it means to be "a Jew with the Jews" is going to vary from time to time and place to place and, as Paul himself found, the same Christian fellowship may have to relate to different people in different ways, at the same time even within the same city. The tension between these twin imperatives of responding to God and reaching out to neighbour (especially when our various neighbours are quite diverse) is evident through many of the arguments Paul uses in *I Corinthians* and may underlie some of the apparent inconsistencies in what he says (e.g. the acceptance of women publicly praying and prophesying in *11:5* and the requirement that women remain silent in church in *14:34* or the way he seems to flip and flop this way and that about whether it is acceptable to eat meat that has been offered to idols in *chapters 8-10*). Paul's practice in *I Corinthians* would tend to suggest that doing Christian ethics is a developing response to what God has done for us in Christ Jesus (and the freedoms that brings), but tempered and constrained, at times, by the need to relate to the diverse and deeply-held ethical understandings of others, both within and beyond the Church community.

As I understand it, Paul's balancing of these two rather different imperatives would always put the need to be true to the implications of the Gospel of the Crucified God in first place. Yet, he would be wary of church practices (even those built on the implications of the Gospel) that risked shocking, misleading or seriously alienating potential believers to a point where there was a risk of entirely derailing the Church's mission. Remember, also, his real concern that liberated church members should not "become a stumbling block" to "those [within the church] whose conscience is weak" (*8:9f*).

Still, I reckon that Paul would always expect church ethics to be noticeably closer to the radical demands of the Gospel than even the best of the ethics of the wider society. Paul's churches are failing if they are not endlessly enabling both potential believers and the ethics of their surrounding society to move closer and closer to the implications of "Christ crucified". From this perspective, Paul would surely consider it deeply shocking if, for example, he found an unshakeably racist church carrying on regardless in the midst of a wider society that was seriously struggling to rid itself of its racism, or heard that Christians were responsible for introducing slavery into a society where it had not previously existed.

For Paul, the tensions, the dialogues and the ethical debates in the church are very real, but so, too, are the underlying imperatives of response to God and reaching out to neighbour.

7.   PAUL AND THE SPIRIT

Our final proposal for conversationalists argued that it is the presence of God's Spirit in communities of believers that constrains and guides their reading of Scripture. There are no explicit discussions of this issue in *1 Corinthians*, but the way Paul handles the Old Testament Scriptures allows an important inference. He unselfconsciously applies the Scriptures to himself and the Corinthian believers without any sense of distance. The ancient text is always read as God's word to us today. Indeed, at the end of an extensive passage applying the experience of the Israelites in the Wilderness to the situation of the Corinthian believers, Paul says, "These things happened to them to serve as an example, and they were written down to instruct us, on whom the end of the ages have come" (*10:11*). Paul sees the *whole* purpose of Scripture as being the instruction of believing communities of the followers of Jesus in these end times. But how are such communities to read the Scriptures aright? Surely, it is the Spirit of God who must guide them; the same Spirit that leads them in prophesying and speaking in ecstatic tongues and interpreting what is said (*12:4-11*). Paul, I would argue, finds the role of the Spirit so obvious that he does not need to spell it out. For Paul, right interpretation of the Scriptures cannot occur without the presence of God's Spirit; as he says of his own efforts at interpretation and application, "I think that I, too, have the Spirit of God" (*7:40*).

6.3   I Corinthians as a 21st Century text

In *1 Corinthians* it is clear that Paul is no solitary, uninvolved philosopher writing a theoretical treatise on right and wrong, nor is he a Christian legislator laying out a comprehensive God-given code of behaviour. He is a pastor responding to particular problems and pressures, a committed friend inviting those he loves to think again and change their ways. There is a wonderful air of improvisation about the way he handles and applies both the Jewish Scriptures and the Christian Gospel, a scent of fresh creativity hanging over his diverse arguments, the invigorating breeze of the provisional about much of what he concludes. Paul vividly illustrates the art of being a Christian Conversationalist engaged in lively debate with others in the Church in response to the call of God – a debate riddled with the particularities of setting, experience and personality.

To return to an earlier image,[230] Paul is no hard-hatted structural engineer building a vast reinforced highway of solid ethics all the way from Scripture text to church practice. In *1 Corinthians* he emerges as much more of a skilled ORIENTEER, improvising creative ethical arguments to work his way from Scripture and Gospel to practical guidance for daily living for the believers in Corinth. But wherever he gets to, he always seems to use "Christ crucified" like a compass to keep his ethical bearings whilst choosing the details of his route in the light of his mighty passion for sharing the love of God with others. As he travels across country, the Spirit of God is his constant unseen companion and the Scriptures themselves are a God-given map of HIS world, of his "TODAY". It is over the 'map' provided by the Jewish Scriptures and the Christian Gospel that he and the Corinthian Christians endlessly bicker and argue as they try to establish where they are and where they should go in this bewildering ethical forest with its constant risk of sinking slowly into a moral quagmire. Here is the setting where Paul and his church "enter into God's conversation" – not on some pure, transcendental ethical plane lit by heavenly light, but deep in the darkening forest of a morally challenging world where every decision affects their chances of survival and (even with God's help) there's always a risk of getting lost.

So what are *we* to do with *I Corinthians*, as we read it as Scripture some two thousand years later? With Richard Hays, I would reject the all-too-common idea that we can rubbish and resist Paul's methods and approach even whilst we take his ethical conclusions and put them on a pedestal.[231] This snatch of part-conversation between Paul and the Christians of Corinth is given to us to help us grapple with our own ethical dilemmas. Paul's inclusive, conversational way of 'doing' ethics has to be a central part of what he offers us. Paul's oft repeated call to imitate what he does (*e.g. I Corinthians 11:1*) surely means "Do what I do" not just "Do what I say".

As I see it, *I Corinthians* (read as Scripture) offers us an invitation to join a later stage of the same conversation that Paul once shared with God and the Christians of Corinth. It summons us to share in our own debates with God, with each other and with Paul (and the rest of Scripture) as we explore the ethical implications of the friendship of God for us today. But just as Paul developed his ethical understanding in the face of the real issues confronting the church in 1st Century Corinth, we have to develop, adjust and extend our own ethical understanding in the face of the dilemmas and issues of our 21st Century world. Yet, we don't simply start with a blank page. We work not only with the Scriptures and Gospel that Paul knew, but also in the light of Paul's own arguments and conclusions. More than that, we are also resourced by the developing stream of competing insights and ideas that has filled the intervening generations. But, like Paul and the Corinthians and every intervening generation, our own contributions to the conversation will be significantly shaped by our own story, our own setting and our own baggage.

Yet, always and always, we are still working out the implications for life and action of "Christ crucified" and seeking that that should be the only source of offence when we try to interest and intrigue our neighbours with the Christian Gospel.

Even within the Bible, even within such a directly ethical text as *I Corinthians*, we have found a world of conversation, an atmosphere of debate, a possibility of real growth and development in ethical understanding as new dilemmas are faced, even a sense that there is always more to each issue than has yet been addressed. Indeed, a world where the church is always at risk of getting it wrong, a world where there are still, even after Paul has spoken, "no answers at the back of the book"[232]. Yet shaping and directing all this diverse vitality are the implications of the cross for the life of the church and the world and the endless need to make the Gospel message and its messengers as winsome as possible to the real people who may hear it. Paul's challenge is still for church practice to be moving closer and closer to the radical ethics of the crucified and risen Jesus. The need for the church to 'make sense' to the wider society in which it finds itself may, at times, restrict that progress in some ways as Paul is also intent on taking as much of that wider society as possible along with him on the road that leads to Jesus. Still, I don't think Paul ever anticipated a situation where church practice might (in any respect) be further from the ethics of Jesus than the norms of the society in which they were set.

So, what has happened since Paul wrote to the Corinthian Christians? How has the conversation developed?

CHAPTER SEVEN

OUR DEVELOPING CONVERSATION

7.1 A Reformable Revelation?

What has happened to God's conversation in the near two thousand years between Paul and ourselves? In what ways has it changed, adapted and developed? Has it basically stood still, or moved on or degenerated, or done a bit of each?

I have neither the space nor the knowledge to lead you through a comprehensive review of how the whole conversation has gone down the centuries. Instead, we will consider, as an example, the disturbing history of Christian attitudes to issues of race and ethnicity, especially Christian attitudes to the Jewish people. This should remind us just how unsavoury Christian ethics can get and allow us to consider whether and how later generations can question the established "Bible-based" Christian opinions which they have inherited. Then, to investigate the details of the process, we will look at three selected moments when accepted opinion was powerfully challenged, two of them from the arguments about slavery in the 18th and 19th Centuries, the third from the arguments about apartheid in the 20th Century. In each case we will be listening out for the ways the conversation has developed, or ideas have changed. We will be seeking evidence of the way this conversation works in practice.

In all our examples from Christian history we will be looking at the way God's conversation **DEVELOPS**. Just about everyone would agree that even between the world of the rural, Galilean Jewish followers of Jesus and the world of Paul's Graeco-Roman, multi-racial, urban churches there has been some sort of development in the faith, largely engineered by the change of language and the hugely different cultural context. Equally, the subsequent changes in various Christian societies and their expectations and norms over the past two thousand years have also led to further developments of one sort or another in the content and character of God's conversation. Yet, there is real disagreement about the exact nature and permissible extent of those developments. Richard Longenecker, in his book on New Testament Social Ethics[233], sorts the rich variety of possible models into three broad approaches. These three approaches differ in what they believe to be reasonable and acceptable development in Christian doctrine and ethics.

First, he identifies an approach that accepts **NO REAL CHANGE**. To be valid, later formulations must be substantially the same as their earlier foundations. What appear to be innovations are 'only more precise explications and applications of what was already implicit earlier'[234]. In this view, Biblical truth is essentially timeless, and equally and obviously accessible in each new cultural setting and epoch. Longenecker sees this as the basic approach of some of the Alexandrian Fathers (e.g. Clement and Origen), but also suggests that it is to be seen in the 20th Century in Catholic, Reformed and Puritan circles that are 'more traditionally oriented'[235].

Second, he recognises another general approach that accepts both 'continuity with a foundational core' and '**GENUINE GROWTH** in conceptualisation and expression'[236]. He likens this idea to the relationship between a growing plant and its original seed. This analogy allows that 'real growth always involves genuine innovations of structure (e.g. the stalk, leaves and flower of a plant are not just reproductions of the original seed), yet that growth is always controlled and judged by what is inherent in the seed itself'[237]. Here Biblical truth will be seen to develop genuinely new forms in new settings, but forms that can always be related back to the forms evident in the Bible itself. God's conversation can involve real innovation, but is always rooted in and connected with the authoritative conversations we find within the Bible. Longenecker traces this approach back to the Antiochian Fathers (e.g. Chrysostom and Theodore) but suggests that it 'has come to characterise the methodology of the more constructive and moderate theologians of our day, whatever their particular confessional stance'[238].

Third, he sees yet another approach that '**EMPHASISES THE INNOVATIONS** in the growth of doctrine and minimises any necessary propositional connection with the foundation core'[239]. This approach is happy to let the conversation wander where it will, shaped by the pressures of new situations and contexts, without any need to refer back to the details of what has gone before. The reality and helpfulness of progress are unquestioned. For this Longenecker finds no ancient precedents, but in the 20th Century he sees it underlying the work of many, including Rudolf Bultmann and his followers.

Those who have travelled through the earlier chapters of this book with me will not be surprised to learn that I have real problems with the first and third of the approaches Longenecker has observed. With Longenecker himself[240], I prefer the second approach.

I find the **first** approach (No real change) altogether too confident in our ability to establish a timeless, cross-cultural understanding of "the truth" against which the offerings of each new generation and setting may be judged and assessed. No-one, I would argue, can be that confident that they have disposed of all their 'baggage'. We considered the case in Chapter One that the Reformation should not be seen as a straightforward rediscovery of timeless truth. Yes, it was in a real sense a return to taking the Bible, the Gospel and its God seriously. Yet, Luther's attitudes to peasants, Popes and Jews (for example) all betray a world view shaped by his cultural roots that we surely find hard to accept today. In an age that reveres universal suffrage and exists after Auschwitz and Vatican II, Luther's unquestioned attitudes can easily strike us as being crudely elitist, harshly intolerant and woefully anti-Semitic. Of course, we must accept that Luther's ideas were not untypical of his day and age (nor are ours of our own times), but that is exactly my point. The Reformation was, truly, a "re-formation" of the faith, its doctrines and its ethics were shaped *both* by the Bible *and* by its own time and place. There is real change and development in the ongoing conversation with God.

On the other hand, I find the **third** approach (with its emphasis on unbridled innovation) far too confident about the onward march of progress. The Reformation, with its deliberate 'back-tracking' on the evolving doctrine and ethics of the late mediaeval church, powerfully contends that not all doctrinal and ethical developments are legitimate and progressive. The Reformation is an acknowledgement that the church can make mistakes. It shows us that the conversation between God and church can be diverted into deeply unhelpful places from which some sort of 'going back' will be necessary. And the only basis for engineering such back-tracking is an ongoing relationship with the text of the Bible. So, we can never leave the Bible behind. There will always be a normative weight to the Gospel story and the experiences of the new churches recorded in Acts and the Epistles. Again, the God we meet and the way we do it must always be linked back to the God we meet in the divers texts of the Old Testament. We may be endlessly in dispute with each other about the exact nature of the Bible's authoritative role in shaping the ongoing conversation, but we must never leave it behind or consider it outmoded or irrelevant.

So, unsurprisingly, I would opt for the **second** approach Longenecker has identified; the organic growth approach which he himself prefers. This account not only fits better with the history of Christian ethics, but with the Bible itself. Quite simply, I can't help seeing a sort of organic growth in doctrine and ethics *within* the developing collection of Scriptures that make up the Bible. This complex book records for us an evolving relationship between God and people; sometimes with harsh moments of sudden inevitable change, sometimes by ongoing dispute and discussion. The Exodus, the Babylonian Exile and 'Good' Friday all represent real moments of wrenching crisis that take the Biblical understanding of God and the ethical implications of seeking to respond to that God to entirely new places. Thereafter, the long disputes about the acceptance of Gentile believers into the church demonstrates a hugely significant process of organic development in doctrine and its ethical implications.

So, I wish to use the following brief sketches of significant ethical disputes in the course of Christian history to try to make the case for a broad, organic directionality in Biblical Ethical development over the last 2,000 years. Yet, I will also argue for a clear recognition that the church can get it *wildly* wrong and that significant 're-formations' will be necessary. For me, the general direction of the development of Biblical Ethics through Christian history is shaped by the central relationships that I believe the Bible seeks to set up. I will argue for the endless importance of the offered friendship of God in Christ and the summons that it brings with it to share the same friendship of God with those around us (God and Neighbour).

In this context, I am intrigued by the way Longenecker proceeds to develop a structure for his own consideration of "New Testament Social Ethics for Today"[241]. He builds his whole approach around *Galatians 3:27-28* :

> As many of you as were baptised into Christ have clothed yourselves with Christ. There is no longer Jew or Greek, there is no longer slave or free, there is no longer male and female; for all of you are one in Christ Jesus.
>
> *Galatians 3:27&28 NRSV*

Here Longenecker finds a clear statement of the ethical implications of the cross. This saving act centred on the public degradation, pain and humiliation of the Son of God changes everything. It undercuts all structures of hierarchy within humanity that count some people more valuable or more worthy than others. It even clears away the great hierarchy of holiness at the heart of the Jewish Scriptures. This idea of concentric circles of increasing holiness is probably developed most clearly in the last eleven chapters of Ezekiel where there is a sort of geography of increasing holiness as you move inwards from the lands of the other nations through the restored holy land of Israel and Judah, into the Holy City of Jerusalem, then into the Great Temple, and ultimately find the centre point in the most sacred space at the heart of the Temple - the Holy of Holies. *Galatians 3:27-28* effectively argues that the death of Jesus on the cross implies a far more radical change than the ripping apart of the curtain that closed off that most holy space (*Mark 15:37f*). It implies that the death of Jesus does more than make the whole Temple in Jerusalem shockingly irrelevant (the daring idea which had resulted in the stoning of Stephen, according to *Acts 7:48ff*). Jesus' crucifixion also permanently abolishes the distinction between Jew and Gentile in a way that even the Jewish Churches still centred on Jerusalem would struggle and struggle to accept (*see Acts 10, 11 & 15 and Galatians 2*). Indeed, *Galatians 3:27-28* seems to accept that there is a radical equality of all humanity before the cross ("for all have sinned" (*Romans 3.23*)) and that that radical equality should find active expression in the human relations and ethical principles of the people of God. In a way that parallels the central importance of "Christ crucified" in Paul's ethical arguments in *1 Corinthians*[242], *Galatians 3:27-28* sees the outworking of the implications of the cross as being the central engine for the development of all Christian Ethics.

Longenecker argues that we should take these two brief verses from Galatians as the basic key to opening up a specifically-Christian social ethics. Following a number of other scholars, he argues that these verses may not be just a passing comment by Paul in a particular letter; rather, they could well have been a widely-used early baptismal confession that Paul is quoting here, expecting easy recognition. This, Longenecker implies, could be the basic creed-like summing up of the implications of faith in Jesus that was used in the first churches all across the eastern Mediterranean region. Moreover, it could well have been an important part of the preparation for baptism or of the baptismal service itself; that hugely significant moment of public commitment in the life of each new believer[243]. Longenecker then plots the working out of the implications of this apparent confessional statement across the subsequent two thousand years of church history. He accepts that the church has often taken substantial wrong turnings in its developing social ethics, but that the challenge of these verses has remained undiminished, endlessly calling for a better response. He also argues that these simple, bald declarations of the implications of what Jesus has done are far from being exhausted. They *still* require much more debate, development and application in our own day and age.

Clearly, this approach fits well with our earlier idea of the implications of "Christ crucified" being the more significant of the two central dynamics in the ongoing ethical conversation and practice of the church[244]. But I would like to keep beside it, as a subsidiary but still important dynamic in the debate, the need to keep the Gospel message as attractive as possible in successive contemporary cultural contexts[245]. I view Paul's ideal as being a church whose practice endlessly seeks to draw closer to the ethics of Jesus, but never completely loses touch with what the surrounding society sees as reasonable.

What I don't think Paul envisaged is the possibility that the ethical arguments raging in the wider society would prophetically challenge the church by inadvertently picking up and emphasising aspects of the ethical implications of the Gospel that the church itself has left in abeyance. Yet it seems to me that this has happened again and again in Christian history... but I'm getting ahead of myself. So, let us now, as an example, follow the course of one particular part of the ongoing conversation (race and ethnicity), then look quickly at three selected close-ups of moments of meaningful change in the history of Christian Ethics. What will we find?

7.2 Unfinished business?

The confessional statement in *Galatians 3:27-8* claims that through Jesus the distinction between "Jew and Greek" is abolished. The radical equality of all before the cross means that, regardless of ethnic or cultural difference, all are equally valued by God, so all should be equally valued by one another. The same point is also at the root of Peter's pronouncement to the household of Cornelius in *Acts* that "I truly understand that God shows no partiality, but in every nation anyone who fears him and does what is right is acceptable to him." (*Acts 10:34f NRSV*). It sounds as if the whole matter is settled. Admittedly, both *Galatians 1-3* and *Acts 9-15* bear witness to considerable church debate, even division, on the matter[246]. Yet the declarations of Peter in *Acts 10:34f* and Paul in *Galatians 3:27f* and the eventual apparent agreement of Peter, Paul, James and the Council of Jerusalem on the matter (*Acts 15*) should surely have left the Jew / Gentile issue done and dusted.

Sadly, most of Christian history tells a rather different story. So, how did this happen?

Just about every book in the New Testament bears witness to some aspect of the tussle between the growing band of followers of Jesus and the followers of the more traditional strands of Judaism for 'ownership' and 'interpretation rights' over the Jewish Scriptures (soon to be redefined by the Church as "The Old Testament")[247]. The Church is clearly bidding for recognition as a central part of God's chosen people. This is not surprising when they see themselves as the followers of the Messiah. Yet the arguments in the New Testament are still largely internal discussions between people who see themselves as Jews. When Jesus is portrayed in *Matthew 23* as vigorously objecting to the attitudes of the Pharisees, when Stephen in *Acts 7* shocks the Jewish leaders in Jerusalem with his close Scriptural (i.e. Old Testament) argument against the centrality of the Jerusalem temple, when Paul offers in *Galatians 3* an extended Scripture-based argument about who can be considered to be the Children of Abraham, then we are still in a world where Jews who follow Jesus are arguing with other Jews.

But even within the pages of the New Testament, as Gentile membership grows in the churches outside Palestine, these internal Jewish arguments about theology begin to take on a Jew/Gentile dimension. This tendency was probably exacerbated by Paul's insistence that Gentile believers in Jesus do *not* need to become circumcised Jews in order to become followers of Jesus[248]. This insistence was clearly rooted in Paul's understanding that the cross effectively abolished any distinction of value between Jews and Gentiles. That is why he is so passionate about Gentile rights of direct access to God, without having to become Jews first. Yet, Paul would surely be equally adamant that Jews do not need to become like Gentiles. He shows ample evidence of his own continuing sense of Jewishness. Indeed, as his story is told in *Acts*, he makes a point of preaching *first* to the Jews and *then* to the Gentiles in each new town that he visits, even though this keeps arousing fierce opposition, imprisoning and whippings.

Still, it does not appear to have taken very long for the arguments recorded in the New Testament to be re-read with a distinct ethnic bias, as Jews became less and less common within the increasingly successful, largely-Gentile churches of the Roman Empire. By the second Christian century the outright supremacy of Christians over Jews became a more and more frequent theme of Christian apologists. Alongside this, new ways of reading "the Old Testament" as a reassuringly Christian document began to develop. Richard Longenecker sums it up like this:

> Christians began claiming for themselves all the heroes, all the promises, and all the blessings of the Old Testament – leaving for the Jews all the sinners, all the curses, and all the judgements. In so doing, the complementary poles of promise and judgement in the prophets' preaching were split apart: every promise was seen as applicable to the Church, and every judgement read as descriptive of the Jews. Such an interpretive procedure, of course, as Rosemary Ruether observes, "turns the Jewish Scriptures, which actually contain the record of Jewish self-criticism into a remorseless denunciation of the Jews, whilst the Church, in turn, is presented as totally perfect and loses the prophetic tradition of self-criticism"
>
> Richard N Longenecker. "New Testament Social Ethics for Today"
> (Eerdmans, Grand Rapids, 1984) p41f

This tendency to think in terms of a good "us" and a bad "them" may well be a natural human trait[249], but it is surely the root idea underlying ethnic chauvinism and racism, the key legitimating idea behind all the awfulness of racial abuse, racial violence, legislated exclusion, imperial expansion, even mass pogroms, death camps and gas chambers. To read the Bible in these terms is not only to fly in the face of one of the central implications of the cross (its implicit abolition of exactly such imbalancing distinctions (*see Galatians 3:27-28*)) it is also to open the door to a disastrously awful way of seeing that inevitably colludes with enormous quantities of hatred, violence and evil.

Sadly, Bible interpretation for much, even most, of Christian history has been woefully content to allow, even affirm, this 'Christian GOOD - Jewish BAD' dichotomy.[250] It has long given some sort of house room to an implicit anti-Semitism that has condoned persistent discrimination and allowed repeated eruptions into savage acts of violence and 'ethnic cleansing'. Then, as Europeans began to travel to other lands, this apparently 'Bible-based' acceptance of Christian cultural superiority provided a ready basis for ideas of European racial superiority that all too easily excused the wholesale expropriation of other peoples' land and property and even the development of a vast, racially-based slave trade.

This gruesome way of reading the Bible, its dogged persistence through most of Christian history and the widespread evils it so easily condones and enables leave me deeply troubled. If we were looking for proof that the Church can get things wildly wrong, we need look no further. This European Christian anti-Semitism in particular and European Christian racism in general leave the Church looking deeply flawed as bearer of the love and justice of God[251]. It would seem that we Christians are in no position to claim obvious ownership of the moral high ground on this issue. That also leaves us open to the contention that a church that could get something like this so badly wrong for so long (despite what it says in the Bible) could get just about any moral issue misconstrued and not even notice it.

But wait. What gives me (and you) the right to question ethical values and ways of reading the Bible that have persisted through most of Christian history? Is it possible that, as some would maintain, we are selling out to the secular morality of our own age or becoming victims of the latest ethical fashion? What are the roots of our moral outrage at the racism and anti-Semitism in the history of the church? Who is 'being Biblical'? Is it us or the pious, Bible-believing racists of Christian history?

To question the basis of our objections to the Church's history of anti-Semitism and racism may, to some, seem quite absurd, but the issue is a real one. We need to be clear about the basis on which we can, as Christians, resist, even overturn, the church's long-established interpretations of the Bible. The argument we have developed all through this book offers us at least **FIVE REASONS** why we may decide to overturn the settled acceptances of past generations of believers – five reasons rooted in the very nature and contents of the Bible itself:

✦ **THE ENDLESS RIGHT TO QUESTION WHAT HAS GONE BEFORE**
– the Bible seems determined to offer each new generation a fresh opportunity to engage directly in conversation with God. Biblical ethics is not a finished, immovable monument. Rather, it is God's endless challenge to wrestle like Jacob *(Genesis 32:24-30)* with God, with the Bible, with our own experience and with each other.[252]

✦ **THE LESSONS OF HISTORY** – The Bible itself runs along at the interface between history and theology. Traumatic events like the wilderness wanderings and the Babylonian exile clearly impacted on Israel's developing grasp of who God is. Similarly, huge events of the last two hundred years, such as Auschwitz, and the horrors of the Atlantic slave trade and the struggle against apartheid must be allowed to impact on our understanding of theology, ethics and Bible. God is still most likely to be met and understood right in the thick of life's battle.[253]

✦ **THE CROSS AS COURT OF APPEAL** – For Christians, the cross is the central event that exposes the very heart of God's intentions for us all. Whatever the textual basis in the Bible of any ethical decision, it may at anytime be reviewed *(as Galatians 3:27-28 makes clear)* in the light of the cross.[254]

✦ **THE RECOVERY OF SILENCED VOICES** – The Old Testament prophets show a real commitment to the voiceless, the exploited and the marginalised. Jesus follows this up by endlessly searching out the irreligious and the desperate. Taken together, they imply that recovering of silenced voices must always be an important part of developing and redeveloping truly Biblical ethics. We need to listen to the previously unheard, even, perhaps especially, when this might embarrass or deeply unsettle the church.[255]

✦ **THE ONGOING WORK OF GOD'S SPIRIT** – The endlessly untameable God of the Bible will always have much more for us to learn, even though not a single word is to be added to the text. Uncovering the challenging richness that is there is a central part of the work of God's Spirit in our midst.[256]

It is on these grounds, not on the grounds of following fashion, that I believe that Christians can adjust, or even repudiate, some of the ethical stances maintained by previous generations. It is on these grounds that many, many Christians (including me) would wish to repudiate the racism and anti-Semitism that has marred the history of the church. It is on these grounds that we would see this repudiation, and the repentance of the church's past failures that it clearly requires, as profoundly Christian and seriously Biblical. It is on these grounds that we would call for a practical humility on the part of the whole church as it seeks to judge moral and ethical issues, a humility that will always allow that we may be mistaken.

So, the history of European Christian anti-Semitism and European Christian racism warn me simultaneously of our need to be bold and our need to be cautious. We surely need to be bold in our willingness to question and debate even the most settled and long-standing of the church's ethical teachings. For we are invited to take a full part in God's ongoing conversation, not simply to listen and receive. Indeed, we have a responsibility to take an active part - humbly, honestly and hopefully. Yet, at the same time, we need to be cautious. We need to acknowledge that we have as much baggage as any previous generation and that there is no guarantee that our baggage will help us see more clearly or that our preferences and perceptions will take us closer to God's truth than before.

Moreover, we need to be both bold and cautious because the struggle to overcome Christian anti-Semitism and Christian racism is far from over. Ask the African Caribbean Christians who settled in Britain during the last fifty years, or their black British children and grandchildren whether racism has been overcome in the British churches. Ask Maori or Pacific Island Christians about New Zealand churches, or black South African Christians about the churches of South Africa. In practice, we all have a long way to go. In Britain and Australia, for example, both Christians and others are currently being challenged to confront the racism in our attitude to asylum seekers. In the United States there are challenging issues around attitudes to Hispanic 'illegals' and the developing question of 'reparations' for chattel slavery. In New Zealand and Canada and South Africa (as well as Britain, Australia and the United States) there are still huge issues embedded in national histories that seem to be far from any sort of final, fair resolution.

Even anti-Semitism, even after the unbridled horror of the Holocaust, remains a deeply challenging and perplexing issue. The whole history of the modern state of Israel (including British involvement in how it came about) and the current desperate plight of the Palestinian people provide a complex of ethical challenges and dilemmas from which the churches cannot walk away unscathed. Indeed, the United Nations World Conference against Racism in Durban in 2001 left the world, perhaps especially the rich nations of the West, with a huge unfinished agenda of lingering, even growing, racial injustices. Where is the voice of Jesus in these contemporary debates and issues?

The bold claim that the cross means there is no longer any difference of value between "Jew and Greek", that we found in *Galatians 3:27-28*, still provides enormous unmet challenges to 21st century churches and Christians. Yet, I do not believe that the issues of racism and anti-Semitism are untypical in this respect. Rather, I think the case can be made that Biblical ethics in general is 'unfinished business'.

Indeed, I suspect we could, with the support of other Bible passages, claim that the cross implies other significant instances of the levelling of value. Some of these have only begun to look 'obvious' and have significant ethical force comparatively recently. Yet, I believe that, because of the cross, there is no longer a defensible difference of *value* before God between:

✦ Adult and Child *(Mark 10:13-16)*,
✦ Rich and Poor *(Luke 6:20-26)*,
✦ Ruler and Subject *(Matthew 27:27-37)*

In each of these areas the wider world may have been a significant prompt to the church, helping us to take the issues seriously[257]. However, I would resist any claim that we are abandoning the Bible and succumbing to worldly 'fashion'. Even in the Old Testament the people of God could be led to a richer understanding of the truth by people from beyond their own circle. Ruth the Moabite gave the clan of David a major lesson on what it meant to be faithful to God *(Ruth 1-4)*. The Assyrian citizens of Nineveh taught Jonah about repentance and acceptance *(Jonah 3 and 4)*. If you have overslept for an important appointment, it does not matter who woke you, only that you are now awake and active.

So, from a Christian perspective, I would see the current focus on taking children much more seriously as people (including the new openness about child protection issues) as something to be warmly welcomed - a long overdue unpacking of the implications of what Jesus said in *Mark 10:13-16* and what Paul said in Galatians 3:27f.

I would see Christian involvement in the Jubilee 2000, Drop the Debt and Fair Trade campaigns[258] as the beginnings of a renewed attempt to take the all-but-forgotten Old Testament teachings on Jubilee and on the sin of usury[259] seriously, with the full backing of Jesus *(Luke 6:20-26)* and Paul *(Galatians 3:27f)*.

I would see the ideas of democracy and universal suffrage as entirely in keeping with what Jesus did to kingship on the cross *(Matthew 27:27-37)* and where we all now stand as a result *(Galatians 3:27f)*.

In other words, I see a continuing development in the outworking of the ethical implications of the cross evident across the centuries and still inviting an ongoing process of exploration and re-valuing. Yet, I also see a continuing risk that each new generation is just as capable of missing important implications of the cross as it is of uncovering implications that their forebears in the faith had previously failed to see.

So, seeking to live Biblically in the 21st Century still involves risk, and challenge, and painful repentance, and mighty disagreements, and a prayerful seeking after the guidance of God. I do not reckon any part of our ongoing ethical conversation with God is sorted, finalised or complete. I suspect that God has always intended for our ethical debates to go on and on and on. I think that Biblical ethics will always be unfinished business.

7.3   **Moments of meaningful change**

We have taken an overview of the history of Christian anti-Semitism and racism, as an example of the broad sweep of the history of the church's Biblical ethics. Now, by contrast, we take a close-up, even microscopic, look at three particular moments of change to try to see how ethical change actually happens. The first two are taken from the history of slavery and the ethical and Biblical arguments mustered in favour of its abolition in the 18th and 19th Centuries. The third close-up comes from the theological arguments about apartheid in 20th Century South Africa.

I.   *WAS GOD AGAINST THE ATLANTIC SLAVE TRADE?*

The confessional statement in *Galatians 3:27-8* is clear that the distinction between slave and free is abolished by the cross. Yet there is no explicit condemnation of the contemporary institution of slavery in the New Testament and no clear proposals for its abolition, even within the tiny urban church communities that Paul and others seek to develop. Perhaps that is why such a vast and ugly inhumanity as the Atlantic slave trade and its resultant slave-holding colonies could later be developed by the citizens of Britain and other 'Christian' countries. Perhaps the developed sense of European superiority (whose roots we considered in the previous section, 7.2) was also a factor that allowed Christian people to accept or ignore their steady development and expansion of this great evil. I cannot speak authoritatively about this. Rather, let me offer you a brief close-up of Biblical interpretation in the heart of the 18th century abolitionist movement in Britain – a glimpse of a moment when the church was beginning to read the weight of the Bible evidence in a new way.

Let us join **OLAUDAH EQUIANO** (1755-1797), a remarkable Christian campaigner for the abolition of the British Atlantic slave trade near the end of the 18th Century. To my shame, I have had a copy of *"The Interesting Narrative of the Life of Olaudah Equiano or Gustavus Vassa, the African, Written by Himself"*[260] in my bookcase for some twenty-five years, but I only read it last year. This significant and very readable autobiography, published in 1789 (with John Wesley as one of its listed pre-publication subscribers) is his central contribution to the abolitionist cause – it is also a well-told and powerful personal story. Equiano began life contentedly in an Ibo village in Eastern Nigeria, but was taken away by raiders at around the age of 10, sold to slave traders and shipped across the Atlantic in chains. After many years serving as a slave on various ships, chiefly plying between the Caribbean and the Eastern seaboard of the United States, he gradually put together enough money to buy his own freedom. After many other adventures, including serving on an Arctic expedition, and his conversion to a strong personal Christian faith, he became a significant activist on the British abolitionist scene.

Clearly, Equiano is aware that his personal story, all the more powerful for being so simply and straightforwardly told, is his strongest argument for the abolitionist cause. Its evident humanity is impossible to deny and highlights the awfulness of the world in which he has survived despite everything. Yet, as R S Sugirtharajah has pointed out[261], Equiano skilfully uses a wide range of Bible allusions in telling his story and unpacking its meaning and significance. Here is, in effect, a previously-silenced voice that is now uncovering the meanings of Scripture from the point of view of an African and a sometime slave.

He notes that many of the customs of his native Ibo people (including circumcision of boys on the eighth day) are similar to those of the Hebrews in the Bible[262], using this to subtly reposition his people away from any notion that they might be savages, rather presenting them as people of God. He also subtly connects his own story and the plight of his people to the stories of Jacob and Moses. Elsewhere he caps off an extended argument against any idea of European superiority with a well-chosen quotation from Paul's speech in Athens (*Acts 17:26*). He offers this advice to "the polished and haughty European[s]":

> If, when they look around the world, they feel exultation, let it be tempered with benevolence to others, and gratitude to God, 'who hath made of one blood all nations of men for to dwell on all the face of the earth'
>
> *O. Equiano, "Interesting Narrative" (Penguin, 1995) p.45*

Again, he tells us how a Mr Drummond, a dealer in slaves, once told him how he had cut off a slave's legs for running away. Equiano (still a slave himself at this time!) responded by saying to Drummond that "the Christian doctrine taught us to do unto others as we would that others should do unto us".[263]

Yet, for us, the most interesting of Equiano's Biblical arguments against slavery (to which Sugirtharajah[264] helpfully draws our attention) are his comments on *Paul's Letter to Philemon*. These occur in a letter Equiano wrote to a London newspaper in 1788[265]. His letter was a response to the publication of a book entitled "*Scripture Researches on the Licitness of the Slave Trade*" by the Revd Raymund Harris. In particular, it responded to the Reverend gentleman's use of *Paul's Letter to Philemon* to claim Biblical support for the acceptability of slavery and the slave trade, as then practised.

You may recall that Paul's letter was a sort of cover note for the return of the slave Onesimus ('useful') to Philemon, his Christian owner. Onesimus had somehow turned up in Rome (perhaps as a runaway?). There he had become a Christian and been very useful to the imprisoned Paul. Still, Paul is now sending him back to Brother Philemon, a prominent Christian who is his legal owner. Mr Harris has clearly found in this story ample proof that Paul would have had no particular problem with Christians being intimately involved with the practices of the Atlantic slave trade and the colonial slavery it supplied.

Equiano forcefully begs to differ. He protests against Harris' use of Paul's letter to support the vast evils of the Atlantic trade when "the whole tenor of [the letter] is in behalf of the slave"[266]. Pointing out that Onesimus is sent back "no longer as a slave but as more than a slave, a beloved brother" (Philemon v.16 NRSV), Equiano continues:

> "in other texts, where St Paul recommends submission to servants for conscience sake, he at the same time enjoins the master to entertain such a measure of brotherly love towards his servant, as must be entirely subversive of the African trade, and West India slavery. – And though St Paul recommends Christian Patience under servitude; yet at the same time he plainly insinuates, that it is inconsistent with Christianity. – ... The dignity of Christ's kingdom doth not admit of Christians to be slaves to their brothers."
>
> Olaudah Equiano, letter of 1788, "The Interesting Narrative and Other Writings"
> (Penguin Books, 1995) p.335

I am mightily moved by what Equiano says – I want to shout "AMEN!" and rush off to write a supporting letter to the paper that has published these stirring words. Yet, I think we should note that the text of *Paul's Letter to Philemon* and the purpose for which it was written do not, of themselves, clearly establish Paul's anti-slavery credentials. After all, Paul is sending a slave back to his owner (even if he does plead for Christian kindness). To make his case, Equiano has to call on what Paul says "in other texts" and even there he has to make the stretching claim that Paul "plainly insinuates" the inconsistency of slavery with Christianity. So, how, exactly, does Equiano think that Paul "plainly insinuates"? He finds anti-slavery credentials at the heart of Paul's theology, in the implications of 'Christ crucified'. He argues that Paul thought it "derogatory to the honour of Christianity, that men who are bought with the inestimable price of Christ's blood, shall be esteemed slaves, and the private property of their fellow-men."[267] Effectively, Equiano is using the equality before the cross which we found in Galatians 3:28 to settle the ethical ambiguities of *Philemon*. He is subsuming any authority to be found in Paul's cautious moral practice within a greater authority that he finds in the same Paul's radical theology of equality and inclusivity at the foot of the cross.

Intriguingly, Equiano also provides a further argument as to *why* Paul counselled slaves to show quiet submission, rather than "absolutely declare the iniquity of slavery". Openly to have denounced slavery in Paul's day would have "occasioned more tumult than reformation". Indeed, in the case of the slaves themselves such a stance would have led to "more striving for temporal than spiritual happiness"[268]. In other words, he clearly thought that Paul had grasped the full ethical implications of the gospel yet had held back from a thorough implementation. Moreover, Equiano considers that Paul held back in this way to avoid provoking a level of civil disruption that might seriously derail the church's urgent spiritual mission.

Just as intriguingly, Equiano, who had extensive experience of being a slave himself, sees no reason for such a holding back in his own day and age. Presumably, the risk of derailing the church's mission by supporting abolition is now so small, in comparison to what he knows of the vast evil of the 18th Century institution, that it can be ignored. The only issue that Equiano considers is the moral status of slavery itself.

The idea that slavery is a moral evil, which we would surely be reluctant to dispute in the 21st Century, was not nearly so obvious to everyone in 18th Century Britain. That the Bible was opposed to slavery was a case that needed making. For, at that time there must have been many British church people with direct or indirect dependence on the proceeds of colonial slavery and the Atlantic trade. Such people had a major investment in reading the Bible in a way that at least left it neutral on the issue of slavery. Moreover, British society was awash with established white myths about the nature of black people (their supposed laziness, stupidity and fecundity) and riddled with powerful fears of slave revolts and insurrections. For an articulate African (still viewed in much of 18th Century British society as a sort of exotic curiosity) to interpret the Bible in the bold way which Equiano did, and to become an author and write strong letters to the London newspapers about correct Biblical interpretation, was no mean feat. This man took real risks publicly to enter God's conversation and contribute so fearlessly on behalf of the voiceless. Thank God that he did.

For me, Equiano's reading of *Philemon* illustrates TWO crucial aspects of how the ongoing ethical conversation with God rightly develops:

✦ **Firstly**, there is great importance in who Equiano is. The perceptions, arguments and testimony of a former slave represent a crucial, balancing voice in the ethical debate about slavery. To view the matter only from the viewpoint of those who could easily qualify to become slave owners but never to be slaves, is to risk unconscionable distortion. Thus, in this case, Equiano's perspective on *Philemon*, including his perception that the whole tenor of Paul's letter takes the part of the slave, is hugely significant. Without such voices powerfully raised in the debate, the excusing of slavery might never have been effectively challenged. Yet, it is precisely those who speak up with the voice of the marginalised and the silenced who stand in the great Biblical prophetic tradition. There is something of Moses, Amos and Jesus about a contribution to the church's ethical debates which challenges readings that give easy comfort to the powerful at the expense of the powerless.

✦ **Secondly**, there is enormous importance in the form of his central argument. His use of Paul's core theology of the cross to rule out Harris' pro-slavery reading of *Philemon* is of huge significance. He triangulates from 'brotherly love', 'the dignity of Christ's Kingdom' and 'the inestimable price of Christ's blood' to overrule any idea that Paul (or any Christian) could be permanently happy with the idea of slavery. This is to handle Paul's writings with something of the same passion, insight and creativity which Paul himself had employed in interpreting the written Scriptures and oral Gospel in his own day. Moreover, here is a practical example of the sort of argument from the very nature and purposes of God that we have already considered in several places. It is with the moral weight of the loving nature of the crucified and risen Christ that Equiano is able to steer us away from pro-slavery readings of *Philemon*. He demonstrates that the text of the Bible is to be read in the light of the God whom it is written to reveal. Every reading of Scripture, including those that offer us ethical conclusions, must be tested against this vital question, "What sort of God does this reading allow?" Without this sort of approach I fear it might have been hard, even impossible, to claim that God was for the abolitionists. Without this way of reading, the Bible might still be used to justify slavery and the Christian God might have been left implicitly ugly, vicious and partisan.

2. WAS GOD AGAINST AMERICAN CHATTEL SLAVERY?

Now, we move on to the middle of the 19th Century, to the period after 1851. That was the year **HARRIET BEECHER STOWE** began publishing her novel, "*Uncle Tom's Cabin*".[269] It is fashionable nowadays to point up the real and evident weaknesses of Stowe's novel, including the obedient, accepting "Uncle Tom" quality of its main character, but it made an unprecedented impact world wide when it was first published. Indeed, except for the Bible, "*Uncle Tom's Cabin*" had more world wide sales than any other book in the whole of the Nineteenth Century.[270] Written out of a deep Christian conviction, this novel was triggered by the introduction of the Fugitive Slave Act of 1850, which required every United States citizen to turn in runaway slaves. Effectively, this act "made every American complicit in slavery"[271]. Mrs Stowe's sister-in-law urged her to write something to attack the institution of slavery and, in particular, the effects of the new act. Her response was to write "*Uncle Tom's Cabin*".[272]

Even in Britain, Mrs Stowe's book and her subsequent personal appearances on tour had an electrifying effect. Committed abolitionists had been finding it harder and harder to raise public interest in the plight of black slaves in the Americas after the passing of the British Emancipation Act of 1833, which had legislated a limited form of freedom for slaves in the British-controlled West Indies. But *The Times* was soon complaining that *"Uncle Tom's Cabin"* was "at every railway bookstall in England, and in every third traveller's hand" and the presence of Mrs Stowe as a speaker was certain to fill the hall just about anywhere in the land[273]. Some would argue, with C Duncan Rice's *"The Scots Abolitionists, 1833-1861"*, that Mrs Stowe's famous novel confines itself to playing with peoples' sentimentality and sensibility, that she "demanded much emotion but no work"[274]. Yet can we be entirely dismissive of what she is doing? I suspect she is engaged in a crucial part of enabling change in moral and ethical understanding; I think she is enabling people to identify with the plight of "the other". Her characters were never intended to represent fully and effectively every aspect of the nature and potential of African Americans; they are designed to be enslaved people with whose plight distant white people could readily identify. Her characters are meant to open up the radical injustice of the peculiar institution to the imaginations of those who had never given slavery a second thought. Let me offer an extract from Chapter Two of "Uncle Tom's Cabin" as an example:

THE TALE OF GEORGE HARRIS AND HIS OWNER

An EXTRACT from CHAPTER TWO of *"UNCLE TOM'S CABIN"* by Harriet Beecher Stowe

[The slave Eliza] had been married to a bright and talented young mulatto man, who was a slave on a neighboring estate, and bore the name of George Harris.

This young man had been hired out by his master to work in a bagging factory, where his adroitness and ingenuity caused him to be considered the first hand in the place. He had invented a machine for the cleaning of the hemp, which, considering the education and circumstances of the inventor, displayed quite as much mechanical genius as Whitney's cotton-gin.

He was possessed of a handsome person and pleasing manners, and was a general favorite in the factory. Nevertheless, as this young man was in the eye of the law not a man, but a thing, all these superior qualifications were subject to the control of a vulgar, narrow-minded, tyrannical master. This same gentleman, having heard of the fame of George's invention, took a ride over to the factory, to see what this intelligent chattel had been about. He was received with great enthusiasm by the employer, who congratulated him on possessing so valuable a slave.

He was waited upon over the factory, shown the machinery by George, who, in high spirits, talked so fluently, held himself so erect, looked so handsome and manly, that his master began to feel an uneasy consciousness of inferiority. What business had his slave to be marching round the country, inventing machines, and holding up his head among gentlemen? He'd soon put a stop to it. He'd take him back and put him to hoeing and digging, and "see if he'd step about so smart". Accordingly, the manufacturer and all hands concerned were astounded when he suddenly demanded George's wages, and announced his intention of taking him home.

"But, Mr Harris," remonstrated the manufacturer, "isn't this rather sudden?"
"What if it is? – isn't the man mine?"
"We would be willing, sir, to increase the rate of compensation."
"No object at all, sir. I don't need to hire any of my hands out, unless I've a mind to."
"But, sir, he seems peculiarly adapted to this business."
"Dare say he may be; never was much adapted to anything that I set him about, I'll be bound"
"But only think of him inventing this machine," interposed one of the workmen, rather unluckily.
"O yes! – a machine for saving work, is it? He'd invent that, I'll be bound; let a nigger alone for that, any time. They are all labor-saving machines themselves, every one of 'em. No, he shall tramp!"......

George was taken home, and put to the meanest drudgery of the farm. He had been able to repress every disrespectful word; but the flashing eye, the gloomy and troubled brow, were part of a natural language that could not be repressed, - indubitable signs, which showed too plainly that the man could not become a thing.

Here, Mrs Stowe vividly evokes the mindless blighting of human aspirations and potential. Surely we can *feel* the injustice done to George Harris by his self-obsessed and implacable owner? We are invited to step in friendship into the situation of this slave, that we might all join in shouting "NO!" with an unbridled sense of moral outrage. She is enabling distant, certain and untroubled white readers to stand in a place they have never stood – to be momentarily "incarnated" as a mulatto slave. Now, and only now, are they in a position to begin to engage in moral discussion of the issue. Of course, emotion is not enough. There has to be reason and logic and Bible reading and as much clarity and honesty as we can muster. Yet we leave out the emotive and the attempt to stand in the place of the other at our own peril. Harriet Beecher Stowe demonstrates for us the power and importance of enabling stories and connecting emotion. We cannot avoid them if we would truly enter God's conversation to develop our ethical understanding.

Surely God's own decision that Jesus should stand where we stand and face what we face is at the heart of what makes God glorious? Do we think we can make sense of other people's pain and pressures without even an attempt, by the power of our imaginations, to make such a connection? Do we think we can 'do' ethics without engaging with 'the other', putting ourselves in their shoes, trying somehow to expose ourselves to what it might feel like from their side. Mrs Stowe's novel certainly didn't bring slavery in the United States to an end, but she must have helped many in the church to see what they otherwise would have failed to see, by letting them stand, momentarily, where they otherwise would never have stood.

Clearly, she understood this - that our emotions greatly affect our ethical decisions, whether or not we are prepared to admit it. Consequently, ethical change requires us to encounter emotions that we may previously have avoided, not just arguments we have not previously heard. She also realised that story could sometimes be the best vehicle to take us to places we need to go and introduce us to people we need to meet, especially when we have no other way to get there. Harriet Beecher Stowe reminds us that ethical change is a change of heart as well as a change of mind.

What, in essence, she is inviting us to view is the difference between the value we put on 'the other' and the value God puts on them. Even though we would not now wish to consider anyone to be a 'thing', there is often, still, a vast gulf between our valuing and understanding of others and that of God. Surely, Mrs Stowe's point is still relevant?

3.   WAS GOD AGAINST SOUTH AFRICAN APARTHEID?

For our third example of the realities of Christian ethical debate we move forward a century to South Africa in 1985-6 for the final grim chapter in the story of apartheid. At this time, after the declaration of the first 'State of Emergency', the level of state violence and repression, in response to growing unrest, was spiralling upwards. Two groups, acting on the concern within the Christian churches about the growing violence and suffering, produced "**THE KAIROS DOCUMENT**" (1985 and 1986)[275] and "**EVANGELICAL WITNESS IN SOUTH AFRICA**" (1986)[276]. Both these documents engaged in a double critique, maintaining not only that apartheid was a serious distortion of a Biblical world view, but that the position hitherto taken by the 'English-speaking Churches' and many Christians in South Africa (both black and white) was also a significant distortion of what the Bible says.

Let us first review the arguments put forward by *"The Kairos Document"*. This brief booklet offers us three contrasting 'theologies' of the political situation current in apartheid South Africa in 1985-6. It critiques the first two theologies, then argues strongly for the third:

A summary of 'STATE THEOLOGY'
✦   This approach relies on *Romans 13:1-7* to argue that the Bible gives "an absolute and 'divine' authority to the state".

✦   It also uses the idea of 'law and order' to insist on compliance with the laws and the order of the *status quo*, making "state security" a more important concern than justice.

✦   It dismisses anyone opposing the state as an atheistic communist.

✦   Then, it co-opts God as its guarantor (e.g. in the apartheid constitution).

The KAIROS CRITIQUE of 'State Theology'
✦   The critique argues that *Romans 13:1-7*, like all Bible texts, has to be read in its own context. Paul was resisting 'antinomianism', the anarchic idea that the laws of *any* state should *never* apply to Christians; he was not trying to defend tyranny.

✦   "The State's efforts to preserve law and order, which should imply the protection of human life, means the very opposite for the majority of the people, namely the suppression and destruction of life."

- The State is wrongly applying the label 'atheist' to millions of South African Christians.
- The God invoked by the South African State is merely an idol, "a god who exalts the proud and humbles the poor – the very opposite of the God of the Bible".

A summary of 'CHURCH THEOLOGY'
- This approach relies on "a few stock ideas derived from Christian tradition" uncritically and repeatedly applied to the situation in South Africa at that time. 'Reconciliation' and forgiveness are held up as ideals to heal society.
- The State and the white community are endlessly urged to act with 'Justice'.
- All violence is condemned whilst 'Non-violence' is praised.

The KAIROS CRITIQUE of 'Church Theology'
- This critique argues that to appeal for 'Reconciliation' when "one side is a fully armed and violent oppressor while the other side is defenceless and oppressed" is a betrayal of the Christian faith. Without the repentance of the oppressor, any appeal for reconciliation is totally misplaced.
- Again, it is wrong to talk of 'Justice' without acknowledging the in-built structural injustice of the situation. It is wrong to expect the oppressors to produce real reform, without listening to the voices of the oppressed. "Real change and true justice can only come from below, from the people".
- 'Violence' can be a loaded word. Can the violence of the state apparatus and people's efforts to defend themselves be equated? You cannot remain neutral in such a conflict.
- The fundamental problem, exposed by the church's lack of an adequate social analysis, is an approach to spirituality that is decidedly other-worldly and individualistic. Thus, the onset of the political crisis has left much of the church "in a state of near paralysis".

THE KAIROS 'PROPHETIC THEOLOGY'
- A truly prophetic theology would return to *the Bible* to search for a relevant message, reading each Bible passage, so far as possible, in the light of its own context.
- It would also engage in *social analysis* of the times and the underlying causes of the crisis, identifying the structures of injustice and oppression.
- It would not be theoretical or academic, but would result in *a call to action*, identifying God and church with the poor and the oppressed.
- It would speak out against the evils of the time and *confront* them, identifying tyranny, declaring such a regime morally illegitimate.
- It would offer an emphasis on *hope*, rooted in the hope of God's people.
- It would be deeply *spiritual*, seeking to have the mind of Christ.
- It would be thoroughly *pastoral*, denouncing sin and announcing salvation.

"*Evangelical Witness in South Africa*" responds by picking up on many of the telling points made by "*The Kairos Document*", but it is powerfully infused with a real sense of repentance for church failure. The authors and signatories openly own up to the following faults:

CHURCH FAILURES (according to "*Evangelical Witness in South Africa*")

✦   We have been carefully conservative, whereas Jesus was radically subversive.

✦   We have wrongly divided the spiritual from the material.

✦   We have urged reconciliation on the oppressed, without due concern for justice.

✦   We have taught obedience to the state when Christians are called to live in permanent critique of the world.

✦   We have been blind to the evils of colonisation and capitalism, denouncing only communism.

✦   Our evangelism has been distorted, as true evangelism cannot be reduced to either 'spiritual needs' or 'social action', but requires both.

✦   Our moral preaching has been against the sins of the poor, ignoring the sins of the rich and those with power.

If we consider these documents as examples of the development of Biblical ethics, what can we learn? **FOUR** aspects of these attempts to 'do' ethics strike me as particularly important.

✦   **Firstly**, neither of these documents allows us a safe, calm, theoretical theologising. This is Biblical ethics strapped together and put to sea in the midst of a mighty storm. Both documents represent attempts to hold significant "crisis meetings" with God, in the face of vast anguish and pain whilst the townships go up in smoke around them.[277] They are seeking to overcome an effective church paralysis in the face of the surrounding social crisis; a paralysis that threatens to leave the churches and their 'spiritual' world looking increasingly irrelevant as the crisis deepens. The detentions, the deaths and the violence that surround them every day have built up a powerful pressure to review long-accepted church ideas, alter them or even repudiate them. All the risk, difficulty and importance of entering God's conversation is powerfully exposed.

✦   **Secondly**, both documents are committed to a "contextual" approach. That means they try to allow for the context in which a particular Bible passage was written rather that read each Bible text as a sort of disembodied truth[278]. They also see it as important to be acutely aware of the context into which they are seeking to apply the Bible's message. "*The Kairos Document*" talks in various places of how applying the Bible's message requires a thoroughgoing "social analysis"; a clear understanding of how society works, who has power and how they keep it. "*Evangelical Witness in South Africa*" tells how the Western missionary roots of their local evangelicalism have made it 'blind' to the social realities of "western domination and exploitation of the Third World" and how that has resulted in an oppressive culture being transplanted into the church in South Africa. Both documents are adamant that Biblical ethics requires us to take full account of the context of the original text and the context of its intended application[279]. With such contextual awareness in place, they are unafraid to read the Bible directly into their crisis and let the crisis directly interact with the Bible. To ask these church people to find a more calm and reflective place to 'do' ethics would be a bit like asking Paul not to bother writing to the Corinthian Church as it starts to fall apart. They need answers and actions, and they need them now. For them, Biblical ethics is a matter of life and death.

✦ **Thirdly**, both documents are unashamedly developing start-up contributions to a vast ecumenical church conversation, within an even bigger church argument about what God is saying to them and their situation. They also have a particular passion to unleash previously silenced Christian voices into the conversation. They see the majority of black South African Christians as people who, for too long, have been told what to think and say, but whose voices need to be heard and whose pains need to influence the whole debate. Both documents strongly criticise the ethical interpretations of both national and church power elites from the standpoint of the patronised, the exploited and the ignored. Whom did Jesus denounce and whom did he support?

✦ **Fourthly**, there is a considerable amount of admission of church failure, even repentance, involved in these snippets of conversation and a real sense that even the renewed understandings they propose are provisional and likely to be superseded before too long. This is strong argument offered with honesty, not mindless arrogance with settled certainty.

For me, these two South African documents have demonstrated some of the core realities of entering God's conversation. They clearly show how contemporary events and experiences can force significant groups within the church to think again about long-settled ethical conclusions with old, familiar Biblical explanations attached. They emphasise how the dangers of misinterpreting the Bible are vastly increased by a failure to consider carefully the context of each text and the context we ourselves inhabit, the context that inevitably shapes and controls our interpretations. They make a powerful case for the inclusion of previously silenced voices that we may all share aright in God's conversation. They show us the power of honest and sincere repentance as an integral part of the life of the people of God.

It is only fair to add that I have the impression that much of the theology in the churches of South Africa today seems to have settled back into something calmer, even more complacent, than Kairos theology now that the particular crisis of full-blown apartheid has past. No matter how disappointing that may be to some, it is neither surprising nor inexplicable. The conversation has moved along, with new problems and possibilities, as the new South Africa has emerged. Yet, who knows, we may **all** have to return to some of these 'Kairos' arguments in the future. Much of these Kairos critiques of apartheid South Africa still work if you re-apply them to the unjust way the world as a whole is run today.280 Perhaps God has important things to say to us, even if we are not that keen to listen.

7.4 **The struggle continues**

So, what can we claim to have learned from our swift look at samples from the history of Biblical ethics, using first a long lens and then a microscope? The historical examples we have considered have clearly exposed the fallible nature of the church. So, the Christian efforts at being God's people do not look significantly better than the wayward people of the wilderness wanderings and the largely ill-led and often unfaithful Kingdoms of Israel and Judah that preceded them in Old Testament times. Nor do the efforts of the churches across the last two millennia noticeably outclass the inauspicious, fractious beginnings of the church which we found in Corinth in Paul's time. The intriguing and depressing mixture of success, failure, beauty and ugliness which we found in the story of God's people through both Testaments is effectively continued in the ongoing life of the church. God's people are clearly continuing to learn, yet always at risk of significant, sometimes prolonged, failures.

The Bible continues to be available to each successive generation, but in each new context it seems to invite fresh struggles for understanding. Making sense of this same Bible in each new setting always seems to offer new debates that divide loyalties, challenge accepted understandings, threaten further schism. There is some sort of ethical progress here. Though I would read it as a sort of outworking of things implicit in the Bible and in the nature of the God which the Bible seeks to reveal. Yet, as each generation takes up the task, there is nothing inevitable or relentless about this progress. Indeed, humanity seems to have a real gift for inventing new forms of ethical ugliness to undercut or erode every beautiful moment of apparent progress. A particularly distressing factor is the pain and suffering that often seems to be involved before the churches are prepared to re-appraise their ethical understanding or the sense they make of the Bible.

I can't entirely shake off or put aside the following sorts of troubling questions:

+ Did it have to take the Holocaust to expose the evils of anti-Semitism?
+ Did Europeans have to ship millions of Africans across the middle passage before churches could see that slavery was wrong?
+ Did we have to wait until the township schoolchildren of South Africa were getting attacked, detained, and caught up in their own acts of violence before some of the churches would seriously try to stand together against apartheid?

All this is not to deny that there have been profoundly positive aspects to the church's attempts at Biblical ethics down the centuries. There have been powerful tales of acknowledged saints and countless unsung heroes. There have been great moral insights and much practical care and kindness nurtured, defended and advanced in the face of cynical selfishness, greed and exploitation. Indeed, I wonder if some of the better parts of the decidedly mixed inheritance of the West would have been there at all without the church's attempts at being true to Jesus, the Gospel and the Bible.

Yet, I can see little or no evidence that the church has been an unstinting defender of an unchanging set of clear Biblical precepts that have been faithfully handed down intact from generation to generation. Like the story the Bible itself tells, it has been much more like an inherited family friendship. On our side, it has been an unpredictable mixture of waywardness and fresh commitment, obfuscation and insight as generation has succeeded generation. The great, challenging, untiring, conversation with God begun in the Bible has continued ever since. It has rolled on through countless, diverse situations and settings, cultures and challenges. In it the God of the Bible is always present to be met anew, or abused or ignored as we, in our turn, agonise over the dilemmas we face, grapple with the baggage we carry, try to make sense of the world in which we have to live.

Will we, with God's help, be able to help the conversation along?

Our samples from church history offer us some clues. In the light of what we have seen, I would suggest that we can take nothing for granted. Even the most settled parts of our ethical inheritance and the most cherished explanations of Bible meanings can be challenged if the pressures of our own day and age offer us fresh questions or unanswered dilemmas. Let us be bold, but let us be cautious. Let us be bold in what we are prepared to question. Yet, let us be wary of presuming our answers will always be better or our own baggage always more helpful. Let us listen to the insights and ideas of others, but let us particularly seek out previously-silenced voices and give them a right to speak. Let us test each reading to see what sort of God it would allow. Let us be open to the range of interpretive tools we have – reason, logic, argument, imagination, emotion, encounter with others, encounter with God. Let us seek to be honest and ready to own up to where we have been wrong. Let us listen. Let us leave

AFTERWORD

THE VIEW FROM HERE

We have completed our wanderings through the various layers of the "How?" questions, the ones about how we make sense of the Bible today and how we use it to help us construct ethical responses to the world around us. I would not be at all surprised if you have found the whole process more than a little frustrating. For we have not been able to expose any sort of underlying structure or logic to Biblical ethics, or even present agreed rules and regulations that might ensure good practice or allow us to arbitrate in disputes. Instead, we have talked of smuggled baggage, of kitchens full of ingredients but no recipes, of orienteers crashing their way through darkening forests, of an untameable text from an untameable God, of the impossibility of being certain that you've found 'the truth' even if you have. In this respect, the "How?" questions of Biblical ethics remind me of the "How?" questions of science. In both cases, the closer you look, the less certain it all seems. So, what CAN we say about Biblical ethics after all these investigations? Let me offer, by way of summary, a quick list of the six key points that seem to act as the foundations of all I have tried to say:

✦ **THE BIBLE REMAINS STUBBORNLY AWKWARD.** There is a yawning mismatch between the Bible we have and the sorts of paperwork we would produce if we wanted to give clear guidance on behaviour and ethics. I have found myself drawing attention to this again and again. If (as I firmly believe) the Bible is intended to be our 'supreme authority', it cannot be intended to operate in the quasi-legal way we often seem to expect. It must be intended to offer us something altogether different. *(see particularly 4.2 & 5.3.1)*

✦ **WE CANNOT FIND TRUTH ON OUR OWN.** I talk a lot about baggage. Mixing with people from different cultures leaves you little choice but to admit that none of us can get close to being objective (despite the confidence in their own objectivity that educated white men sustained through much of the time between the Reformation and now). To get past our biases and have any chance of a real encounter with the God who is there, we have to work together and work together with people who have seriously different starting points from us. *(see particularly 1.3 & 3.3)*

✦ **GOD MAY HAVE INTENDED BOTH OF THESE FACTORS.** I can't see these complications as a mistake. So, did God deliberately create these awkwardnesses in the nature of reality and the contents of the Bible? Certainly they work against two of our most persistent failings – our tendency to try to domesticate God and our longing for neat and tidy closure. They also swing the basis of our relationship away from legal obedience to gracious and vulnerable friendship, inviting an endless renewal and creating lively community. Both the Bible we have and our inability to be objective seem designed to enable a developing friendship with our God and with God's people. *(see 4.4)*

✦ **ETHICAL ARGUMENTS MAY BE PART OF GOD'S PURPOSE.** The particular awkwardness of the Bible for making clear, logical deductions about ethics and its refusal to lay down obvious rules as to how we might go about it are intriguing. What if our moral and personal development are encouraged and enabled by ethical debate and dispute? What if this is God's means of forcing us to plumb the depths of the issues before us? Then long ethical arguments could be a more important part of what the Bible sought to offer us than clear, decided moral certainty. *(see particularly 5.5)*

✦ **HUMILITY, RESPECT AND CO-OPERATION ARE OUR VITAL TOOLS.** Our judgement is always biased on its own. Our conclusions are always provisional and open to the challenge of others. So, we will need others, we will need their co-operation and their insights. We will also need to own up to things we have got wrong and be prepared to change our minds. Humility, mutual respect and mutual co-operation must surely be the very essence of our approach. Only with these tools can we work together on uncovering God's will for us in our setting, in our day and age. *(see particularly 6.2)*

✦ **ETHICS IS NOT THE GOAL; THE BIBLE IS NOT AN END IN ITSELF.** It is altogether too easy to get caught up in the ins and outs of a particular ethical dilemma and lose sight of the core purposes of the Bible. By means of this vast text we are invited to join a passionate conversation in which we may personally encounter the God of relationship and rescue. The very awkwardness of the text also seems intent on encouraging us to share God's emerging friendship with others. It seems to me that it is these relationships that are the very heart of the matter. The Bible is but a glorious means to these yet more awesome ends. *(see particularly 4.4)*

Between them, these six points support just about all of the things I have sought to address. They explain for me how we can be left facing vast ethical chasms like the one at the heart of church debates about homosexuality and yet how both sides can be sincerely seeking God's truth in the Bible. They give me good reason to urge patience and humility and respect and co-operation on everyone involved. They give me hope that progress can be made, though we may all be surprised as to some of the places that God is leading us. Yet, they allow me to invite friends on all sides not to be distracted from the vast and glorious message of God's passionate concern for them, but also for those who seem to stand far from them.

As for me, I have now spent two and a half years living with the evolving contents of this book. Because of that, I have also had to live with a special closeness to the big, beautiful, complex, frustrating, challenging, God-bearing text which we call the Bible. Somehow, despite or indeed because of its vast and complex awkwardness, I have fallen in love with it all over again. Standing here, I find myself far more in awe of the God who shaped, inspired and co-ordinated it all. I also find myself ever more privileged to be called to be a friend of this amazing God. I am simultaneously elated and humbled by my own invitation to commit all of my life to the ongoing conversation with God and with God's people.

What about you?

Copyright Acknowledgements

FOOTNOTES

INTRODUCTION - ASKING THE "HOW?" QUESTIONS

1   I build my analogy here (and throughout this chapter) on an idea of Eugene Peterson on p.8 of his Foreword to Dyck, E. 'The Act of Bible Reading' (Paternoster Press, Carlisle, 1996).

2   United Reformed Church Reports to Assembly 2000, Mission Council Report, Resolution 14, p.39.

3   United Reformed Church Reports to Assembly 2000, Mission Council Report, Resolution 15, p.42.

4   United Reformed Church, "Human Sexuality Report 1999" (United Reformed Church, London, 1999), Working Group Report 'A', The Nature of Biblical Authority, pages 41-56. With regards to the reports produced by other churches in the Reformed Communion, I found the following Reports in store in the basement of our denominations offices in London:
CHURCH OF SCOTLAND
"Human Sexuality", extracted from the Report of the Board of Social Responsibility, May 1994 and "The Interpretation of Scripture", Report to the General Assembly of 1998 by the Panel on Doctrine
THE UNITING CHURCH IN AUSTRALIA
"Uniting Sexuality and Faith", The Uniting Church in Australia Assembly Task Group on Sexuality, July 1997
THE PRESBYTERIAN CHURCH OF AOTEAROA NEW ZEALAND
"Unity and Diversity" Report of Commission and Other Papers, PCANZ General Assembly, 1999.

CHAPTER ONE – SEEING WITH "REFORMED" SPECTACLES

5   for example, Chapter 4 'Medieval Interpretation' in Bray, Gerald "Biblical Interpretation past and present" (Inter Varsity Press, Leicester, 1996).

6   translated in "Luther's Works vol.25" (Concordia Publishing Co., Saint Louis, 1972) p.4.

7   Roger Lundin 'Interpreting Orphans: Hermeneutics in the Cartesian Tradition' in Lundin, R. et al. "The Promise of Hermeneutics" (Paternoster Press, Carlisle, 1999) pp.6&7.

8   quoted in Cornick, D. "Under God's Good Hand" (United Reformed Church, London, 1998).

9   McGrath, A., "Reformation Thought, an Introduction" 3rd edition (Blackwell, Oxford, 1999) p.162.

10   Ozment, S. "The Age of Reform, 1250-1550" (Yale University Press, New Haven & London, 1980), p.327.

11   Chadwick, O. "The Reformation" (Penguin Books, Harmondsworth, 1964) p.57f

12   Not 'everyone' could read, Not 'everyone' could afford a Bible, even in the towns, but great barriers to availability of Bibles and freedom to comment on stories and texts had come crashing down. Texts and stories from the Bible could be quoted and discussed on the street and no-one could stop it.

13 Ozment, S. "The Age of Reform, 1250-1550" (Yale University Press, New Haven & London, 1980), pp.340-351.

14 Lindberg, C. "The European Reformations" (Blackwell, Oxford, 1996) pp.217ff.

15 Chadwick, O. "The Reformation" (Penguin Books, Harmondsworth, 1964) p.60.

16 Chadwick, O. "The Reformation" (Penguin Books, Harmondsworth, 1964) p.190.

17 Hill, C. "The English Bible & the Seventeenth-century Revolution" (Penguin, Harmondsworth, 1994) p.13.

18 Cornick, D. "Under God's Good Hand" (United Reformed Church, London, 1998) p.23.

19 Calvin, J., "Institutes of the Christian Religion", an English translation forms volumes 20 & 21 of the Library of Christian Classics, edited by McNeill, J. T. & trans. F. L. Battles, (Westminster Press, Philadelphia, 1960), Book 1, Chapter 7.

20 see previous note (above).

21 Parker, T. H. L., "Calvin's New Testament Commentaries" (SCM Press 1971, London), & Bray, Gerald, "Biblical Interpretation past and present" (Inter Varsity Press, Leicester, 1996) pp.178f.

22 Cornick, David "Under God's Good Hand" (United Reformed Church, London 1998) p.20, *also* Parker, T. H. L. "Calvin's Preaching" (Westminster/John Knox Press, Louisville, 1992).

23 Bray, Gerald, "Biblical Interpretation past and present" (Inter Varsity Press, Leicester, 1996) pp.201ff.

24 Cornick, D. "Under God's Good Hand" (United Reformed Church, London, 1998) p.22f.

25 for example, his comments on the genealogies of Jesus given in Luke and Matthew's Gospels
in Calvin, J. "A harmony of the Gospels" Vol. 1, pp. 51ff. (English trans., St Andrews Press, Edinburgh, 1972).

26 There is a discussion of the Sadolet & Calvin letters in Soskice, J. M., "The Truth looks different from here", pp.43-77 of Reagan, H. & Torrance, A. (eds.) "Christ & Context" (T & T Clark, Edinburgh, 1993).

27 Parker, T. H. L., "Calvin's New Testament Commentaries" (SCM Press 1971, London), & Bray, Gerald, "Biblical Interpretation past and present" (Inter Varsity Press, Leicester, 1996) pp.58f.

28 Aylmer, G. E., "Rebellion or Revolution?" (Oxford University Press, Oxford, 1987), Chapter 4, p.78ff.

29 Cornick, D. "Under God's Good Hand" (United Reformed Church, London, 1998) p.51f, *also* McEwen, J. S., 'How the Confession came to be written', pp.6-16 in Heron, A. I. C. (ed.), "The Westminster Confession in the Church today" (St Andrews Press, Edinburgh, 1982).

30 Cornick, D. "Under God's Good Hand" (United Reformed Church, London, 1998) p.52

31 Ferguson, S. B., 'The Teaching of the Confession' in Heron, A. I. C. (ed.), "The Westminster Confession in the Church today" (St Andrews Press, Edinburgh, 1982) p.28.

32 Hill, C. "The English Bible & the Seventeenth-century Revolution" (Penguin, Harmondsworth, 1994) p.198.

33 Hill, C. "The English Bible & the Seventeenth-century Revolution" (Penguin, Harmondsworth, 1994) p.199.

CHAPTER TWO: BETWEEN THEN & NOW - ENLIGHTENMENT & REACTION

34   McKim, D. K. ed., "Historical Handbook of Major Biblical Interpreters" (Inter Varsity Press, Leicester, 1998) p.259.

35   Middleton, J. R. & Walsh, B. J., "Truth is stranger than it used to be" (SPCK, London, 1995) p.10.

36   we meet Robert Boyle & Peter Pett courtesy of Jacob, J. R., "Restoration, Reformation and the Origins of the Royal Society", pp.155-175 of HISTORY of SCIENCE vol. 13, (1975).

37   Newton himself seemed more fascinated with making sense of the numbers in the Book of the Prophet Daniel than applying unfettered reason to the Bible; he worried away at the Daniel numbers and their possible meaning on and off through most of his career as a scientist.

38   Reventlow, H. G., "The Authority of the Bible and the Rise of the Modern World" (Eng. trans. SCM Press, London, 1984) pp.294ff and 354ff.

39   Schweitzer, A. "The Quest of the Historical Jesus" (Eng. trans. A & C Black, London 1910) p.5.

40   Rogerson, J. "Old Testament Criticism in the Nineteenth Century" (SPCK, London, 1984) pp.138-144.

41   Kummel, W. G., "The New Testament - the History of the Investigation of its Problems" (Eng. trans. SCM Press, London 1973) pp.133ff.

42   Hafemann, S. J. "F. C. Baur" p. 285-289 in McKim, D. K. ed., "Historical Handbook of Major Biblical Interpreters" (Inter Varsity Press, Leicester, 1998).

43   Clements, R. E. "Julius Wellhausen" in McKim, D. K. ed., "Historical Handbook of Major Biblical Interpreters" (Inter Varsity Press, Leicester, 1998) pp.380-385.

44   United Reformed Church "Basis of Union", quoted in United Reformed Church, Human Sexuality Report 1999, 'Rpt A', pp.41.

45   Barton, J. ed., "The Cambridge Companion to Biblical Interpretation" (Cambridge University Press, Cambridge, 1998).

46   Brueggemann, W. "Theology of the Old Testament" (Fortress Press, Minneapolis, 1997), p.14f.

47   Schweitzer, A. "The Quest of the Historical Jesus" (Eng. trans. A & C Black, London 1910) p.398.

48   from an account of Campbell in Albert Peel's "These Hundred Years: a History of the Congregational Union of England and Wales, 1831-1931" (London, 1931) p 220, quoted in Watson, J. R., "The English Hymn, a critical and historical study" (Oxford University Press, Oxford, 1997) p.490.

49   see the article on Briggs by T. H. Olbricht pp.294ff in McKim, D. K. ed., "Historical Handbook of Major Biblical Interpreters" (Inter Varsity Press, Leicester, 1998).

50   see the article on Robertson Smith by J. A. Dearman pp.359ff in McKim, D. K. ed., "Historical Handbook of Major Biblical Interpreters" (Inter Varsity Press, Leicester, 1998).

51   see the article on Wellhausen by R. E. Clements pp.380ff in McKim, D. K. ed., "Historical Handbook of Major Biblical Interpreters" (Inter Varsity Press, Leicester, 1998).

52   thus Bray, G. "Biblical Interpretation past and present" (Inter Varsity Press, Leicester, 1996) pp.555f.

53   Here, and in what follows, I am indebted to the accounts of Warfield and his opinions in Bray, G. "Biblical Interpretation past and present" (Inter Varsity Press, Leicester,

1996) pp.555-561, McGrath, A. "A Passion for Truth - the intellectual coherence of evangelicalism" (Apollos / Inter Varsity Press, Leicester, 1996) pp.58, 108 & 166-169 and Jack B. Rogers "The Authority and Interpretation of the Bible" in McKim, D. ed. "Major themes in the Reformed Tradition" (Eerdmans, Grand Rapids, 1992) p.58-65.

54   Presbyterian and Reformed Review, 4:277-221 (1893), reprinted in the posthumously printed collection, Warfield, B. B., "The Inspiration and Authority of Scripture" (Presbyterian & Reformed Publishing, Philadelphia, 1948, p.217.

55   despite what Warfield says, this goes way beyond the expectations of Augustine and Calvin, who allowed that God could, where appropriate, 'accommodate' what he said to 'what was known' in the times the text was written, or even to the purposes of the text. See, for example, Calvin's comments on the genealogies of Jesus given in Luke and Matthew's Gospels in Calvin, J. "A harmony of the Gospels" Vol. I, pp.51ff. (English trans., St Andrews Press, Edinburgh, 1972), where Calvin 'allows' the discrepancies in the number of generations given by Matthew and Luke to be because Matthew "felt free to omit some names" as he was rounding out the numbers of generations to better illustrate his interpretation of the theological meaning of the different sections of the genealogy.

56   thus, in Hodge, A. A. and Warfield, B. B., "Inspiration", Presbyterian Review 2, (April 1881) - though as Jack B. Rogers tells it in his article on "The Authority and Interpretation of the Bible" in McKim, D. ed. "Major themes in the Reformed Tradition" (Eerdmans, Grand Rapids, 1992) p. 61, Warfield added that no error could be proved unless it could be shown to be in the original text of the Bible. Rogers comments, "Since the original manuscripts were all lost, Warfield seemed to have an unassailable apologetic stance." On another tack, David H. Kelsey argues that for Warfield his theory acted more like one of Thomas Kuhn's 'paradigms' in the physical sciences (Kuhn, T. S., "The Structure of Scientific Revolutions" Univ. Chicago Press, Chicago,1962 especially chapters 6-10), in which case it would be likely to take the pressure of a vast number of apparently conflicting facts before the theory would be abandoned - a few conflicting facts could always be treated as 'difficulties to be adjusted to it" rather than refutations. (Kelsey, D. H., "The Uses of Scripture in Recent Theology" SCM, London, 1975, p.22 & note 20 on p.31).

57   see section 1 of the Introduction above.

58   In various articles Warfield regularly makes a case that Bible authors had a concept of Biblical Inspiration that could be described as 'plenary', that is inspired throughout, but, as I read his case, there is still a gap between this and his particularly severe concept of inerrancy, inherited from Turretin, relying on a very mimetic understanding of the nature of truth in a text (which appears to come from the way the Scottish Common Sense Philosophers understood language to operate - see McGrath, A. "A Passion for Truth - the intellectual coherence of evangelicalism" (Apollos / Inter Varsity Press, Leicester, 1996) p.169). Then, having established to his own satisfaction that his doctrine of what Scripture must be like is the exact doctrine that can be presumed to lie behind the text EVERY time Scripture makes some reference to how it sees itself, he proceeds to declare ALL the rest of Scripture to be beyond the purview of the argument - Scripture's actual nature and contents must NOT be considered at all. To argue on the grounds of WHAT IS IN SCRIPTURE as to the nature of the revelation is, for Warfield, to

argue against his already established 'Scriptural' doctrine of Scripture. Thus, to argue from what Scripture is like with a view to suggesting any change in his doctrine of Scripture is to say that Scripture's own ipso facto inerrant definition of itself is wrong and therefore to declare all Scripture a lie, not to amend the doctrine of Scripture at all. See, for example, Warfield, B. B. "The Real Problem of Inspiration" Presbyterian and Reformed Review, 4:277-221 (1893), the most extensive relevant treatment reprinted in the posthumously printed collection - Warfield, B. B., "The Inspiration and Authority of Scripture" (Presbyterian & Reformed Publishing, Philadelphia, 1948). Clearly, to make all of this stick he has to have established that first crucial step that 'what I [B. B. W.] say Scripture is' is in fact IDENTICAL with 'what Scripture says Scripture is' whenever it talks about it. I am not persuaded.

59 Bray, G. "Biblical Interpretation past and present" (Inter Varsity Press, Leicester, 1996) p.557.

60 Brueggemann, W. "Theology of the Old Testament" (Fortress Press, Minneapolis, 1997), p.14.

61 cited in Jack B. Rogers "The Authority and Interpretation of the Bible" in McKim, D. ed. "Major themes in the Reformed Tradition" (Eerdmans, Grand Rapids, 1992) p.61, see also McGrath, A. "A Passion for Truth - the intellectual coherence of evangelicalism" (Apollos/Inter Varsity Press, Leicester, 1996) p.169.

62 Bray, G. "Biblical Interpretation past and present" (Inter Varsity Press, Leicester, 1996).

63 for example, the extended argument of John Goldingay, a noted English Evangelical Old Testament scholar, in Chapter 19 of his book "Models for Scripture" (Paternoster, Carlisle, 1987) pp.261-283.

64 for a summary see, Brown, R. E. "An Introduction to the New Testament" (Doubleday, New York, 1997).

CHAPTER THREE - READING AND MAKING SENSE TODAY

65 see section 2.1 above.

66 Daniel 5:1-31.

67 Middleton, J. R. & Walsh, B. J., "Truth is stranger than it used to be" (SPCK, London, 1995) p.20ff.

68 for example, Roger Lundin 'Interpreting Orphans: Hermeneutics in the Cartesian Tradition' in Lundin, R. et al. "The Promise of Hermeneutics" (Paternoster Press, Carlisle, 1999) p.6ff.

69 Certainly, it was an assumption that happened to be incredibly creative for science as it investigated the workings of the physical aspects of the world. Yet, it has always been a distortion, especially when applied to aspects of the human world or even aspects of the natural world open to 'anthropomorphic' ways of seeing (that is ways of seeing based on comparison with the ways humans are thought to behave).

70 for example, "Dances with wolves", or Clint Eastwood's "The Unforgiven".

71 Anderson, W. T. "Reality isn't what it used to be" (Harper & Row, San Francisco, 1990), quoted as the heading of their ' Chapter Two' by Middleton, J. R. & Walsh, B. J., "Truth is stranger than it used to be" (SPCK, London, 1995).

72 Middleton, J. R. & Walsh, B. J., "Truth is stranger than it used to be" (SPCK, London, 1995).

73 Middleton, J. R. & Walsh, B. J., "Truth is stranger than it used to be" (SPCK, London, 1995) p.42.

74 Middleton, J. R. & Walsh, B. J., "Truth is stranger than it used to be" (SPCK, London, 1995) p.43.

75 Middleton, J. R. & Walsh, B. J., "Truth is stranger than it used to be" (SPCK, London, 1995) p.46-49.

76 Middleton, J. R. & Walsh, B. J., "Truth is stranger than it used to be" (SPCK, London, 1995) p.54f.

77 Lundin, R. "The Culture of Interpretation: Christian Faith and the Postmodern World" (Eerdmans, Grand Rapids, 1993) p.250, as quoted in footnote 37 on page 209 of Middleton, J. R. & Walsh, B. J., "Truth is stranger than it used to be" (SPCK, London, 1995).

78 Roberts, J. M., "The Triumph of the West" (BBC Books, London, 1985).

79 Let me make it clear that I have NOT attempted to read the works of Ricoeur, Gadamer Foucault and Derrida, even in English translation. Time and their reputation for writing dense, difficult texts have been my two main enemies in this. Indeed, I have struggled to read and understand those who would be interpreters of their ideas. The account that follows relies on six interpretations of recent ideas in hermeneutics (though I do not agree with everything that I understand them to be saying) These are: Craig M. Gay "The Sociology of Knowledge and the Art of Suspicion" in Dyck, E. 'The Act of Bible Reading' (Paternoster Press, Carlisle, 1996); Roger Lundin 'Interpreting Orphans: Hermeneutics in the Cartesian Tradition' in Lundin, R. et al. "The Promise of Hermeneutics" (Paternoster Press, Carlisle, 1999); Middleton, J. R. & Walsh, B. J., "Truth is stranger than it used to be" (SPCK, London, 1995); Anthony Thiselton "Biblical Studies and Theoretical Hermeneutics" in Barton, J. 'The Cambridge companion to Biblical Interpretation' (Cambridge University Press, Cambridge, 1998) ; Anthony Thiselton "Communicative Action and Promise in Interdisciplinary, Biblical and Theological Hermeneutics" in Lundin, R. et al. "The Promise of Hermeneutics" (Paternoster Press, Carlisle, 1999); Loren Wilkinson "Hermeneutics and the Postmodern Reaction Against "Truth"" in Dyck, E. 'The Act of Bible Reading' (Paternoster Press, Carlisle, 1996).

80 see chapter One, section Three and all of Chapter Two, above.

81 Moses, W. J., "Afrotopia - the Roots of African American Popular History" (Cambridge University Press, Cambridge, 1998) pp.106-113.

82 Calvin seems to be well aware of our potential for biased judgements. Commenting on Luke 13:1-9, he writes: "The chief value of this passage springs from the fact that we suffer from the almost inborn disease of being overstrict and severe critics of others whilst approving of our own sins." - Calvin, J. "A Harmony of the Gospels Matthew, Mark & Luke" (1555 - English Translation by T. H. L. Parker, 1995, The Paternoster Press, Carlisle vol. II, p.94).

83 Roger Lundin 'Interpreting Orphans: Hermeneutics in the Cartesian Tradition' in Lundin, R. et al. "The Promise of Hermeneutics" (Paternoster Press, Carlisle, 1999) p.57.

84 Roger Lundin 'Interpreting Orphans: Hermeneutics in the Cartesian Tradition' in Lundin, R. et al. "The Promise of Hermeneutics" (Paternoster Press, Carlisle, 1999) p.57.

85 Craig M. Gay "The Sociology of Knowledge and the Art of Suspicion" in Dyck, E. 'The Act of Bible Reading' (Paternoster Press, Carlisle, 1996), p.89ff.

86 Craig M. Gay "The Sociology of Knowledge and the Art of Suspicion" in Dyck, E. 'The Act of Bible Reading' (Paternoster Press, Carlisle, 1996), p.92.

87 Robert Allan Warrior, "A Native American Perspective: Canaanites, Cowboys and Indians" in Sugirtharajah, R. S., ed. "Voices from the Margin - Interpreting the Bible in the Third World" (SPCK, London, 1991), p.287-295.

88 Sadly, this admonition comes in the midst of an acrimonious correspondence whilst Cromwell's invading English army sought a way to capture the Scottish capital. Both Cromwell and the Kirk's Assembly seemed to vie with each other to see who could be the more arrogant and unbending. The complete text of Cromwell's letter is given in Abbott, W. C., "Writings and Letters of Oliver Cromwell, volume 2, 1649-1653" (Harvard University Press, Cambridge, Mass., 1939) pp.302-303.

89 Loren Wilkinson "Hermeneutics and the Postmodern Reaction Against "Truth"" in Dyck, E. 'The Act of Bible Reading' (Paternoster Press, Carlisle, 1996).

90 Olthuis, J., "A Cold and Comfortless Hermeneutic or a Warm and Trembling Hermeneutic: A Conversation with John D. Caputo", Christian Scholars Review 19, no.4 (1990) pp.345-362, as quoted in Loren Wilkinson "Hermeneutics and the Postmodern Reaction Against "Truth"" in Dyck, E. 'The Act of Bible Reading' (Paternoster Press, Carlisle, 1996), p.138.

91 The Westminster Confession (1647), Chapter One, section nine - reprinted in Thompson, David M. (ed.) "Stating the Gospel - Formulations and Declarations of Faith from the Heritage of the United Reformed Church" (T & T Clark Ltd., Edinburgh, 1990) p.14.

92 Roger Lundin 'Interpreting Orphans: Hermeneutics in the Cartesian Tradition' in Lundin, R. et al. "The Promise of Hermeneutics" (Paternoster Press, Carlisle, 1999) p.60 see also Anthony Thiselton's article in the same volume. Here they are evidently also in accord with Gadamer and Ricoeur.

93 as quoted in Lundin 'Interpreting Orphans: Hermeneutics in the Cartesian Tradition' in Lundin, R. et al. "The Promise of Hermeneutics" (Paternoster Press, Carlisle, 1999) p.61.

94 MacIntyre, Alasdair "After Virtue – a study in moral theory" (Duckworth, London, 1981) ch.15, p.204ff.

95 Wendel, F. "CALVIN - the origins and development of his religious thought" Eng. Trans. (Collins, Glasgow, 1963) pp.26-37.

96 Wendel, F. "CALVIN - the origins and development of his religious thought" Eng. Trans. (Collins, Glasgow, 1963 notes (p.27) that Calvin's Seneca commentary is "a work that deserves to arrest attention by its erudition and style, and, no less, by the author's employment of the method which had been perfected by Valla, Erasmus, Bude and others." He then notes (p.28) that Calvin himself "asserts in his preface that he has found all kinds of things in Seneca which Erasmus had not noticed".

97 Parker, T. H. L., "Calvin's New Testament Commentaries" (SCM Press 1971, London)

98 for example, the whole argument of Kendall, R. T., "Calvin and English Calvinism to 1649" (Oxford University Press, 1981, Oxford) – reissued in 1997 by Paternoster Press (Carlisle) in their Paternoster Biblical and Theological Monographs Series. Also, Torrance, J.B., 'Strengths and Weaknesses of the Westminster Theology' pp.40-55 in Heron, A. I. C. (ed.) "the Westminster Confession in the Church Today", (The Saint Andrews Press, Edinburgh, 1982).

99 see section 2.3, above.

100 Olthuis, J., "A Cold and Comfortless Hermeneutic or a Warm and Trembling Hermeneutic: A Conversation with John D. Caputo", Christian Scholars Review 19, no.4 (1990) pp.345-362, as quoted in Loren Wilkinson "Hermeneutics and the Postmodern

Reaction Against "Truth"" in Dyck, E. 'The Act of Bible Reading' (Paternoster Press, Carlisle, 1996), p.138

101 Niebuhr, H. R. "Christ & Culture" (Harper & Row, New York, 1951).

102 see Chapter Two, section Three above.

103 "The Kairos Document - Challenge to the Church" Revised 2nd Edition, (Skotaville Publishers, Braamfontein, Johannesburg, 1986), produced with the full support of "thousands of signatories".

104 "Evangelical Witness in South Africa - Evangelicals critique their own theology and practice" by 131 listed signatories ("Concerned Evangelicals", Dobsonville, SA, 1986).

105 of course, Jesus was challenged by the Syro-Phoenecian woman on this point (Mark 7:24-30), but he didn't take shelter in his Jewishness, he took the criticism fair and square.

106 the last two lines of each verse in the hymn by George Rawson (1807-1889), "We limit not the truth of God", which Congregational Praise claims is based on the parting words of Pastor John Robinson to the Pilgrim Fathers.

CHAPTER FOUR - SEEING THE BIBLE WITH FRESH EYES

107 see Section 1.3 above.

108 for example, Richard B. Hay's account of the varied use of Scripture by five representative ethicists in Part Three of his book "The Moral Vision of the New Testament" (Harper Collins, 1996, New York and T & T Clark, 1997, Edinburgh).

109 reprinted in Thompson, David M. (ed.) "Stating the Gospel - Formulations and Declarations of Faith from the Heritage of the United Reformed Church" (T & T Clark Ltd., Edinburgh, 1990) p.14.

110 it is only fair to point out that opinions vary wildly as to the exact nature of the relationship between the printed text of the Bible and the authoritative Word of God that it carries/contains. Intriguingly, the wording of the quoted statements from the Westminster Confession (1647) and the Basis of Union of the United Reformed Church (1972) both allow a wide selection of possible interpretations of the way the Bible conveys 'The Word of God' with the ministering help of the Holy Spirit. However, it is not my intention, at this point, to get involved in that particular debate. My point here is simply the broad agreement within the Christian Churches that the Bible (with the help of the Holy Spirit) is the place to look when we seek the Word of God (no matter how we may view the nature of the relationship between the Bible and the Word of God).

111 behind and beyond all the issues about how we use the Bible that I am seeking to explore in this book is another whole range of issues about the origins and extent of the 'canon' (the list of accepted books) that constitute the Old Testament and the New Testament and the related issues of the divergence between the accepted Canon of the Bible in the Catholic, Orthodox and Protestant traditions. I will not be considering these issues in the present book, but I acknowledge they are real and important issues. For some discussion of these matters see, for example, Part Two of John Goldingay's book "Models for Scripture" (Paternoster, Carlisle, 1987) pp.83-198.

112 Carr, David "Untamable Text of an Untamable God" Interpretation, Oct. 2000, p.355.

113 Albert Schweitzer, "The Quest of the Historical Jesus" (Eng. trans. A & C Black, London, 1910) p.4.

114 The scientist in me would like to do some research at this point to establish a clear evidence base for this important assertion. Time is, again, the enemy. I can simply ask, do you agree?

115 The Westminster Confession of Faith (1647), Chapter One, Section Five, reprinted in Thompson, David M. (ed.) "Stating the Gospel - Formulations and Declarations of Faith from the Heritage of the United Reformed Church" (T & T Clark Ltd., Edinburgh, 1990) p.13.

116 for example, the first chapter of Gillingham, Susan E., "One Bible, Many Voices" (Eerdmans, Grand Rapids/Cambridge, 1998).

117 Ruthven, Malise "Islam- a very short introduction" (Oxford University Press, Oxford, 1997) pp.32-8.

118 For example, Barrett, C. K., "Acts & the Pauline Corpus" Expository Times, 88, (1976-77), pp.2-5.

119 see Chapter Two, section 3, above, also Parker, T. H. L., "Calvin's New Testament Commentaries" (SCM Press 1971, London), & Bray, Gerald, "Biblical Interpretation past and present" (Inter Varsity Press, Leicester, 1996) pp.58f.

120 Carr, David "Untamable Text of an Untamable God" Interpretation, Oct. 2000, p.349-353, who gives various examples from the book of Genesis.

121 the oft-repeated phrase for a metanarrative used in the BBC radio series written by Douglas Adams, "The hitchhiker's Guide to the Galaxy" and in the subsequently published five-volume 'trilogy' with the same title.

122 the texts of both of them appear in the United Reformed Church's hymnbook "Rejoice and Sing" as numbers 759 & 760.

123 Calvin, J., "Institutes of the Christian Religion" volumes 20 & 21 of the Library of Christian Classics, edited by McNeill, J. T. & trans. F. L. Battles, (Westminster Press, Philadelphia, 1960).

124 Calvin, J., "Institutes of the Christian Religion" volumes 20 of the Library of Christian Classics, edited by McNeill, J. T. & trans. F. L. Battles, (Westminster Press, Philadelphia, 1960), p.6, 'Subject matter of the present work', from the French edition of 1560.

125 this example is taken from the 'Excerpts from the Preamble, Questions and Formula prescribed in the 1929 Basis and Plan of Union for the Ordination and Induction of Ministers' reproduced as an Appendix on p.148f of Heron, A. I. C. (ed.) "the Westminster Confession in the Church Today", (The Saint Andrews Press, Edinburgh, 1982).

126 The classic example is surely the Chalcedonian Definition that has largely fallen out of church liturgical usage, probably because it is so layered with responses to a whole range of Christological disputes on points that would never have occurred to most 20th or 21st Century Christians. For an English translation, see Stevenson, J. (ed.), "Creeds, Councils and Controversies" (SPCK, London, 1966), p.337.

127 both the Westminster Confession (1647) and the Savoy Declaration (an amended version of the Westminster Confession altered to represent Congregationalist perceptions of the faith in 1658) can be found reprinted in Thompson, David M. (ed.) "Stating the Gospel - Formulations and Declarations of Faith from the Heritage of the United Reformed Church" (T & T Clark Ltd., Edinburgh, 1990).

128 The Statement of the Nature, Faith and Order of the United Reformed Church (used at ordinations and inductions as a confession of the faith of the United Reformed Church) explicitly allows for doctrinal development within our tradition. At one point

it states clearly that "we affirm our right and readiness, if the need arises, to change the Basis of Union and to make new statements of faith in ever new obedience to the Living Christ". similarly 'the Preamble, Questions and Formula prescribed in the 1929 Basis and Plan of Union for the Ordination and Induction of Ministers' of the Church of Scotland talks of 'claiming the right, in dependence on the promised guidance of the Holy Spirit, to formulate, interpret or modify its subordinate standards...' see the 'Excerpts from the Preamble, Questions and Formula prescribed in the 1929 Basis and Plan of Union for the Ordination and Induction of Ministers' reproduced as an Appendix on p.148f of Heron, A. I. C. (ed.) "the Westminster Confession in the Church Today", (The Saint Andrew Press, Edinburgh, 1982).

129 Isaac Watts' well-known hymn "Our God, our help in ages past, our hope for years to come, our shelter from the stormy blast, and our eternal home" – probably in most English language hymnbooks, e.g. no. 705 in "Rejoice and Sing".

130 Personal communication.

131 I would accept that this may have been part of the intended purpose of some of the Bible's constituent parts - see, for example, the book of Deuteronomy - but it cannot be taken to be the obvious purpose of every Bible book and certainly, as I have argued in section 5.2, can hardly be taken to be the one unified purpose of the-Bible-as-a-whole.

132 also, the discussion of Mark 7:1-2 & 5-13 in Chapter 4, part 3, subsection 3 "The Importance of Suspicion", above where Jesus denounces the self-deceiving legal meticulousness of Pharisees using the idea of 'Corban' to avoid caring for their parents.

133 Carr, David "Untamable Text of an Untamable God" Interpretation, Oct. 2000, p.349-353.

134 see section 2.2, above.

135 see section 2.3, above.

136 see section 1.3, above.

137 Brueggemann, Walter "Theology of the Old Testament" (Fortress Press, Louisville Ky, 1997) p.63.

138 Eichrodt, Walther "Theology of the Old Testament" 2 vols., (Eng. Trans. Westminster Press, Philadelphia, 1961, 1967).

139 Brueggemann, Walter, "Theology of the Old Testament - a prompt retrospect", Chapter 21 of Linafelt, Tod and Beal, Timothy K. (eds.) "God in the Fray - a tribute to Walter Brueggemann" Fortress Press, Minneapolis Mn 1998) p.38. Whilst Brueggemann is here (and elsewhere) appreciative of Eichrodt's key idea, seeing it as "in his time, an immense gain", it is only fair to point out that he is rightly wary of its over application as an organising principle for Old Testament Theology, wondering whether Eichrodt's use of this idea gives "excessive" closure (see Brueggemann's comments in his "Theology of the Old Testament" (Fortress Press, Louisville Ky, 1997) p.41.

140 as in Walter Bruggemann's phrase "there are no answers at the back of the book" - Brueggemann, Walter "Theology of the Old Testament" (Fortress, Louisville Ky, 1997) p.63.

141 Walter Brueggemann's "The Message of the Psalms" (Augsburg, Minneapolis, 1984) offers an intriguing division of the Psalms into the broad categories of "Psalms of Orientation", "Psalms of Disorientation" and "Psalms of Re-orientation" that illustrates how important re-appropriation of the faith is in the Psalms. Indeed, re-appraisal and re-appropriation of the faith because of dissonance between the inherited tradition and the experience of the psalmist is surely one of the key aspects of the spirituality of the Psalms.

CHAPTER FIVE – HOW DO WE DECIDE WHAT GOD WANTS US TO DO?

142   Bauckham, R., "Scripture and Authority Today" (Grove Booklet B12, Cambridge, 1999), p.5. Much of what follows in this section (section 5.2) is based on the clear & succinct argument of Bauckham's booklet.

143   Bauckham, R., "Scripture and Authority Today" (Grove Booklet B12, Cambridge, 1999), p.6.

144   Schweitzer, A. "The Quest of the Historical Jesus" (Eng. trans. A & C Black, London 1910) p.5.

145   see section 2.2 above ("Assured results" of Higher Criticism).

146   Bauckham, R., "Scripture and Authority Today" (Grove Booklet B12, Cambridge, 1999), p.6.

147   Bauckham, R., "Scripture and Authority Today" (Grove Booklet B12, Cambridge, 1999), p.8. See, also, above section 3.2 (What's happening now?)

148   see above, section 4.4 (What might the Bible be trying to say), sub-section 3 (Finding Friendship).

149   in the ongoing story of the wilderness wanderings from Exodus to Joshua the people of Israel really don't seem to get this point, preferring to operate with a truculent mix of reluctantly-offered obedience and outright rebellion. But note the great re-statement of the terms of God's case on the lips of Joshua in Joshua 24:2-28.

150   see Rogerson, J., 'The Old Testament and Christian Ethics' in Robin Gill (ed.) "The Cambridge Companion to Christian Ethics" (Cambridge University Press, Cambridge, 2001) p.30.

151   The law contained in the Mishnah, Tosephta and Talmuds is taken to be oral law given to Moses on Mount Sinai at the same time as the written law contained in the Pentateuch, but passed on orally until these documents were written many hundreds of years later.

152   Janet Tollington (personal communication) has helpfully pointed out that we must not crudely equate the Jewish idea of 'Torah' with a modern court-administered law code. Reading some of the Psalms that praise God's law (e.g. Psalm 119) should make that clear. There is a much richer idea here. Janet puts it like this: "Torah is a gift from God, a great blessing, guidance about a way of life, which if followed will enable someone to deepen his/her relationship with God and thereby experience yet more blessings".

153   see Ruthven, M. "ISLAM, A Very Short Introduction" (Oxford University Press, Oxford, 1997) pp.39-41.

154   Jones, G. 'The authority of scripture and Christian ethics' in Robin Gill (ed.) "The Cambridge Companion to Christian Ethics" (Cambridge University Press, Cambridge, 2001) p.25, also Bauckham, R., "Scripture and Authority Today" (Grove Booklet B12, Cambridge, 1999), 11.

155   Chapter Four, section two (What have we got in the Bible?), sub-section 3 (A kitchenful of ingredients but no recipe).

156   a 'Grand Narrative' (otherwise known as a 'metanarrative') is a story that seeks to explain the meaning of 'the world, the universe and everything' in terms that are important and controlling for a particular culture. Postmodernism has famously been defined by Jean Francois Lyotard as, "an incredulity towards metanarratives" – quoted by Middleton, J. R. & Walsh, B. J., "Truth is stranger than it used to be" (SPCK, London, 1995), p.70.

157 for the phrase 'sacred canopy' as a description of the role of faith in life see Peter Berger's "The Sacred Canopy" (Doubleday, Garden City NY, 1967).

158 Lundin, Roger 'Interpreting Orphans: Hermeneutics in the Cartesian Tradition' in Lundin, R. et al. "The Promise of Hermeneutics" (Paternoster Press, Carlisle, 1999) p.3ff.

159 Middleton, J. R. & Walsh, B. J., "Truth is stranger than it used to be" (SPCK, London, 1995) p.52ff

160 our stated aim – see section 1 of the introduction, above.

161 see Chapter Four, section 4.2, (What have we got in the Bible?) subsection 4 (A strange rule book)

162 see Chapter Four, section 4.4 (What might the Bible be trying to say?)

163 Chapter Nineteen ('Of the Law of God') of the Westminster Confession (1647) singles out the Ten Commandments as the part of the Law of Moses that continues to have the weight of 'obligation' for Christian believers. Whilst it recognises that there are many ceremonial laws (that continue to prefigure Christ and 'his graces, actions, sufferings and benefits') and judicial laws, these are now 'abrogated' and 'expired', respectively. The Westminster Confession is reprinted in Thompson, David M. (ed.) "Stating the Gospel - Formulations and Declarations of Faith from the Heritage of the United Reformed Church" (T & T Clark Ltd., Edinburgh, 1990), Chapter 19 is on page 30.

164 If my memory of a newspaper article serves me right, this law appeared in an interesting judgement in a South African court case in 2000. A Christian School had sought the right to use corporal punishment on its pupils, citing verses from the Law of Moses in the Bible. The judgement included the argument that as the judge could not conceive that the school would wish this law about stoning stubborn sons to be applied today, he could not apply the other law the school wished applied either – he threw out their case.

165 Bauckham, R., "Scripture and Authority Today" (Grove Booklet B12, Cambridge, 1999), pp.16 & 17.

166 we may not agree which commands are to be treated in which ways and we may have inherited ready explanations that apply to particular commands and how we treat them, but it is my contention that a careful examination of what each of us believed would show that we all employ a variety of different strategies for making sense of each apparent command in the Bible. It also seems unlikely that most of us could produce an entirely convincing explanation why we treat some commands in one way and others differently, apart from our inherited theological preferences and learned arguments.

167 Theissen, G., "The Social Setting of Pauline Christianity" (Eng. Trans. Fortress Pr., Philadelphia, 1982).

168 Meeks, Wayne, "The First Urban Christians – the social world of the Apostle Paul" (Yale U P, New Haven, 1983) and other works.

169 for example, some of the works listed in the Bibliography of Anthony Thiselton's commentary – Thiselton, A. C., "The New International Greek Testament Commentary – The First Epistle to the Corinthians" (Eerdmans, Grand Rapids MI & Paternoster, Carlisle, 2000) pp.xxix – xxxiii.

170 the comments of Richard Bauckham in Bauckham, R. "The Bible in Politics: How to read the Bible politically" (SPCK, London, 1989) Ch. 1.

171 for example Mark 7:1-2 & 5-13 and Chapter Three, Section Three, Subsection Three (the importance of suspicion) above, where Mark 7:1-2 & 5-13 is discussed.

172 thus, the noted Christian Ethicist Paul Ramsey (1913-1988) in a letter to James Gustafson, quoted on p.93 of Siker, J. S., "Scripture & Ethics – twentieth century portraits", (Oxford UP, New York NY, 1997).

173 Siker, J. S., "Scripture & Ethics – twentieth century portraits", (Oxford UP, New York NY, 1997).

174 Hays, R. B., "The moral vision of the New Testament" (Harper Collins, New York NY, 1996 and T & T Clark, Edinburgh, 1997), Pt. 3, pp.207-312.

175 Hays, R. B., "The moral vision of the New Testament – Community, Cross, New Creation - a Contemporary Introduction to New Testament Ethics" (Harper Collins, New York NY, 1996 and T & T Clark, Edinburgh, 1997).

176 Hays, R. B., 'Moral Vision...' p.1.

177 Hays, R. B., 'Moral Vision...' p.xi.

178 Hays, R. B., 'Moral Vision...' p.2.

179 Hays, R. B., 'Moral Vision...' 3.

180 Hays, R. B., 'Moral Vision...' 3.

181 Hays, R. B., 'Moral Vision...' p.xiii.

182 Hays, R. B., 'Moral Vision...' p.xi.

183 Hays, R. B., 'Moral Vision...' p.3.

184 Reinhold Niebuhr, Karl Barth, John Howard Yoder, Stanley Hauerwas and Elizabeth Schussler-Fiorenza – see Chapter Twelve of Hays, R.B., op. cit..

185 Hays is careful not to claim too much for his method, declaring his aim as "to describe a frame-work for New Testament ethics within which the constructive improvisation of moral judgements can take place." – Hays, R. B., 'Moral Vision...' p.6. Yet, I have a lingering suspicion that the very carefulness and structure of Hays' 'framework' may give some of his readers the impression that he is offering something much more substantial and 'scientific' - a secure method for constructing Christian Ethics. I fear this may be so, despite the very real caveats he himself scatters all through his text.

186 Hays, R. B., 'Moral Vision...' p.189.

187 Hays, R. B., 'Moral Vision...' p.198.

188 Hays, R. B., 'Moral Vision...' p.298.

189 Hays, R. B., 'Moral Vision...' p.298.

190 Hays, R. B., 'Moral Vision...' p.304.

191 Hays, R. B., 'Moral Vision...' pp.296-8.

192 Hays, R. B., 'Moral Vision...' p.306.

193 This strongly echoes what was said about John Calvin in Chapter One, Section Three (Calvin & the unified Word of God), above.

194 Bauckham, R. "The Bible in Politics: How to read the Bible politically" (SPCK, London, 1989) Ch. 1.

195 Thiselton, Lundin and Weinsheimer, who in their turn cite both Ricoeur and Gadamer – see Roger Lundin 'Interpreting Orphans: Hermeneutics in the Cartesian Tradition' in Lundin, R. et al. "The Promise of Hermeneutics" (Paternoster Press, Carlisle, 1999) p.60 see also Thiselton's article in the same volume.

196 Olthuis, J., "A Cold and Comfortless Hermeneutic or a Warm and Trembling Hermeneutic: A Conversation with John D. Caputo", Christian Scholars Review 19, no.4 (1990) pp.345-362, as quoted in Loren Wilkinson "Hermeneutics and the Post-modern Reaction Against

"Truth" in Dyck, E. 'The Act of Bible Reading' (Paternoster Press, Carlisle, 1996), p.138.

197 see the argument of Loren Wilkinson's footnote 21 on page 178 of Dyck, Elmer "The Act of Bible Reading", (Inter Varsity Press, Downers Grove Il., 1996 & Paternoster Press, Carlisle,1997).

198 Rogerson, J. W., p.18 of 'Discourse Ethics and Biblical Ethics', pp17-26 of Rogerson, J.W. et al., "The Bible in Ethics", (Sheffield Academic Press, Sheffield, 1995).

199 see above Chapters 1-3, but especially Chapter Three, Section Three (And what can we learn from the text?), Subsection Three (The Importance of Suspicion).

200 see above, Chapter Three, Section Three (And what can we learn from the text?), Subsection Four (The Liberation of Listening).

201 this whole section of the argument is closely paralleled by that of Stephen E. Fowl and L. Gregory Jones in their book "Reading in Communion – Scripture and Ethics in Christian Life", (SPCK, London, 1991).

202 West, Gerald O., 'Local is Lekker, but Ubuntu is Best: Indigenous reading resources from a South African Perspective', pp.37-51 in Sugirtharajah, R. S. (ed.) "Vernacular Hermeneutics" (Sheffield Academic Press, Sheffield, 1999).

203 My limited understanding of Postcolonial Theory suggests that it has real concerns about this, hence the wide influence of Gayatri Spivak's essay "Can the subaltern speak?" as cited in Bart Moore-Gilbert's "Postcolonial Theory – Contexts, Practices, Politics" (Verso, London & New York NY, 1997) p.79ff.

204 thus Walter Brueggemann, "To build, to plant – a commentary on Jeremiah 26-52", (Eerdmans, Grand Rapids MI & Handsel, Edinburgh, 1991) p.113.

205 see the previous footnote, Brueggemann, op. cit. p.113.

206 The Westminster Confession (1647), Chapter One (Of the Holy Scripture), section five, reprinted in Thompson, David M. (ed.) "Stating the Gospel - Formulations and Declarations of Faith from the Heritage of the United Reformed Church" (T & T Clark Ltd., Edinburgh, 1990), p.13.

207 the titles of the first 2 subsections of Chapter 4, Section 2 (What have we got in the Bible?), above.

208 Rex Mason's exciting "Propaganda and Subversion in the Old Testament" (SPCK, London, 1997)

209 note the apposite comments of the United Reformed Church Biblical Authority Working Party on the role of 'patterns' and 'schemes' in ensuring incommensurable outcomes to competing exegetical efforts – to which they trace the whole basis of disagreement in the United Reformed Church's sexuality debate – see above, Introduction.

210 although, as Richard Hays clearly found, it may not be as 'objective' and 'scientific' as you may have hoped – see, above, in this chapter, Section Three, subsection Three (Can we find a reliable method?)

211 Longenecker, Richard N., "New Testament Social Ethics for Today" (Eerdmans, Grand Rapids, 1984), especially Chapter One.

212 Longenecker, 'N. T. Social Ethics...', p.9.

CHAPTER SIX – CONFLICT IN CORINTH – A CASE STUDY

213 Theissen, G., "The Social Setting of Pauline Christianity" (Eng. Trans. Fortress Pr., Philadelphia, 1982).

214 Meeks, Wayne, "The First Urban Christians – the social world of the Apostle Paul" (Yale University Press, New Haven, 1983) and other works.

215 for example, some of the works listed in the Bibliography of Anthony Thiselton's commentary – Thiselton, A. C., "The New International Greek Testament Commentary – The First Epistle to the Corinthians" (Eerdmans, Grand Rapids MI & Paternoster, Carlisle, 2000) pp.xxix–xxxiii.

216 Murphy-O'Connor, Jerome, "St Paul's Corinth" (The Liturgical Press, Collegeville Mn, 2002) – a collection of passages from classical authors about Corinth (with commentary) and a digest of relevant archaeological studies of Corinth that all contribute to our understanding of the city of Corinth in the time of St Paul.

217 Thiselton, A. C., "The New International Greek Testament Commentary – The First Epistle to the Corinthians" (Eerdmans, Grand Rapids MI & Paternoster, Carlisle, 2000) pp.1-29.

218 Theissen, G., "The Social Setting of Pauline Christianity" (Eng. Trans. Fortress Pr., Philadelphia, 1982).

219 the title of the first section of the Introduction of Hays, Richard B., "First Corinthians – Interpretation Bible Commentary Series" (John Knox Press, Louisville Ky, 1997) p.1.

220 Hays, Richard B., "First Corinthians – Interpretation Bible Commentary Series" (John Knox Press, Louisville Ky, 1997) p.130.

221 there is a succinct analysis of this argument in Wayne Meeks', "The Moral World of the First Christians" (Westminster Press, 1986 & SPCK London, 1987), pp.132-136.

222 Meeks, Wayne, "The Moral World of the First Christians" (Westminster Press, 1986 & SPCK London, 1987), p.131.

223 Hays, Richard B., "First Corinthians – Interpretation Bible Commentary Series" (John Knox Press, Louisville Ky, 1997) p. 213.

224 Hays, Richard B., "Echoes of Scripture in the Letters of Paul" (Yale University Press, New Haven & London, 1989), p.162.

225 Hays, 'Echoes...', p.160.

226 Hays, R. B., "Echoes of Scripture in the Letters of Paul" (Yale University Press, New Haven & London, 1989)

227 Hays, 'Echoes...', p.160.

228 Hays, 'Echoes...', pp.183-188.

229 Hays, 'Echoes...', p.191.

230 see the opening paragraph of Chapter Five, section five, 'Seven proposals for conversationalists'.

231 Hays, Richard B., "Echoes of Scripture in the Letters of Paul" (Yale University Press, New Haven & London, 1989).

232 Brueggemann, Walter "Theology of the Old Testament" (Fortress Press, Louisville Ky, 1997) p.63.

CHAPTER SEVEN – OUR DEVELOPING CONVERSATION

233 Longenecker, R. N., "New Testament Social Ethics for Today" (Eerdmans, Grand Rapids, 1984) p.24ff.

234 Longenecker, 'N. T. Social Ethics...', p.24.

235 Longenecker, 'N. T. Social Ethics...', p.25.

236 Longenecker, 'N. T. Social Ethics...', p.25.

237 Longenecker, 'N. T. Social Ethics...', p.25.

238 Longenecker, 'N. T. Social Ethics...', p.25.

239 Longenecker, 'N. T. Social Ethics...', p.25.

240 Longenecker, 'N. T. Social Ethics...', p.26.

241 the title of Richard N. Longenecker's short but lucid book – "New Testament Social Ethics for Today" (Eerdmans, Grand Rapids, 1984).

242 see above, Chapter Six, section Two, subsection Six, "Paul's twin imperatives".

243 we have no means of knowing how widely the three-fold formula of Galatians 3:28 was, in fact, used at baptisms or in the preparation of candidates for them. However, Richard B. Hays, in his 'Interpretation' commentary on 'First Corinthians', (John Knox Press, Louisville Ky, 1997) p.122f, describes Galatians 3:28 as "Paul's baptismal catechesis". He, too, clearly finds the trace of something widely known in Paul's churches and connected with baptism. Indeed, he finds an implicit echo of the three-fold idea of Galatians 3:28 in the form of Paul's argument in I Corinthians 7:17-24.

244 see above both Chapter Five, Section Five, subsection six ('Affirm God's underlying purposes') and, for the particular importance of this idea in I Corinthians, see above, Chapter Six, Section Two, subsection six ('Paul's twin imperatives').

245 see above the sections listed in the previous footnote.

246 Philip Esler makes a powerful case that the disagreement and division may have been far more acrimonious than Acts is prepared to let on, see Esler, Philip, "Community and Gospel in Luke-Acts, the Social and Political Motivations of Lucan Theology" (Cambridge University Press, Cambridge, 1987), pp.71-109. Yet, the text we have presents us with an agreement in Acts 15 that seeks to settle once and for all the dispute about ethnicity and value.

247 throughout this section (7.2) I have found Steve Motyer's booklet "Antisemitism and the New Testament" (Grove Books, Cambridge, 2002) helpful, also the argument in Chapter Three of Longenecker, R. N., "New Testament Social Ethics for Today" (Eerdmans, Grand Rapids, 1984).

248 This insistence must have been a sort of prerequisite for a successful Christian mission to Gentiles, for adult male circumcision cannot have been a very attractive requirement for would-be converts to Christianity.

249 remember what Calvin said whilst commenting on Luke 13:1-9, "we suffer from the almost inborn disease of being overstrict and severe critics of others whilst approving of our own sins." - Calvin, J. "A Harmony of the Gospels Matthew, Mark & Luke" (1555 - English Translation by T. H. L. Parker, 1995, The Paternoster Press, Carlisle vol. II, p.94).

250 a very real failing that it does not seem at all easy for even the late twentieth century church to put right, see Shawn Kelley's recent "Racializing Jesus – Race, ideology and the Formation of Modern Biblical Scholarship" (Routledge, London & New York, 2002).

Being Biblical

251 Remember, also, the shameful Christian attitudes to 'infidels' or 'non-believers' in the times of the crusades. Surely there was a disturbingly racist component to these deeply negative attitudes and their resultant behaviour – behaviour that still casts a cloud over relations between Christianity and Islam?

252 relevant arguments are to be found in Chapter 4, section 4, part 6 – 'Always Anew' and Chapter 5, section 5, part 5 – 'Keep talking about ethics', above.

253 relevant arguments are to be found in Chapter 4, section 4, part 6 – 'Always Anew', above.

254 relevant arguments are to be found in Chapter 5, section 5, part 6 – 'Affirm God's underlying purposes' and Chapter Six, section 2, part 6 – 'Paul's twin imperatives', above.

255 as would seem to be the case with regards to the voicing of child abuse issues for so many churches in Europe and the English-speaking world at the present time – but note also the relevant arguments that are to be found in Chapter 3, section 3, part 4 – 'The liberation of listening' and Chapter 5, section 5, part 2 – 'Admit our need of others', above.

256 relevant arguments are to be found in Chapter Five, section 5, part 7 – 'Allow for the role of God's Spirit' and Chapter 6, section 2, part 7 – 'Paul and the Spirit' above.

257 as has surely, also, been the case in relation to the position of women and various aspects of racism, despite these issues being explicitly listed in Galatians 3:28.

258 'Jubilee 2000' and 'Drop the Debt' are international campaigns to encourage Western countries and their international institutions to release developing countries crippled by massive debt servicing bills from those debts in return for a commitment to use the money saved in development and education programmes. They have been widely supported by churches in the UK through Christian Aid, our shared agency for international aid and developement issues. Jubilee 2000 was explicitly based on the idea of a Jubilee remission of outstanding debts found in Leviticus 25 and Deuteronomy 15. The 'Fair Trade' campaign is about exposing the unfairness of the world trade system and its bias to the commercial needs of richer countries.

259 Usury is the idea of taking an interest payment on a loan – the very basis of Western Capitalism – but forbidden in the Pentateuch. It seems to have been Calvin who 'opened the floodgates' by rejecting the view that interest on capital was inherently wrong. But in the last decade or so Christians have begun to look again at the whole issue of the ethics of moneylending. See, for a brief introduction to all of this, Susan L. Buckley's Grove Booklet, "Usury Friendly? – The Ethics of Moneylending – A Biblical Interpretation" (Grove Books, Cambridge, 1998).

260 there are various editions of this remarkable work first published in 1789 in print at present. It forms part of Equiano, Olaudah, "The Interesting Narrative and Other Writings" edited by Vincent Carretta (Penguin Books, Harmondsworth, 1995), it is also available as a Norton Critical Edition, edited by Werner Sollors, (W. W. Norton & Co., New York & London, 2001)

261 Sugirtharajah, R. S., "The Bible and the Third World – Precolonial, Colonial and Postcolonial Encounters" (Cambridge University Press, Cambridge, 2001) pp.75-87.

262 Equiano, O. "The Interesting Narrative and Other Writings" (Penguin Books, Harmondsworth, 1995) p.41.

194 Footnotes

263 Equiano, "The Interesting Narrative..... p.105, quoting Matthew 7:12.

264 Sugirtharajah, R. S., "The Bible and the Third World – Precolonial, Colonial and Postcolonial Encounters" (Cambridge University Press, Cambridge, 2001) p.82f.

265 this letter is reproduced for us in Equiano, O. "The Interesting Narrative and Other Writings" (Penguin Books, Harmondsworth, 1995) p.335f.

266 Equiano, O. "The Interesting Narrative and Other Writings"... p.335.

267 Equiano, O. "The Interesting Narrative and Other Writings"... p.336.

268 Equiano, O. "The Interesting Narrative and Other Writings"... p.336.

269 Stowe, Harriet Beecher, "Uncle Tom's Cabin" (Norton Critical Edition edited by E. Ammons, W.W. Norton, New York and London, 1994 – published in serial parts in 1851-2, first published as a complete book, 1852).

270 Ammons, E., Preface to Stowe, Harriet Beecher, "Uncle Tom's Cabin" (Norton Critical Edition edited by E. Ammons, W.W. Norton, New York and London, 1994).

271 Ammons, E. Preface,..... p.viii.

272 Ammons, E. Preface,..... p.viii.

273 Rice, C. Duncan, "The Scots Abolitionists 1833-1861" (Louisiana State University Press, Baton Rouge and London, 1981) see pages 173-188.

274 Rice, C. D., "The Scots Abolitionists.... p.175.

275 "The Kairos Document - Challenge to the Church" Revised 2nd Edition, (Skotaville Publishers, Braamfontein, Johannesburg, September 1986), the first edition had been produced in September 1985 and used for widespread consultation, the resulting second edition was largely the same as the first, except for a major reworking of the chapter on Prophetic Theology. This was in response to widespread requests to make the Bible basis of Prophetic Theology clearer, including the provision of far more Bible references.

276 "Evangelical Witness in South Africa - Evangelicals critique their own theology and practice" by 131 listed signatories ("Concerned Evangelicals", Dobsonville, SA, July 1986), a response to the first edition of the Kairos Document developed by a group of evangelicals based in the Johannesburg and Pretoria areas, but in consultation with others across South Africa prior to publication.

277 "Evangelical Witness" mentions security force attacks on two schools and a subsequent attempted vehicle burning by schoolchildren that all happened within a few hundred yards of the church where they met, whilst they were meeting. Its authors note in their preface the reality of their dilemma, "If we failed to intervene in the legalized brutal violence of the security forces what right do we have to intervene in the counter-violence of the young people?"

278 This approach allows, for example, the sort of reappraisal of Romans 13:1-7 which is broadly shared by the two documents.

279 This is certainly not to rule out the significance of the interpretive history of the text (in various intervening contexts), simply to emphasise the particular value of our best reconstructions of the original setting of the text and a full awareness of the setting into which we seek to apply it now.

280 Forrest, Martin, unpublished sabbatical report, for further information contact the author at The Manse, Southend, Argyll, UK.